To Catch a Tartar

DATE DUE

WITHDRAWN
UTSA Libraries

To Catch a Tartar
A Dissident in Lee Kuan Yew's Prison

FRANCIS T. SEOW

with a foreword by
C.V. DEVAN NAIR

Monograph 42/Yale Southeast Asia Studies
Yale Center for International and Area Studies

Yale University Southeast Asia Studies
James C. Scott, Chairman
Marvel Kay Mansfield, Editor

Consulting Editors
Hans-Dieter Evers, Universität Bielefeld
Huynh Sanh Thông, Yale University
Sartono Kartodirdjo, Gadjah Mada University
Lim Teck Ghee, Institute for Advanced Studies, University of Malaya
Alfred W. McCoy, University of Wisconsin
Anthony Reid, Research School of Pacific Studies, Canberra
Benjamin White, Institute for Social Studies, The Hague
Alexander Woodside, University of British Columbia

Library of Congress Catalog Card Number: 94-060647
International Standard Book Number: paper   0-938692-56-9
                                        cloth   0-938692-55-0

© 1994 by Yale University Southeast Asia Studies
New Haven, Connecticut 06520-8206
Second impression

Distributor:
Yale University Southeast Asia Studies
P.O. Box 208206
New Haven, Connecticut 06520-8206
U.S.A.

Printed in U.S.A.

*Lovingly dedicated to
the memory of my late wife, Rauni Marjatta Kivilaakso
and to my mother, Pang Siew Peck
and my sister, Clare Seow-Looi*

Contents

Foreword		*ix*
Acknowledgements		*xxxi*
Maps of Singapore		*xxxiv*
1	An Historical Background	1
2	Prologue	8
	Whitley Detention Centre	8
3	Salad Days	13
4	May 21, 1987	67
5	Pavilion Intercontinental Hotel	81
6	May 6, 1988	102
	The Trap Sprung	106
7	The Search	111
8	In the Eye of Harry—The Interrogation	121
9	At the General Hospital	146
10	Still in the Eye of Harry—Interrogation Continued	149
11	Devan Nair and the Asylum	161
12	The Closing Society	173
13	Dr. Toh Chin Chye *et al.*	195
	Tan Boon Teik	197
14	Cell L-9, Block L	205
	Valley Wing	209

15	Security	212
	Counsel's Visits	214
	Family Visits	215
16	Method of Recording	220
17	Period of Rehabilitation	226
18	On the Eve of the Day	236
19	A Summer Bird—July 16, 1988	239

Epilogue	243
Appendix I—Statement of Ex-detainees of Operation Spectrum	258
Appendix II—Floor Plan of Centre and Cells	262
Appendix III—Statement of Grounds of Detention	264
Appendix IV—Representations	268
Appendix V—An Open Letter to Lee Kuan Yew	273
Index	283

Foreword

Before reading Francis Seow's manuscript, I had decided that I would decline his request for a foreword. My political days are definitively over—and for more reasons than either friends or foes imagine. Apart from a series of reflective essays (in preparation) on the making of an ideal (in which I too had been privileged to share), on its unmaking (which I watch in helpless pain from the sidelines), and on the dubious—to say the least—political and social aftermath of phenomenal economic success, I had, and still have, no intention of becoming involved in promoting the political views or program of any individual or group, whether within or without Singapore.

After reading through the manuscript, however, I realized that I would never again be able to look at my face in the mirror without flinching, if I said no to Francis, at least in regard to this particular piece of writing by him. For this was no political harangue by one of Singapore's leading opposition figures, excoriating the political or economic program of the powers-that-be, and pleading the virtues of his own political cause. On the contrary, central to this book is a grim account of how a citizen of Singapore was treated while under detention without trial under the republic's internal security laws.

As an ex-detainee myself, who had undergone in two separate spells a total of five years of political imprisonment in the fifties under the British colonial regime as an anticolonial freedom fighter, I recalled that I was never treated in the shockingly dehumanizing manner in which Francis was by the professedly democratic government of independent Singapore. Indeed, my fellow-detainees and I had as legal counsel a brilliant lawyer and vocal freedom-fighter by the name of Lee Kuan Yew, who has publicly borne witness to the comfortable circumstances in which we lived under detention, and how he was freely able to visit us, without supervision, to discuss, among other things, strategies for bringing the colonial rule of our jailers to an end.

Francis's account of his seventy-two days of detention by Prime Minister Lee's government confronted me yet once again with acutely poignant questions: What has the nation come to? And what malefic hidden persona has emerged in Lee Kuan Yew of today? Surely, this cannot be the same man, whom I and several other starry-eyed anticolonial revolutionaries in the fifties and sixties had jubilantly accepted as our captain in the grim, heroic struggles of those early days to create what we expected would be a new Jerusalem? Alas, it took us thirty years to realize that we had been treading on air.

Mr. Seow's book is an eye-opener, that is, for those whose eyes still require to be opened. Mine too, for that matter. Nobody is blinder than a captain's inveterate hero-worshipper. And none probably as wilfully, self-righteously closed to unfolding reality as I was. Indeed, until fairly recently, I had believed that the People's Action Party (PAP) government, by which I had once sworn, had all along been tolerably civilized and humane in its treatment of political prisoners. Yet another scale had to fall from my eyes, the latest in a series of scales which had already fallen earlier, and which I will deal with in my own book.

The economic transformation wrought by the PAP government in Singapore is there for all the world to see. The towering skyline of the island city state, the great vistas of new high-rise apartments which have replaced the sordid sprawling slums and malarial swamps of only three decades ago, the magnificent international airport at Changi about which all visitors rave, the world's latest and, perhaps, best mass rapid transit system, the clean and green garden city—all and more—quite rightly evoke the envy and admiration of foreign visitors, especially those from developing countries with much less to boast of by way of efficient development-oriented governments.

I would be the last person to denigrate the material achievements of Singapore, for the good reason that I was also a member of the ruling team responsible for them. Like other members of the PAP old guard, I saw the creation of a solid socioeconomic base as a vitally necessary springboard for the realisation of human ends and values. At least for me, and for the others in the anticolonial movement like me, the human agenda was primary. In short, the urgent, organized, disciplined drive for economic growth and technological progress was powered by noneconomic aspirations and ideals.

We looked at the sad fate of other multiracial and multireligious developing countries and recognised that life's highest rewards and fulfillments were beyond the reach of societies riven by sterile, senseless class and ethnic strife, and cursed by a corrupt polity, inefficient production, material poverty, and hungry bellies. Modern technology and management systems would be the necessary means to advance the human agenda. Alas, we failed to foresee that human ends would come to be subverted for the greater glory of the material means, and our new Jerusalem would come to harbour a metallic soul with clanking heartbeats, behind a glittering technological facade.

History bears abundant witness that idealists generally come to grief. They awaken high human aspirations and hopes and ignite the liberating fires of revolution. The pains and humiliations of foreign subjection and exploitation are scorched, and, for a brief, blazing period, men transcend themselves in the inspiring vision of a great common future. The revolution triumphs—but idealists become expendable thereafter. One by one, sooner or later, they are eased out. And the revolution is inherited by cold, calculating powerbrokers at the head of a phalanx of philistines.

Lee Kuan Yew's earlier speeches echo the great themes of freedom fighters everywhere. As the several irrefragable quotes Seow offers in his book testify, Lee too had once waxed eloquent about liberty, freedom, harmony, justice, and the dignity of man. But reading Lee Kuan Yew today, or listening to him, one realizes how brazenly he has abandoned the positions which had so convincingly persuaded an earlier, revolutionary generation of Singaporeans, both old-guard colleagues and the population at large, to confirm him in the captainship of party and nation. We had taken him at his powerfully eloquent word. If Lee had then given even the mildest hint of the apostate he was to become, he would have received short shrift from the revolutionary following who had put their trust in him.

Those who order, systematise, and govern in the aftermath of revolutions often become votaries at covert and pernicious altars. Ineluctably, the Olympian gods are displaced and a Titan holds sway, with lamentable results. The march of the human spirit is first arrested, then retarded.

What we launched as the independent republic of Singapore succeeded, as the world knows, all too well, only to discover that in the eyes of Lee Kuan Yew, means had become ends in themselves. First principles were stood on their heads. Economic growth and social progress did not serve human beings. On the contrary, the primary function of citizens was to fuel economic growth—a weird reversal of values. The reign of Moloch had begun. Not an unfamiliar phenomenon to those who browse in the pages of history. My old-guard colleagues and I might have been wiser men and women if we had read our history with greater comprehension than we do now. Alas, one cannot alter the past.

The inevitable drift to totalitarianism begins with the typically symptomatic thesis of the progenitors: "Society as No. 1, and the individual, as part of society, as No. 2." The words are Lee Kuan Yew's, speaking to Singapore journalists in Canberra, ACT, on November 16, 1988. He was dutifully echoed by Goh Chok Tong, the First Deputy Prime Minister, (now Prime Minister), when he announced this as one of the pillars of the government's new goal of "a national ideology" for Singapore. Portentous words, given the current morbidities in the republic, which include the account given by Francis Seow in the following pages of his seventy-two days of detention and interrogation by the guardians of "national security," the Internal Security Department. Seow learned at first hand what happens to the individual as No. 2, when subjected to society as No. 1 in the shape of his jailers and interrogators in the Whitley Detention Centre.

"The individual, as part of society," is a marginal improvement on Mr. Lee's egregious penchant for referring to fellow-citizens as "digits" of the development process. You are either a productive "digit," or an inefficient one. And "digits," like robots, if they are to be functionally useful, have to be programmed. So one need not be surprised that Singapore's political programmers should now be working on a "national ideology," in addition to the social and genetic engineering already in the works. Shades of Huxley's *Brave New World*!

History bears irrefutable witness to the self-evident truth that no harmony is possible between the individual and society where either seeks aggrandisement at the expense of the other. The mutual need for each other, for mutual completion and fulfillment, is frustrated if one seeks to devour the other. Invariably, the end result is material and spiritual impoverishment, stagnation and death, for both individual and society. The equation is infallible, whether the nation concerned is eastern or western, although Lee Kuan Yew pretends that Confucius would have sanctioned the outrages he has perpetrated in Singapore. Which, as those who decline to traduce history for political ends will appreciate, would be an unwarranted insult to the memory of that venerable figure, whose proverbial wisdom laid primary emphasis on character-building enhancement of the human spirit and of social mores—not their mutilation.

The tree is known by its fruits. The supremacy of the state over the individual which those inclined to totalitarianism always propound has invariably meant, in practice, the immolation of the individual at the altar of an impersonal, faceless, and conscienceless deity, sanctified by the grandiose term: "the organized community." But the voices which issue from the iron throat are recognisably those of the political élite in power. They spell out the implacable social "imperatives" which override the rights of the individual. And in the name of these imperious mandates, the social juggernaut driven by political roughnecks grinds the hapless individual under its wheels. Francis Seow was one such victim. Another was Chia Thye Poh, whose lengthy incarceration has been compared to the experience of Nelson Mandela. It would be invidious to mention others by name, for either their spirits have been broken, or they remain subject to tongue-tying restrictions.

Seow survived the ordeal. Because he is a free man outside Singapore, he becomes the first ex-detainee to place on record the ordeal of arrest and detention without trial in Singapore. In doing so, he has rendered a signal service to all Singaporeans, as indeed to all sane and humane men and women everywhere. But they must know that he will have to pay a heavy price for his pains in the shape of repeated or fresh calumnies and of rearrest should he choose to return to Singapore. Indeed, this will be in addition to the price he has already paid for raising his voice against Moloch. It is a rare kind of courage which would take on so perverse and formidable an adversary.

I am able personally to confirm the brutal fact that exile, for whatever reason, uprooted from one's entire milieu of life, culture, and career, from friends and relatives, is, to put it bluntly—unremitting spiritual agony. Nonetheless, an ordeal certainly preferable to the *individual as No. 2* suffering systematic asphyxiation by *society as No. 1*. And writing this foreword, I am cruelly aware that I am, in effect, finally and irretrievably burning my boats with my country and a people whom I love and served over the greater part of a lifetime. But what would you? Exile, pensionless to boot, at least ensures the survival of the integrity of the person.

The story, Francis Seow tells, is a grisly symptom of a high-seated (rather than deep-seated) political malaise afflicting Singapore. History will indict Singapore's *éminence grise*, now Senior Minister and Secretary-General of the ruling party, Lee Kuan Yew, as the source and bearer of what, despite transient and misleading appearances to the contrary must, without radical political surgery, turn out to be a terminal condition.

I may be wrong in believing that the point of no return has already been passed, for currently it does appear that a population rendered politically comatose over the years will be unable to bestir itself sufficiently—apart from surreptitiously immobilizing subway trains by stuffing well-chewed chewing gum into their doors—to cancel the blank cheque it has given to the Singapore government.

However, I am also aware that we live in times when reality keeps exploding in the faces of the experts. It has more than once exploded in mine, not to speak of Francis Seow's. There is no guarantee that one day it will not explode in Lee's own face, or in the faces of those who will inherit his creed and style of power. Gorbachev, Ceausescu, and Honecker are only the more visible among the many who, in the very recent past, succumbed to invisible, vast, and powerful undercurrents which suddenly surfaced, ensuing in utterly unforeseen, convulsive change in the sprawling Soviet Empire and eastern Europe, leaving all the world's normally voluble geopolitical pundits and pontiffs flummoxed.

Some believe that the necessary inspiration for surgical intervention to rescue Singapore from terminal risk might arise from within the republic's own undoubtedly intelligent establishment. A good number of professionals and civil servants *do know*, and will privately acknowledge—looking over the shoulder, of course—what has gone grievously wrong with the once promising Singapore experiment. In the strictest privacy, they readily admit that, if there is any country in Southeast Asia which, by virtue of economic success and of probably the best educated population in Asia after Japan, can afford a more relaxed style of government, tolerant of free expression and dissent—that country is Singapore. They *appreciate* that the people of Singapore are certainly intelligent enough to discern where their best interests lie, and run no risk of falling prey to rabble-rousing politicians with easy panaceas and quick fixes.

Indeed, they vividly *recall* that an earlier, less educated generation of Singaporeans had, after listening to open public arguments and debates, repeatedly rebuffed at the polls slogan-shouting demagogues who clearly did not know the social and economic priorities of a small island nation with absolutely no natural resources to boast of, dependent on neighbouring Malaysia even for its water, and entirely dependent on the stability of export markets for comfortable living. Finally, they *know* that the source of the overweening authoritarianism—so entirely contra-indicated by one of the most vibrant and successful economies in Asia—issues from the increasingly obsessive fixations and bizarre values of one man—Lee Kuan Yew.

But it remains to be seen whether knowledge goes with moral courage and the will to action. I confess that, with every passing year, I have come to fear that the point of no return has already been reached and passed. For Singapore's *grey eminence* lords it over the republic from the top of a tower of undeniable previous achievement. He had been the superb captain of a superb team which had led a highly responsive and intelligent population out of a savage and sterile political wilderness into outstanding economic success and internationally recognized nationhood.

Today every member of that superb team has been eased out of power and influence in the name of political self-renewal, while Lee himself has ensured that he presides, as Secretary-General of the ruling party, not as he once did, over equals who had elected him, but over a government cabinet and a judiciary made up entirely of his appointees or nominees. In relation to old guard leaders, Lee had been no more than *primus inter pares*. He had perforce to deal with his equals, and they were fully capable of speaking their minds. Once, in the early days of the PAP, in sheer exasperation, I myself had responded to him with a four-letter word and thought no more about it.

Today, Lee no longer deals with his equals, but with his chosen appointees, who did not earn power the hard way, but had it conferred on them. They are highly qualified men, no doubt, but nobody expects them to possess the gumption to talk back to the increasingly self-righteous know-all that Lee has become. Further, the bread of those who conform is handsomely buttered. Keep your head down and you could enjoy one of the highest living standards in Asia. Raise it and you could lose a job, a home, and be harassed by the Internal Security Department or the Inland Revenue Department, or by both, as happened to Francis Seow.

Nonetheless, one must hope, even against hope, that the daunting challenge is not evaded by intellectually honest and spiritually courageous members of the Singapore establishment. The inevitable alternative is clearly the abortion of what began as the Singapore miracle. An abortion *and* a treachery. For not many societies return whole from the graveyard of elementary human rights and decencies.

Admittedly, Lee is right in talking of the remarkable economic transformation we wrought in Singapore, an achievement at once collective and individual. The people of Singapore well deserve the material success for which they worked so hard. But, all the same, they have reaped a baleful harvest. Lee bakes a bitter bread. The relish of greater material well-being gives way to the acrid taste of ill-being along other equally vital, if less tangible dimensions, beyond the gauge of the GNP, the only measuring rod Lee knows. As his career progressed, he revealed, in increasing measure, enormous blind spots.

"Transformation" is quite the wrong word for qualitative aberrations which have occurred in the noneconomic areas of life in Singapore. On reading Seow's manuscript, the word which leaps to mind is "transmogrification," or the grotesque metamorphosis that has overtaken the perception and treatment of the individual in the republic.

My thoughts go back to my own arrest by the British colonial authorities in Singapore in the fifties. I have already indicated that my experience as a political prisoner under a British colonial administration had nothing in common with what Seow went through. I can come to only one conclusion. The colonial Special Branch were saints compared to Lee Kuan Yew's Internal Security outfit. The end result of our struggle for political freedom and independence turns out to be not a progression in terms of respect for human dignity, but a surreptitious regression into barbarity.

Few can appreciate how painful a contemplation from the sidelines Seow's account is for those like me who had spent a good part of our active lives helping to launch modern Singapore. Contrary to Lee's pretensions, Singapore is not only his baby. It's our baby as well. But under Lee's exclusive charge, the miracle child suffocates today beneath a pile of heavy swaddling. Small wonder therefore that a disturbing number of Singaporeans have chosen to emigrate from Lee's utopia to less strait-jacketed places like Australia, New Zealand and Canada. According to government figures, the exodus reached 4,000 families in 1989, around 16,000 people. The London *Economist* observed:

His (Lee's) statistically-inclined government may well reflect that, proportionally, the exodus from Singapore, which faces no threat from China, was not far below the flight from Hong Kong last year.[1]

Lee himself appears to be the only person who does not seem to have got the message. In his National Day Rally speech in 1989, he affected incredulity—even turning lachrymose—that so many Singaporeans should choose to opt out of his paradise. Nobody present could summon the gumption to tell him that to discover the reason why, all that he need do was look into the mirror.

For Lee's entire approach to government pointedly ignores some crucial ingredients of nation-building. Full employment, well-fed digestive tracks, clean streets, and decent homes are not the be-all and end-all of good government. They are only a necessary beginning—an essential foundation from which to aspire for greater human ends. Like people elsewhere, Singaporeans also have keen nonmaterial appetites, the satisfaction of which will not brook permanent denial. For these are fundamental urges which return after every banishment.

A new and better educated generation, increasingly open to the great winds of change blowing all over the world, is bound to intensify the search for an invigorating image of desire and hope, a liberating political formula, a more satisfying life scheme and scene than are available under the present pervasive system of coercion and control. Also, in this day and age, ideas and hopes increasingly scorn border check-points and censorship laws.

A society burdened by a multitude of prohibitions must come to suffer that stifling of innovation and creativity which comes of excessive regulation. Singaporeans today have to memorise an exhaustive list of prohibitions. But they are without a comparable list of what they are free to do.

Certainly citizens of a civilized community need to cultivate that sense of order and discipline which has served Singapore's economic success so admirably thus far. But where a sense of social responsibility goes unnourished by an equally vivid sense of individual rights, and of participation and involvement in the entire

---

1. *The Economist*, March 10–16, 1990.

political and legislative process, there the human spirit is bound to shrivel under the deadening touch of authoritarianism. Indeed, what has become increasingly evident to Singaporeans is Big Brother's total lack of trust and confidence in the good sense and judgment of his citizens. Hence the hectoring speeches by ministers, and worse, the ubiquitous voice of the oracle telling everybody else, including government ministers who perform under his watchful eyes, what is good for them.

The obvious danger is that if ever Singapore is faced with a serious economic downturn, as is entirely possible given the republic's overwhelming dependence on increasingly volatile export markets, the current disturbing brain drain may be expected to gush into a massive exodus. And that would be a sad end for what began as the most promising experiment in socioeconomic growth in Southeast Asia.

Lest it be considered that I have revised my views about the conditions of my own detention, after having parted company with Lee Kuan Yew, I will quote here from the statement I made on behalf of the People's Action Party of Singapore at the meeting of the Bureau of the Socialist International held in London on 28–29 May 1976, with the approval of Prime Minister Lee. I said:

> In 1950 I joined the Anti-British League, an underground auxiliary of the Malayan Communist Party. I spent, in two separate spells, a total of five years in British prisons. I am not in the least bitter. Indeed, I look back nostalgically to my years of incarceration, for they were years of intensive reading and self-education. On the whole, my fellow detainees and I were well-treated. One of the few complaints we had was that the British allowed us radio sets which were doctored to receive only Radio Singapore. We wanted to listen in to Peking and Moscow as well.
>
> We were in touch, through easily bribable camp warders, with the communist underground in Singapore. We were instructed to go on a hunger strike and to protest against "ill-treatment and torture." When some of us pointed out that there was no ill-treatment and torture, our chief fellow detainee told us that "it was a revolutionary *duty* to expose the imperialists, through whatever means were available." Our anticolonial zeal being greater than our commitment to truth, we swallowed whatever qualms we had and embarked on a six-day hunger strike. It had the required effect, not upon the British—

who were quite unmoved—but as far as underground communist propaganda in Singapore was concerned, for our hunger strike was extolled as an example of our heroism and of the vileness of the imperialists. ...

I was reminded of this episode when I read the Dutch Labour Party paper about the torture of detainees. ...

I also happen to know a good deal about both prisons and detention camps in Singapore. For, soon after Lee Kuan Yew formed the first PAP Government in May 1959, I persuaded him to set up a Prisons Inquiry Commission, for I had not liked what I had seen of the demeaning conditions of imprisonment imposed by the British authorities: not on political detainees, but on convicted prisoners. For example, on the approach of a British prison officer, every convict had to kneel down on the floor, with his head down. *That* aroused my ire, and it still does, when I think of it.

I was appointed Chairman of the Prisons Inquiry Commission, which included two British academics from the University of Malaya in Singapore—the late Dr. Jean Robertson and Professor T.H. Elliott. The recommendations my Commission made, to humanise prison conditions, still form the nominal basis for the administration of prisons and detention centres in Singapore. The International Red Cross has had access to our prisoners, detainees, and places of detention. You will appreciate that the Red Cross is not allowed in several other countries, and I can confidently challenge any country in the world to boast a more efficient prison system than the one we have in Singapore.

This explains why I read with wry amusement the absurd allegations of ill-treatment, torture, and inhuman conditions in our prisons and detention centres, made by our communist united front group in Singapore, and faithfully repeated in the Dutch Labour Party paper.

Today I am obliged to eat a good number of the words I uttered in London in 1976. A humbling obligation, and therefore good for the soul. I have no difficulty, of course, reaffirming that my fellow detainees and I were well treated in British colonial centres of detention. That was a fact of direct personal experience. Not so, apparently, the conditions political detainees were subjected to in the seventies. I had then accepted, all too gullibly, that these were humane and civilised purely on the word of the powers-that-be. I was not the only credulous Singaporean to do so.

There is no better teacher than painful personal experience. I know today that in this matter, as in several others, my trust and confidence were grievously misplaced. I am certain now that if any of these detainees had brought themselves to write of their experiences as Seow has done, their accounts would not have been greatly dissimilar. If anything, going by what Seow learned from other detainees whom he had represented as legal counsel, some of them went through much worse ordeals. I can also appreciate today that the Internal Security Department has means of ensuring that detainees do not speak up during guided tours of detention centres for Red Cross representatives.

Seow's account of the horrendous process of interrogation he underwent, the freezing coldness of the soundproof interrogation room (*"The floor was like a slab of ice, which rapidly drained away the body's heat"*), an air-conditioner blower duct on the ceiling which directed a continuous and powerful cascade of cold air down at the spot where, barefooted, he was made to stand, the sudden paroxysms blasts of cold air sent him into, the total darkness save for the powerful spotlights trained on him, the obscenities, shouts, and threats he had to endure, all left me stupefied.

Sleep deprivation, for instance, is a fiendishly effective means employed by Singapore interrogators to thoroughly disorient the detainee, so that he may be suitably readied for abject "confessions" which would later be copiously presented by the government-controlled media as a "statutory declaration." One cannot think of any other country in the civilized world where "statutory declarations" exacted under duress from political prisoners are published and unabashedly palmed off on the public as gospel truths.

I found acutely disturbing the following paragraphs in the book at page 122 *et seq.*:

> As I walked through the doors of the interrogation room, a freezing coldness immediately wrapped itself around me ....
>
> I had lost all sense of time. I had been standing there under the pitiless glare of the spotlights. I felt the urge to go to the toilet. I told them. Two Gurkha guards appeared and escorted me to the toilet. Having stood almost motionless at one spot for so long I had great difficulty in walking. I found myself rooted to the ground—a term more descriptive of the reality of the situation than a mere figure of speech. My limbs were stiff all over. I was unsteady. The two Gurkha guards on either side of me supported me under my arms. I staggered out of the interrogation room, half carried by them, along the dark corridors up two flights of stairs to the ground level of Block C,

along a corridor, to a toilet located in an empty cell in Block D. I blinked at the unexpected harsh light of day. I was quite shocked. The urge to go to the toilet was forgotten for a moment. I asked one of the two Gurkhas for the time of day, ... It was 11:30 in the morning. I was astounded. I then realized that I had been standing in the interrogation room for about sixteen hours warding off questions thrown unremittingly at me. It seemed incredible to me that I could have stood at one spot, almost motionless, for that length of time. I recalled with shame that, when my detainee-clients had previously complained to me that they had been deprived of sleep and forced to stand for as long as 72 hours at a stretch, without sleep, I had great difficulty in believing them. I thought that they were exaggerating; but incredibly, I, too, was, undergoing a somewhat similar experience! ...

I noticed, too, dried sunburnt blisters peeling from the skin of both arms. I could not at first comprehend how I could have acquired them until I realized that I had been burnt by the powerful rays of those spotlights, which had also dried up the moisture in my eyes. Cold rashes had broken out all over my atrophied limbs under my clothes. Unlike many people who are sensitive to sunburn, I am susceptible to cold rashes. It was always troublesome for me whenever I had perforce to travel abroad during winter. In this instant case, as if signaled by a faithful built-in thermometer, the rashes broke out in chilling confirmation of the coldness of the room. My interrogators had swaddled themselves up in warm winter clothes and left it, time and again, whenever they could no longer withstand the wintry cold.

As a prisoner of the British, my fellow detainees and I had simply refused to be interrogated. We told our captors that we would only speak as free men. We were left alone after that. We experienced no soundproof room, no brutal interrogation and sleep deprivation for hours on end, no air-conditioner blower duct directing a powerful and continuous cascade of cold air at the spot where the barefoot detainee stood on *"a floor like a slab of ice,"* no spotlights, no threats and obscenities shouted in our ears, no absolutely solitary confinement throughout the period of detention, indeed none of the things which Mr. Seow had to undergo at the hands of the rulers of free, independent, and, professedly civilized Singapore.

After the statutory period of 21 days' solitary confinement,[2] my fellow-detainees and I were allowed to live together in camp

---

2. It suddenly dawned on me after reading Francis Seow's manuscript that the statutory limitation of 21 days on the length of solitary confinement no longer exists, either in the current Internal Security Act or in the regulations which govern the

conditions, whether in Changi Prison or, even better, on salubrious St. John's Island. Our lawyer, Lee Kuan Yew, was freely allowed to visit and talk to us, without Special Branch supervision, and to plan with us the downfall of the British colonial power. So free were we as political detainees to pursue our own interests and studies that we light-heartedly referred to our places of detention as "St. John's" University and "Changi" University.

Mr. Lee *knows* all this. It surely cannot be termed progress in freedom and humanity to arrest and treat his own political prisoners so brutally, and with far less reason than the British had to detain me and my revolutionary comrades. After all, we had made no secret of the fact that we were committed to the violent overthrow of the British colonial power. But Seow and others like him certainly did not aim to overthrow the elected government of Singapore by unconstitutional means. Even if they did, Lee and his government would still stand convicted of the kind of inhumanity of which "the perfidious British colonialists" (as we referred to them in those days) were not guilty.[3]

The government's assertion that it does not ill-treat detainees strains credulity. Seow's readers will find extraordinary (to put it mildly) Brigadier General Lee's (Lee Kuan Yew's son and Singapore's Deputy Prime Minister) statement in an interview with the BBC World Service:

> The Government does not ill-treat detainees. It does however *apply psychological pressure* [italics mine] to detainees to get to the truth of the matter ... the truth would not be known unless psychological pressure was used during interrogation.[4]

Systematic sleep deprivation, continuous interrogation over sixteen hours by strident, foul-mouthed intelligence officers, while standing barefoot in flimsy clothing on a cold cement floor in a freezing

---

accommodation and treatment of detainees. Seow's own 72 days of detention were in entirely solitary confinement apart, of course, from the unsolicited "companionship" of his interrogators. Apparently, other much longer-term detainees spent unconscionable months in solitary confinement.

3. Not always. I recall that some Chinese-speaking detainees in the same colonial period told me that they had been rather badly beaten by officers of the British Special Branch.

4. *The Straits Times*, Friday, April 22, 1988.

room under the skin-blistering and eye de-moisturising glare of spotlights, unlimited solitary confinement, are at once both *physical* and *psychological* ordeals.

Mr. Seow quotes to potent effect a comment by Jerome A. Cohen, a prominent legal representative of Asia Watch, while on a visit to Singapore at the time. Mr. Cohen

> ... found deeply disturbing both the use of psychological torture and what he called a pervasive Singaporean, if not Asian view that "if you haven't hit somebody, it isn't torture." Psychological disorientation is evil whether it happens in South Africa, the Soviet Union, China, Singapore or the United States. Yet here they seem almost proud of their psychological tactics—of breaking down the defenses of people in captivity. They need to be more sensitive to the definition of what constitutes cruel and unusual punishment.

One can understand why the Singapore government hurriedly withdrew its initial offer (made inadvertently by junior ministers when Big Brother happened to be out of town) to appoint a judicial Commission of Inquiry to examine public allegations of ill-treatment by nine ex-detainees in April 1988. They were rearrested instead, and it came as no surprise that some of them duly signed, while in renewed custody, "statutory declarations" withdrawing their earlier allegations, and asserting that they had not been ill-treated. Much more convenient, certainly, for Lee and his government, than a judicial Commission of Inquiry, which would publicly examine and pronounce on charges made from the witness stand by free men and women, subject to no constraints but those of conscience and of cross-examination by defence and prosecution alike.

The circumstances of Seow's arrest and the subsequent ordeal of interrogation and detention provide occasion not only for grave disquiet over the brutal mistreatment of detainees. (They certainly put paid to any continued pretense on Lee Kuan Yew's part that he walks in the company of civilised statesmen.) It raises another question—perhaps the most crucial one—in my own mind. I may explain, even if the effort proves, as it certainly will, an unflattering commentary on some of my own past judgments of person and events.

I had once publicly supported the need for the Internal Security Act when the democratically elected PAP Government was engaged in a life and death struggle against a murderous communist united front movement, committed to the violent overthrow of constitutional government. In subsequent years, I had continued to believe that the Act was justified given the volatile geopolitical milieu in which Singapore had to survive. Never had it occurred to me that the PAP government was capable of the gross abuse of the draconian powers conferred by the Act. And never was I more wholly wrong, and my confidence so grievously misplaced.

What an unconscionably long time some people take to learn that power really does corrupt, especially its exercise when placed outside the purview of an impartial third party—like an independent judiciary. No statesman was ever more resoundingly correct than Thomas Jefferson when he warned:

> In questions of power, let no more be heard of confidence in man, but bind him down from mischief by the chains of the constitution.[5]

Alas, because he was not stopped in time, Lee Kuan Yew has proceeded to alter the laws to bind down the judiciary and the media instead.

The crucial question is this. What internal or external dangers threaten Singapore so gravely today to justify the need of a law like the Internal Security Act, allowing, as it does, indefinite detention without trial? None that anyone acquainted with the current political and economic situation in Southeast Asia can think of. None at all that cannot be more effectively dealt with by sensible democratic political process, under the ordinary laws of the land.

There is no longer a communist insurrectionary movement in Malaysia committed to the violent overthrow of lawfully constituted governments in Singapore and Malaysia. There is no communist united front movement left in Singapore. By all accounts, communist potential in the area has been decisively scotched by economic, political, and geopolitical developments. The Communist Party of Malaysia, a sad and bedraggled relic of a once truly formidable movement, which it took all the military and political skills of the British and subsequent Malaysian governments to defeat, finally laid down their arms on December 2, 1989, after signing peace

---

5. Kentucky Resolutions, November 1798.

agreements with the Malaysian and Thai governments, and thus brought to a formal close 41 years of armed conflict.

When this was announced, the first Prime Minister of Malaysia, the late Tungku Abdul Rahman, promptly and publicly recalled the pledge he had given in the free Malaysian parliament to the effect that the internal security laws providing for the arrest and detention without trial of suspected subversives were directed solely at the communist insurrectionary movement, and would be repealed once the insurrection was overcome. He therefore called for the outright abolition of the Internal Security Act since the communist threat to constitutional government had ceased to exist. Not so Lee Kuan Yew whom the London *Sunday Telegraph* reported as saying: "I don't see myself repealing it."[6] Do Confucian conformity and stability require powers of detention without trial?

In Singapore, by the early seventies, we had decisively debunked and defused a once powerful communist united front movement, which is no longer in evidence. I should know, because I was right out in the front line of that battle, among the foot soldiers, in constant danger of life and limb, leading the free trade unions—now, under Lee's surrogates, no longer free. The economic, social, and administrative successes we registered clearly do not provide fertile soil for violent insurgency of any kind. With the notable exception of Singapore, everywhere else economic success, even of much less magnitude than we can boast of, has invariably been accompanied by more relaxed political climates and styles. Not so under Lee.

Success has been followed by an even further tightening of the screws. Indeed, even the insurrectionary communists of the fifties and sixties, with their unconstitutional resort to armed violence, civil riots, and strikes, were dealt with under laws and custodial treatment more benign and civilised than were constitutional law-abiding dissenters like Seow, and other social workers and professionals arrested and detained in Singapore in recent times. Neither were they obliged to produce abject statutory declarations "confessing" their numerous "misdeeds." Much can be said of the defects and shortcomings of previous British colonial regimes in Singapore.

---

6. *The Sunday Telegraph*, 28 October 1989.

But these did not include the systematic and ruthless crushing of the human spirit at which Lee's Internal Security boys excel. One can appreciate now why he proudly refers to them as "professionals."

Only recently, yet another striking departure from decent civilized practice occurred. Detention without trial is no longer subject to judicial review in Singapore. The government on January 25, 1989, amended the Internal Security Act to place its powers of detention without trial beyond challenge in the courts, with retrospective effect into the bargain. And nobody will ever know what takes place behind the walls in the soundproof, freezing rooms of the Whitley Detention Centre, from which issue "statutory declarations" by political prisoners abjectly admitting to a variety of antigovernment offences.

Thus, by means the venerable Confucius would never have condoned, Lee hopes to enforce in his ideal city state the Confucian conformity and respect for authority he so much admires. In these circumstances, it will be a rash Singaporean who, knowing the grave risks he is likely to incur, will dare even to murmur dissent. But alarm bells are already ringing in the night. As already observed, internationally mobile Singaporeans are leaving "the Singapore Miracle" in disturbing numbers to seek their fortunes in more congenial pastures, where they can breathe more freely.

The road to perdition gets rougher and spikier as one goes down it. Relentlessly downhill has forged the predatory road with a vengeance, especially in the last few years. Consider the spate of repressive legislation enacted in a brief three to four years.

Parliament is converted into "a political mine-field," as a pained and shocked Dr. Toh Chin Chye, the founder chairman of the People's Action Party, observed in 1987. A mine-field which blew opposition leader J.B. Jeyaretnam out of the legislative chamber and made certain that he would not be able to contest another election for at least five years. An even worse fate has befallen Francis Seow.

Parliamentary select committees, by hallowed Westminster convention serious and sedate forums to consider public or professional reservations about government bills tabled in Parliament, are transformed into criminal courtrooms where a fiercely prosecuting, browbeating prime minister puts startled witnesses in the witness box for gruelling cross-examination. This was what happened to Francis Seow, the then president of the Law Society, and to members of the Society's governing council. Subsequent legislation ensured that Seow could no longer remain president, and that the Law Society would never again be able to comment publicly on bills before the legislature, on the ground that they were beyond the limited professional competence of the Society. The curious theory was trotted out that politics is only for politicians, not for professional bodies, even though their members are citizens with legitimate concerns about matters of public interest.

Draconian laws were passed to bring to heel foreign journals and newspapers which were critical of what they considered bizarre goings-on in the republic. The *Asian Wall Street Journal* and the *Far Eastern Economic Review* were accused of "meddling in domestic politics," and their free circulation was drastically curtailed. They were told that they were not reporting Singapore to Singaporeans "fairly," as if that were the role of the free international media.

Lee forgets that in the colonial past, his British predecessors were not knocked off balance by free reporting on Singapore by the foreign media, even though they had to deal with an obstreperous population and its equally restive politicians who included, for instance, rambunctious types like Lee Kuan Yew and Devan Nair. In particular, he forgets that his own international reputation as a staunch anticolonial freedom fighter owed a great deal to the free and open manner in which the foreign media covered him and his party's activities.

One could go on *ad lib ad infinitum* about the road Lee Kuan Yew has chosen to travel. My immediate purpose, however, is to paint as vividly as possible, with a few basic strokes, the political context in which Francis Seow's book should be read. I hope I have managed to do this with at least a minimum of adequacy. For there have been other detainees in Singapore whose predicament was, if anything, worse than Seow's was.

There is, for example, Chia Thye Poh. First arrested on October 29, 1966 under the ISA, Chia was banished on May 16, 1989 to the off-shore pleasure island of *Sentosa*. One cannot improve on what

Christopher Lockwood of the London *Sunday Telegraph* noted:

> Exile on Sentosa is a diabolically-crafted alternative. Who can take a prisoner of conscience seriously on a holiday island? With Chia out of jail, he [Chia] fears, world disapproval of his detention will simply evaporate.[7]

But Nelson Mandela was unconditionally freed by President F.W. de Klerk of South Africa—free to begin shaking the evil apartheid system down to its foundations. Chia Thye Poh is incapable of shaking anything. So why this extraordinary vindictiveness?

I recall Lee Kuan Yew once quoting, in euphoric mood, Churchill's resonant words:

> "In war, resolution. In defeat, defiance. In victory, magnanimity."[8]

Lee and his comrades-in-arms were resolute in all the political battles we fought in the early years against the colonialists, the communists, the communalists, and the crooks. But Lee has never yet known defeat. So far he has met only victories, in all of which he has shown himself incredibly vicious. Unlike Churchill, who, incidentally, could not boast anything comparable to Lee's two firsts and a star for distinction in Cambridge, Lee misses human greatness by several million light years.

As was inevitable for one who, in arrogant contempt for soulcraft as a vital ingredient of successful statecraft, recklessly opted for an errant orbit, traced in benighted times past by the trajectory of Moloch.

Lee's major justification for his policies is the example of Singapore's remarkable economic success. But what will haunt generations to come in Singapore and the Southeast Asian region generally are his even more monumental failures. Well did the Bard observe:

> The evil that men do lives after them;
> The good is oft interr'd with their bones.[9]

Ultimately, his most unpardonable failure is the crass betrayal of the ideal which launched the People's Action Party into political

---

7. *The Sunday Telegraph*, 28 October 1989.
8. Winston Churchill, *The Second World War*.
9. *Julius Caesar*, Act III, sc.2, 19.

orbit—that of an equal, multiracial, democratic society which would banish from its midst, for ever and a day, invidious notions of ethnic or religious majorities and minorities. In Singapore there would be no majorities and minorities. There would only be Singaporeans. This was the flaming aspiration on which Lee rode to power on the crest of revolutionary fervour. Today he has defiled the social atmosphere of Singapore with the sordid evil of ethno-centrism, which he had vowed to eradicate, in my company and in that of countless other comrades in the common struggle against colonialism, communalism, and communism. But this is not the place to expatiate on this particular piece of treachery. I will deal with it in my own book.

Lee is gifted with a brilliant brain and an eloquent tongue. But the capricious gods omitted to equip him with the saving grace of that essential wisdom which makes for true greatness. And Singapore thereby missed the infinitely more potent miracle of the political and spiritual success it might so easily have provided, as a practical, living demonstration to the other unhappy, struggling, heterogenous nations of Southeast Asia, not merely of singular economic achievement, but also of the eminent viability of a free, open, sane, and equal multiracial democracy, worthy at once of economic, political, and moral emulation.

As things are, one can only wonder how much longer successful economic performance and a loutish political style can sleep together in the same bed. While one dreams of electronic paradises to come, the other enacts, in political nightmares, vengeful vendettas against foes real or imaginary, mostly the latter. Alas, both must perish in fatal embrace, on the same bed.

C.V. DEVAN NAIR

Acknowledgements

I would be wanting in gratitude if I fail to register the valuable contribution of several persons towards the completion of this book, foremost amongst whom is Miss Doris Gwee Puay Lan, formerly of my law firm. In addition to her onerous work, she cheerfully assumed secretarial duties by transcribing the minutiae of my arbitrary arrest and detention under the Internal Security Act, Cap. 143, after my release from Whitley Detention Centre, Singapore, thus enabling, me over the ensuing months, to mould and shape the form of this manuscript. In this regard, my sons, Ashleigh and André, encouraged me in the prosecution of this undertaking, and gently prodded me into renewed vigour whenever I showed signs of flagging. They shared my feelings that I should tell my side of this melancholy story to the people of Singapore and, through them, to the world. Deprived overnight of accustomed secretarial services, my daughter Annalisa, who was providentially present in America, mitigated the loss of those services by steering me through computer esoterica and overseeing this manuscript through to print.

To C.V. Devan Nair, the former president of Singapore, I am doubly indebted, firstly, for his chivalrous, public defence of me by nailing the base and palpably untrue governmental allegations to the counter, incurring thereby the implacable wrath of a political genius gone awry. There are, regrettably, very few Singaporeans with that rare courage and intellectual, let alone political, honesty to call a spade a spade; wherefore a litigious prime minister dragged a reluctant litigant into a libel suit in the Singapore High Court. Secondly, I am further indebted to him for his authoritative and eloquent foreword.

This story could not possibly have been written in Singapore. I was fortunate to have been invited as a human rights monitor at a propitious moment by the Human Rights Watch to celebrate the tenth anniversary of its founding in New York. I was given official permission by the director, Internal Security Department—a prerequisite of my release from detention—to leave Singapore, but only just.

During my absence abroad, events unfolded ominously in Singapore which were clearly not conducive to my political or physical welfare. The ceremonial opening of parliament (of which I was a non-constituency member) was deliberately delayed until I was disqualified from taking my parliamentary seat by virtue of hasty convictions for alleged income tax offenses obtained against me in my absence and in the absence of my counsel. But, overarching this obscene rush to judgment was the prosecutor's perverse application to stay one single charge, and adjourning it, *sine die*, pending my return to Singapore. He then publicly announced his demand for a custodial sentence, in stark usurpation of judicial power and authority, a serious departure from traditional practice and procedure!

In the circumstances, I opted for the tranquil ivied halls of Yale University in New Haven, Connecticut rather than an economically sparkling island paradise, where a capricious prime minister and his government seemed hell-bent on keeping me out of parliament, and in gaol. This noetic sanctuary provided me with the unique opportunity to complete this manuscript. For this coign of vantage, I am forever thankful to the Human Rights Watch, New York and, more particularly, to its executive director, Aryeh Neier, and deputy director, Kenneth Roth, and to Asia Watch's executive director, Miss Sidney Jones. They have been true friends in need and in deed! Among the other persons who have, in one way or another, facilitated the passage of this book, I would be remiss if I fail to mention my longtime friends, Lee Yang Kwang, and Teo Kwee Chuan.

At the end of my fellowship at Yale University, I moved on to Harvard University, Cambridge, Massachusetts, where I was able to revise and update this book in its final present form, not without the experienced help of my charming editor, Ms. Kay Mansfield.

Last, but by no means the least, I owe an especial debt of gratitude to Professor James C. Scott, Eugene Meyer Professor of Political Science at Yale University, for his great sense and even greater sensibility of my émigré situation there in the spring of 1989, as well as for a splendidly perceptive review of my manuscript. In this connexion, I also owe a similar debt of gratitude to Mrs. Margaret John, Amnesty International coordinator for Malaysia and Singapore, for befriending and guiding my sister Clare in her quest for my release from Lee Kuan Yew's prison, and for her compassionate review of this manuscript.

Map 1 *Singapore in Southeast Asia*

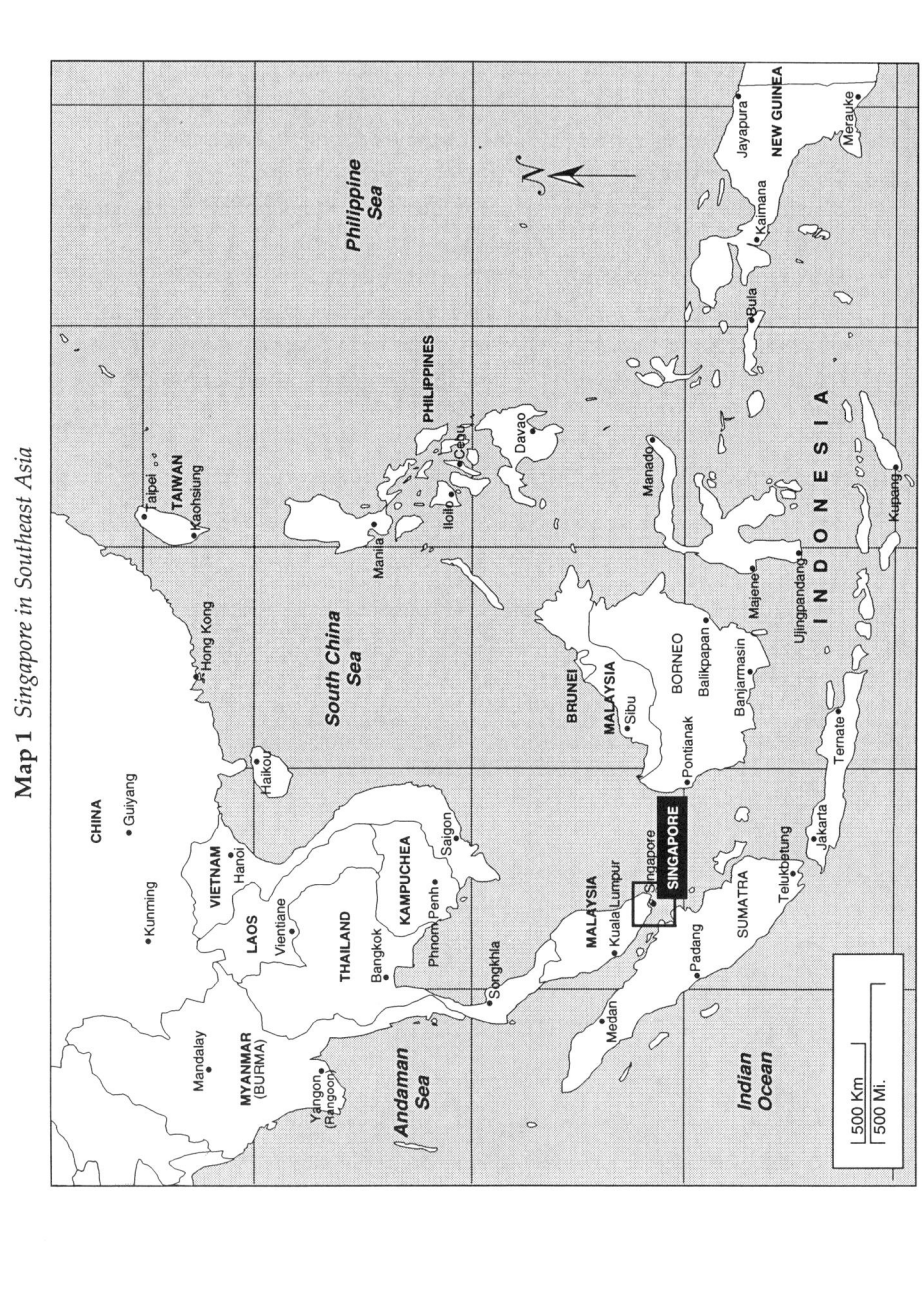

Map 2 *The main Island of Singapore*

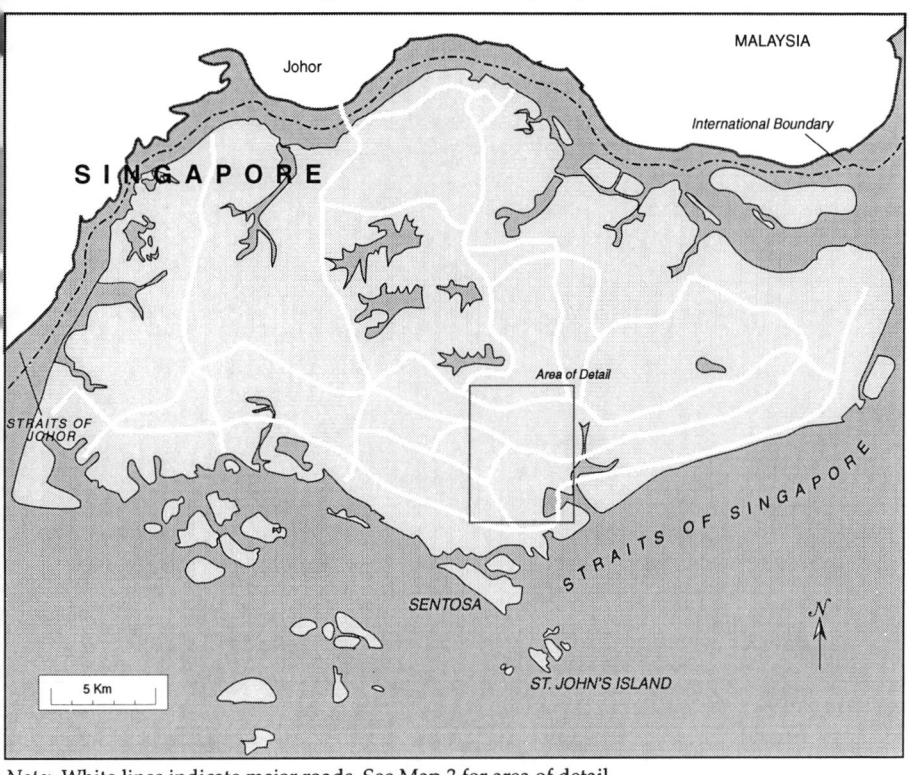

Note: White lines indicate major roads. See Map 3 for area of detail.

Map 3 *Area of detail: downtown Singapore*

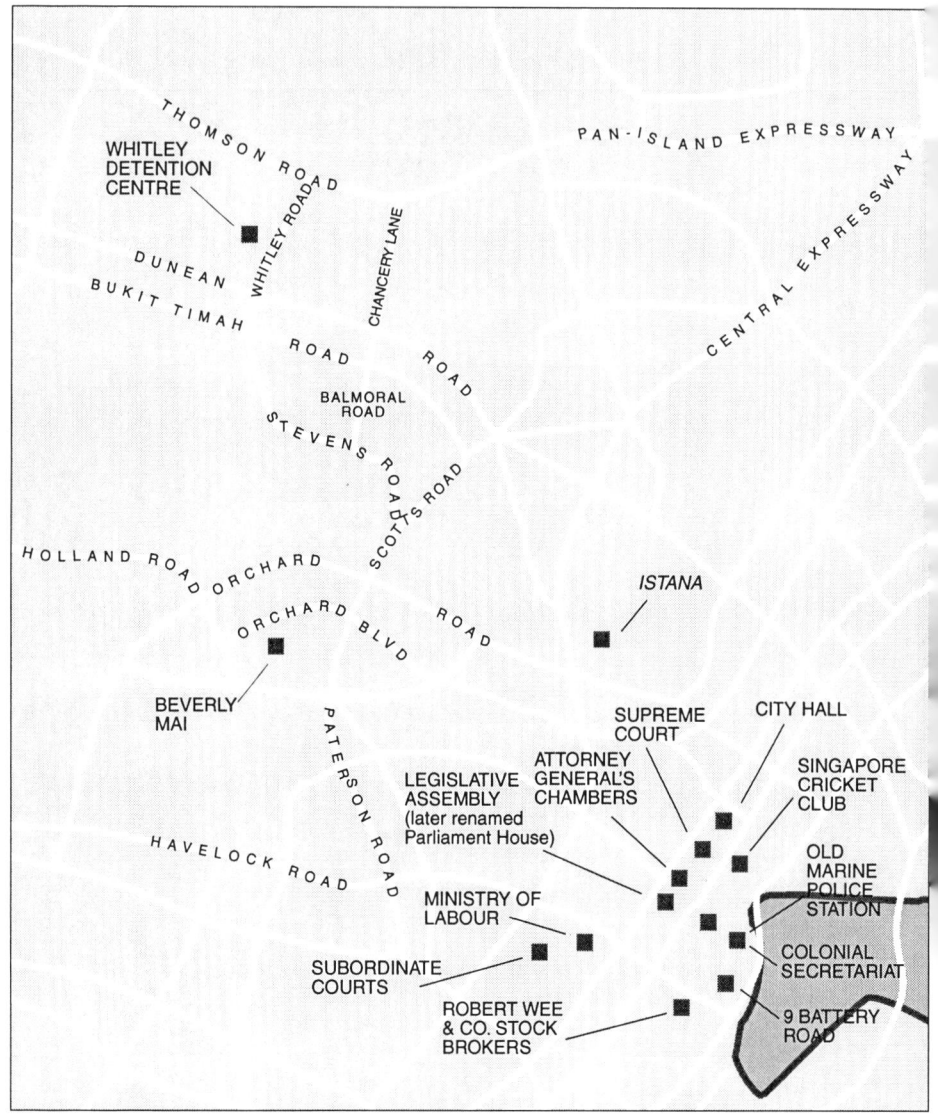

Note: See Map 2 for area's location on Island of Singapore.

1

An Historical Background

> We are blind until we see,
> That in the human plan
> Nothing is worth the making
> If it does not make the man.
>
> Why build these cities glorious
> If man unbuilded goes?
> In vain we build the world, unless
> The builder also grows.
>
> —Edwin Markham, *Man-Making*

On January 29, 1819, escorted by an armed flotilla, an English statesman and visionary, Sir Thomas Stamford Raffles, sailed on the vessel *Indiana* into the tranquil waters of an unprepossessing island at the southernmost tip of the Malay peninsula and, from the deck of his vessel, saw beyond the rat-infested mud flats, swamps, scrubs, and hilly jungles its geostrategic importance. At the time, the island was inhabited by a few Malay fishermen and even fewer Chinese traders. From a thriving port in ancient times, *Temasek*, as it was then known, had declined over the centuries into an occasional haunt of pirates, who preyed upon the trading vessels that plied the surrounding seas. Raffles envisioned the island as a key maritime interchange between Europe and Asia and as a seat of learning, which would attract peoples from far and wide to its shores.

On February 6, 1819, he acquired the island as an outpost for the East India Company from the Sultan of Johore, whose southerly sultanate included tenuous sway over the island of Singapore—the Lion City.

The dispute between the Dutch and the English in Europe had ended, and they marked out between them their spheres of influence in the Far East. From thenceforth, the English would confine their activities to and on peninsular Malaya whilst the Dutch would be left the whole of what is now known as the Indonesian archipelago.

Peace reigned over the area. Attracted by its relative stability and tranquillity and encouraged by British overlords, peoples from the neighbouring countries flocked to the island to seek fame and fortune. Trade flourished. And the population rapidly increased.

In 1826, the Settlement of Malacca and the Prince of Wales Island—better known as Penang and Province Wellesley on the peninsula—were surrendered by the East India Company to the British Crown. The Crown merged them into the Straits Settlements with the main seat of government ensconced in Singapore under a governor who, in addition thereto, exerted great influence over the several Malay sultanates on the peninsula.

World War I did not affect the Straits Settlements or the Malay Peninsula adversely. However, the outbreak of World War II, followed by the Pacific war with Japan in 1941, changed irrevocably the entire situation. Japanese military forces overran British Malaya and captured the so-called impregnable fortress of Singapore. Elsewhere across the Pacific, Japanese armed forces cut a wide swathe of victories, and hitherto seemingly awesome colonial empires crumbled. The landscape of Asia was changed forever.

At the end of the hostilities in 1945, the Straits Settlements ceased to exist as a political entity. Singapore was severed from it. It became a crown colony. Malacca and Penang became part of the short-lived Malayan Union, which bestowed equal political rights and common citizenship on the Chinese and the other races, but, because of Malay hostility towards the Union, a federation of all the Malay States in the peninsula took its place.

In 1955, the United Kingdom government introduced a partially elected legislature in Singapore, but real power still remained with the governor. Elections were held. The Labour Party, as the largest single party returned, was asked to form the government. Its Jewish leader, David Saul Marshall, a flamboyant criminal lawyer of Iraqi origin with a mercurial temperament, formed the Labour Front government, a coalition with the Malayan-based UMNO-MCA Alliance. A new left-wing party, a unified front of social democrats and pro-communist elements known as the People's Action Party (PAP) which was launched in 1954, captured four seats in the newly constituted legislature. Its leader and spokesman was Harry Lee Kuan Yew, a cold, calculating young Chinese lawyer of rising reputation, who, covered with academic laurels, had recently returned from Cambridge University, England.

In 1959, Singapore was granted limited self-government with a fully elected legislature with full powers to run its own internal affairs, save on matters of foreign policy and defence, (which included internal security) which remained in the hands of the British government as expressed through the governor. In June that year, the general election saw the PAP under Harry Lee Kuan Yew returned with an overwhelming majority to form the government. But Lee Kuan Yew ostentatiously refused to take office unless and until all his pro-communist colleagues, who had been detained without trial by the Labour Front government under the Preservation of Public Security Ordinance (PPSO) (a law enabling the government to detain persons, without trial, for subversive activities) had been unconditionally released from prison. A number of them were accordingly released.

Amongst them was C.V. Devan Nair, who was destined to become the future president of the Republic of Singapore. However, his tenure as such was to prove as uneasy as it was short-lived. He was a founder-member of the PAP and a trusted confidant of Harry Lee Kuan Yew. And, until he fell out with him, enjoyed considerable influence over government policy directions.

In 1961, the inevitable PAP split occurred; the breakaway faction, calling itself the *Barisan Sosialis* (Socialist Front), joined the ranks of the opposition. They comprised many of the selfsame persons for whom Harry Lee had so pretentiously refused to pick up the reins of government, unless they were released from prison.

And whom he was to arrest and put back behind bars with no trace of guilt or irony.

In August 1963, notwithstanding internal opposition to merger, Singapore became a constituent state within the Federation of Malaysia. Early in February that same year, the Internal Security Council, (consisting of the representatives of the governments of Singapore, Malaya, and Great Britain) had ordered the arrest and detention of over a hundred dissidents, including leading opposition *Barisan Sosialis* members of parliament and trade union activists, "to safeguard national defence and the security of Singapore and the other territories of Malaysia."[1] The mass arrests eased the entry of Singapore into the Federation of Malaysia and crippled a formidable parliamentary opposition. It does not require much imagination to fathom the posture adopted by the Singapore representatives, of whom Lee Kuan Yew was one, at that fateful Internal Security Council meeting.

Under the new constitutional arrangements, the powers hitherto exercised by the governor were transferred to the federal government. But Singapore shrewdly retained for itself certain powers relating to, among other things, finance, education, labour, and communications. This union with Malaya, which was intended "to endure for the next hundred years," was doomed to failure from its very inception owing to the political psyche and ambition of several leading personalities on either side of the causeway. It was a troubled union.

In over zealously promoting Singapore's political philosophy of union with Malaysia, Lee clashed repeatedly with the federal government. Given his abrasive political style, he appeared fractious, belligerent, and insultingly intolerant and provocative in his dealings with federal ministers, which seriously offended the sensitivity of the Malay people. It was not long before tension built on political tension seriously threatened the stability and integrity of the new Federation.

The benign and princely Prime Minister of Malaysia, Tungku Abdul Rahman Putra al-Haj, intervened. Rather than yielding to the

---

1. See *Singapore Year Book*, 1963.

strident cries of the Malay *ultras* to detain Lee under the Internal Security Act for instigating and inciting communal unrest, he decided to boot Lee and Singapore out of the Federation. British Prime Minister Harold Wilson had apparently warned the Tungku that the British government would not take it too kindly if Lee were arrested and detained. Lee later rather overstated the situation: "Mr. Wilson who is a personal friend cannot see me languishing in jail for ever."[2] Thus Singapore became a sovereign and independent nation.

The PAP government opted for a Westminster-style of republican government, with a president as constitutional head of state, within the Commonwealth acknowledging Queen Elizabeth II of Great Britain as Head of the Commonwealth of Nations. It was feared at the time that Singapore would have great difficulty in charting its newly-independent course in the world of nations, given its insignificant size of 225 square miles, the loss of its natural hinterland, and a dearth of natural resources. All it had then was its 1,864,000 people[3] of diverse races and its unique geostrategic position. Notwithstanding those disadvantages, the people of Singapore, coupling courage and determination with foresight and imagination, worked hard under capable leadership to transform the island into a towering economic miracle of Asia.

The PAP government under Harry Lee Kuan Yew has been overwhelmingly returned to power in successive general elections, a political feat probably without parallel anywhere else in the world. Its very success has now turned upon itself. Gone are the days of the open debate or argument to win and retain the hearts and minds of the people. Its long tenure in office has bred an intolerance of the common man and contempt for his opinion and viewpoint. And bred in the durable leader an omniscience, that only he knows what is best for the people, reinforced by his boast that his party and government have collected into itself seemingly all the best brains available in Singapore. He brooks no opposition. Opposition *per se* is a luxury that Singapore cannot afford; but opposition within the parameters laid down by Harry Lee is tolerated, with just one little

---

2. TV Singapura, 14 August 1965 broadcast.
3. *Singapore Year Book* 1965.

snag—the goal posts keep being moved! Democracy has given way to the autocracy of Harry Lee Kuan Yew, which is now masquerading as modern-day Confucianism.

The growth of the island over the years has exceeded even the prodigal imaginations of its founder, Sir Thomas Stamford Raffles. Singapore is today *the* busiest seaport in the world. It has *the* finest international airport. And, notwithstanding oil crises, it is Asia's premier oil refining centre—third largest in the world after Houston and Rotterdam, which is no mean feat considering it does not produce a single drop of oil. Towering buildings reach for the skies. The broad, tree-lined avenues are spectacularly clean. There is no filth. There is no squalor. No strewn litter or garbage offend the eye. It is a garden city. Everything is clean. Everything works. Telecommunications are among the best in the world. Singapore's orderliness and efficiency are legendary. Its people enjoy the second highest income *per capita* in Asia after Japan. And yet, overhanging the dazzling show-piece of cleanliness, progress and efficiency, a climate of fear enshrouds the lives of the citizenry.

Following the massive media clamp down in 1971 by the Singapore government in jailing without trial owners, editors, and journalists allegedly for glorifying communism, fostering Chinese chauvinism, or being bankrolled by foreign interests, *The Australian* editorialized:

> Singapore is a one party State that bears the injuries that all one party States do to themselves. Those who see the power of the Singapore government and the lengths to which Lee Kuan Yew is prepared to go to hang on to it are frightened by what is likely to be the result of it all. In Singapore the question is being asked more often these days: What is the point of being one of the best fed, best administered, best dressed nations in Asia if that nation is also one of the least free?[4]

Since the utterance of those sombre observations, the situation in Singapore has not by any means improved. Instead, it has worsened as this book will bear ample testimony.

Singaporeans, long termed "digits" by the prime minister, are wary to whom they speak their minds. Every criticism or comment

---

4. *The Australian*, Friday, 21 May 1971.

on government policy or action may be construed as a challenge to government by an ungrateful population. That there is an ambience of fear is not denied by the political leadership. Dr. Toh Chin Chye, a former cabinet minister turned critic, belatedly acknowledged, not without bitter irony, the need to check PAP power and accused the government of "administration by intimidation" and conformity of thought:

> People abroad say to me: "You Singaporeans seem to be nervous, always looking over your shoulders." And it's true, Singaporeans are so bloody scared. Nobody wants to say anything. It's always: "Don't quote me." ... They're scared of losing a licence or their jobs .... *Here we're all ball bearings produced by quality control.* [Emphasis added]

A perpetual feeling of insecurity of its political longevity, bordering on a paranoiac dread of the fragility of power, motivates Prime Minister Harry Lee Kuan Yew to root out and ruthlessly destroy any form of dissent by periodically using the communist bogy as a ruse. And, if it is not the communist bogy, it is the American gremlin or some other goblin, which is used as a guise to stamp out any contrary voices of dissent. This is a tale of one such contrary voice.

2

Prologue

> Every prison that men build
> Is built with bricks of shame,
> And bound with bars lest Christ should see
> How men their brothers maim.
>
> —Oscar Wilde, *The Ballad
> of Reading Gaol*

Whitley Detention Centre

Sandwiched between Whitley Road where the Bukit Brown Chinese Cemetery now lies in tranquil desuetude and Mount Pleasant Road along which stand some splendid colonial bungalows, a cluster of unobtrusive low-level buildings nestles snugly on a knoll amidst verdant quietude. The Pan-Island Expressway leading to famed Changi International Airport runs by below it. The cluster of buildings goes virtually unnoticed by the daily procession of rapt commuters between east and west Singapore. Unless one searches diligently for it, it is difficult to find. Even the postman has difficulty in locating it. It is well-isolated from the daily hustle and bustle of life in Singapore. This is the Whitley Detention Centre, which acquired recent notoriety as home to twenty-two reluctant young professionals, Roman Catholic church lay and social workers.

Whitley Detention Centre, the entrance to which is by way of Onraet Road, is the main Internal Security Department (ISD) holding centre.[1] It was built as an interrogation centre sometime in the

---

1. See, generally, "Singapore Inc.'s corporate security service," *Far Eastern*

mid-sixties to hold suspected communists or subversives. Its organization and structure were influenced by the British and, later, by the Israelis, who were somewhat drolly described as "Mexican agricultural advisers," to avoid offending the sensitivities of neighbouring countries. The Israelis set up and trained the Singapore armed forces, a select few remained for several years thereafter as military advisers. ISD officers were trained in Britain, the U.S. and Israel. Since its completion, the Centre has played host to unwilling guests, who at one time numbered as many as a hundred or more suspected communists, communalists, and religious zealots.

Not all ISD arrests and detentions attract the attention of the media or are known to the general populace. In March 1984, Kalu Sarkar, an Indian-born physiotherapist and personal friend of President Devan Nair, who had accompanied him during a private visit to Sarawak, East Malaysia, was arrested and detained under the ISA. He was interrogated by ISD officers for several days without the knowledge of the public in, oddly enough, the very same room in the Centre in which I was later to find myself.[2]

Sarkar was then a guest of the president and the first lady and stayed at the *Istana*, the presidential palace. He was rudely awakened from his slumber in the wee hours of the morning and silently taken away from the *Istana*, without the knowledge of the first lady or the heavily-sedated president, who was himself under guard in the Singapore General Hospital. Sarkar was subjected to intense interrogation directed towards *persuading* him to sign a statement confirming the government's account of the president's alleged misbehaviour in Sarawak. Sarkar apparently refused to oblige; and was quietly put on a flight out of Singapore without being able to see the Nair family. Sarkar was the only independent witness then in Singapore to the events in Sarawak.

Only many months later, when the former president visited him in India, did he learn of the brutal treatment to which Sarkar had been subjected when in the custody of the ISD. It makes for a dismal

---

Economic Review, June 30, 1988.

2. See, also, Devan Nair's open letter to Lee Kuan Yew, at Appendix 5; and *White Paper*, Command 8 of 1988, June 29, 1988.

commentary. Besides Sarkar, one other male guest of the president and his wife at the time was also arrested that same night, but was later released after interrogation disclosed a case of mistaken identity. No one knew of either incident then. If a house guest of the first family of Singapore can be terrorized under the ISA in such impudent circumstances, what possible protection can an ordinary citizen hope to have, especially now that the courts have been denied the power of review in such so-called security cases! Further, the veil of secrecy thrown over the Sarkar arrest would have been lifted long ago, if Singapore had a free and vigilant press to call the government to account for its action.

Long-term political detainees, like university lecturer and physicist, Chia Thye Poh, (who has the dubious distinction of being detained for more than twenty-two years) were kept at Moon Crescent Detention Centre, adjoining the egregious Changi Prison. Chia was a member of parliament whose political party, *Barisan Sosialis*, was then in opposition to the longtime PAP government. Together with twenty-one other party members, he was arrested on October 29, 1966 for allegedly orchestrating a major public demonstration against the visit to Singapore of President Lyndon B. Johnson and the U.S. involvement in Vietnam. Some years later, the government belatedly accused him of being a communist, which he steadfastly denied. On May 17, 1989, he was conditionally released from preventive detention, but bizarrely confined on *Pulau Sentosa* (Isle of Tranquillity) a Singapore-island version of Disneyland, opposite the main island of Singapore. Before the island was rechristened by a purposeful government and invested with a new role, it formed part of the strategic defence of the much vaunted impregnable fortress of Singapore, and was known to history by the morbid name of *Pulau Blakang Mati* (Isle Beyond the Dead).

Whitley Detention Centre was gazetted on February 1, 1974, as a prison for purposes of the Prisons Act, Cap. 247.[3] However, the director of prisons has virtually no control or responsibility over it. The maintenance, management, and discipline of the Centre is vested in the Internal Security Department.[4] It makes for grim irony

---

3. *Gazette Notification* S.62, February 1, 1974.
4. See the *Internal Security (Detained Persons) Rules*, 1960, as amended. Cf. *Prisons*

that the Centre should take its name from Major N.H.P. Whitley, M.C., a war hero, and an illustrious judge of the Supreme Court of Singapore.

The Internal Security Department (ISD) is the successor in name of the Special Branch, an internal security outfit first established in 1919 by V.G. Savi, later chief constable, Fife, Scotland, who laid the foundations of the department. "In addition to security work against political movements and suspects the Special Branch concentrated on all racial, religious and social activities, and kept an eye on the trend of events in neighbouring countries."[5] The role of the Special Branch, as spelled out by René Onraet, inspector general of police, Straits Settlements, has not changed. It is still to collect and collate security intelligence and liaise with other friendly security services in the region and elsewhere, so as to enable the commissioner of police to warn the government of any threats to the maintenance of public order from subversive or hostile forces or from racial or religious friction.

The Special Branch or ISD forms an integral major division of the Singapore police force, whose officers and men are freely interchangeable under the Ministry for Home Affairs. But, in practice, they tend to remain in fairly watertight compartments.

The security of the Centre is entrusted to a detachment of Gurkhas drawn from the Gurkha police contingent, based at the Mount Vernon cantonment. It forms a separate and distinct unit of the Singapore police force, although commanded by a retired British Gurkhali-speaking officer from the brigade of Gurkhas of the British Army.

The Gurkhas come from the mountainous Kingdom of Nepal, which is hemmed in between the two great states of China and India. Through its longtime British connexion, Singapore is one of the very few countries that is still able to recruit these mercenaries. The Sultanate of Brunei is another. They have been chosen in preference to the local populace because of their deserved reputation for unswerving loyalty, rigidity in carrying out instructions, and general

---

Regulations, 1938, as amended.
5. *Singapore, A Police Background*, London: Dorothy Crisp and Co., Ltd., 1947.

incorruptibility. Or, in the trenchant words of the prime minister, "one good thing about them is that they execute your order with a determination and summariness which makes law and order all that much more respected,"[6] which partially explains the reason why he has surrounded himself with a round-the-clock Gurkha security screen.

Conversations between Gurkha guards and detainees are frowned upon and are, in any event, compounded by a natural language barrier, which makes it all but impossible to initiate any affinity. The Gurkha guards are rotated weekly, thus derogating any possible rapport being established between captive and captor.

Apart from being good martial material, the Gurkhas, also, make ideal prison guards.[7]

---

6. Speech, Convent of the Holy Infant Jesus, December 11, 1965.
7. See, generally, Flora Lewis, "Gurkhas can solve the UN's problem," *The New York Times*, February 8, 1992.

3

Salad Days

But we either believe in democracy or we do not. If we do, then, we must say categorically, without qualification, that no restraint from any democratic process, other than by the ordinary law of the land, should be allowed. ...

If you believe in democracy, you must believe in it unconditionally. If you believe that men should be free, then, they should have the right of free association, of free speech, of free publication. Then, no law should permit those democratic processes to be set at nought, and no excuse, whether of security, inconvenience to traffic, or inconvenience to police officers, should allow a government to be deterred from doing what it knows to be right, and what it must know to be right. ...

—Lee Kuan Yew[1]

Soon after I completed my pupillage in July 1956 with the durable law firm of Tan, Rajah and Cheah, then located at Raffles Place in downtown Singapore, I told my master, A.P. Rajah, of my desire to join the Singapore Legal Service and, more particularly, as Crown Counsel and deputy public prosecutor in the attorney general's chambers. A.P., a cultured and rare Indian gentleman of the old school, with an engaging dry wit, was then a Progressive Party member in the Legislative Assembly, whose notable career as lawyer, politician, Speaker of Parliament and ambassador, ended in his elevation to the bench of the Supreme Court of Singapore.

---

1. Legislative Assembly Debates, April 27, 1955, vol. 1, cols. 59–60.

With an introductory letter from him to the attorney general in hand, I strode happily late one Saturday morning in July across bustling Raffles Place, along Battery Road towards the General Post Office, and skirted the Malayan Bank Building at Flint Street. As I traversed the narrow Cavanagh Bridge, which spans the malodorous, muddy Singapore River, covered with the flotsam and jetsam of one the world's busiest seaports, a familiar scene greeted my eyes. Wooden lighters and Chinese junks with painted staring eyes, secured to one another by mooring ropes, were bobbing up and down in rhythm to the restless river, which ceaselessly jostled and justled them into myriad aqueous floral patterns. The bobbing boats were linked to *terra firma* by slender, swaying, timber gangplanks, along which grunting, leathery Chinese coolies balancing precariously weighty loads on their bare shoulders staggered from the skittish vessels to unload them onto lorries waiting by the river bank, returning empty-shouldered to perform repeatedly this Olympian trial of strength and balance. The pungent, spicy morning air was punctuated with loud shouts of cautionary instructions from alert overseers. This picturesque riverine scene beloved of artists and photographers is now no more, banished forever by a fastidious, environs-conscious government.

Singapore River was a main commercial artery ever since the foundation of modern Singapore. Further upstream, godowns lined the river banks, where large banking establishments and trading houses warehoused a profusion of goods, imported by their customers on credit and trust releasing them only against payment.

I walked past the Marine Police Station at the river's mouth, where several police motor launches gently heaved with the rise and fall of the water agitated by the lighters, junks, and other motorized boats as they churned noisily along the river. The police station has since been demolished in the name of modernity and the exigency of city planning to make way for fastfood centres and promenades. Hard by the police station, stands the vast imposing Colonial Secretariat building—now cast in the role and trappings of a museum. The Colonial Secretariat, viewed with some awe by the common citizenry in those days, was the seat of colonial power, or, in the translated vernacular of the common people, the seat of the "great man." The other end of the axis of command was Government House Domain at Orchard Road, where, in vice-regal fashion and manner, the governor and his administrative office were ensconced.

From the driveway, I looked up the main flight of steps and, with light steps and great expectation, mounted them. At the top of the landing, upon due inquiry, I was directed by a security guard to the far right end of the building. I walked slowly along the wooden, creaking floor taking in the aura of administrative activity on either side of me. At the end of the corridor, I was met by a slim, dark-haired, fair Chinese woman of indeterminate age, to whom I handed the letter. I later discovered she was married to an Indian. She was the private secretary to the attorney general and was almost a fixture there, having served several other attorney generals before the present incumbent. I was told to take a seat. I looked around the book-lined chambers, trying to absorb the ambience of the cockpit of executive jurisprudence. She soon returned and ushered me into a moderate-sized room.

Exuding spontaneous charm, the tall Caucasian occupant instantly rose from behind his desk to meet me with a warm, ready smile and an outstretched hand. He waved me to a chair. I sat down. He held the letter opened in his hand. He introduced himself as Murray Buttrose, and said he was acting as attorney general in place of C.H. Butterfield, Q.C. (Queen's Counsel), who was then away on home leave. Murray Buttrose was shortly afterwards elevated to the Supreme Court of Singapore as a puisne judge, where he sparkled with judicial distinction. We were to meet often thereafter in court. I prosecuted some of the most celebrated cases in the legal annals of Singapore before him.

He spoke of A.P. with great warmth, that he was a good friend and, if A.P. had said that I was all right, he was sure that I was; but he, nevertheless, asked me a lot of searching questions, both personal and professional. Finally, fully satisfied, he wanted to know when I could start work as deputy public prosecutor. And, before I could answer,

"Would Monday be all right?" he asked, and, added, "I am quite sure that A.P. would not mind, or, would you rather I clear it with him first?"

I was not quite prepared for this swift approval and the sudden rush to work. I said that was not necessary.

"Good! That settles it then. I will see you on Monday. Report here in the morning, and we will show you what you have to do."

I have never had a more pleasant job interview before or since.

On Monday morning I reported for duty. By lunch time, Raffles Place, the legal, financial and commercial heart of Singapore, was throbbing with the news. In the fashionable Robinson's Department Store's restaurant at Raffles Place, the spaciously old-world G.H. Cafe on Battery Road, the more plebeian Longhouse coffee shop at Malacca Street, and at other nondescript watering holes in the city where men of commerce and the professions congregated, I was the focus of envious conversations among members of the legal fraternity. Speculation was rife as to the manner of my *entrée* into the *élite* branch of the Singapore Legal Service.

The attorney general's chambers, or the AG's chambers as it is better known by its acronym, was the *sanctum sanctorum* of the Singapore Legal Service, and, from time immemorial, considered the white man's exclusive preserve. For many local members of the bar, too, had previously applied for positions in the AG's chambers, but had been turned down "with regret." A negative whispering campaign began. It was insinuated that I had got into the chambers through the "back door." Lively reports reached me of amorphous plans by some unsuccessful members of the legal fraternity to approach an opposition PAP assemblyman, one Harry Lee Kuan Yew, to raise in the legislature the gory details of my appointment. I was, in truth, not a little amused. Whether they carried out their foolish threat or not, I did not know nor did I really care. As far as I was concerned, "the world was mine oyster, which I with sword will open."

I was placed under the tutelage of Acting Senior Crown Counsel Tom Mahoney, a battle-scarred but genial Irishman, with an illimitable capacity for the "cup that clears TODAY of past Regrets and future Fears." He was an unalloyed war hero, having been twice decorated with the Military Cross for exceptional courage and bravery in the last World War. Tom, who was head of the crime section, obligingly showed me the ropes in the AG's chambers and imparted invaluable advice. Unlike some other officers, he was genuinely pleased that I had joined the chambers. One of the things he advised me to do as soon as I had settled down was to go and sign the books of the governor and of the chief justice. "It was the done thing," he said. I was not aware of this venerated practice, which traced its origin back to the early days of the "founding" of Singapore and beyond to England. It was customary for a new comer to a district to call on the local residents, and, in their absence, to leave a card behind announcing his presence in the neighbourhood; but in time all that was necessary was to sign the visitors' books of the important local residents. Books were also kept at the bungalows of the attorney general, the colonial secretary, and the financial secretary in the Government House Domain. I could sign them, if I like it; but the books of the first two officials were most important from a law officer's future point of view. After the governor's book had been signed, I could expect, I was told, an invitation from him to dine at Government House.

On an opportune afternoon, I drove to Government House, and, there, outside the gates in the guard-house, where a sentry and a policeman were on duty, was the visitors' book. I signed it and left and then proceeded to 1 Nassim Hill, where, in the vestibule of the chief justice's residence, I signed my name in his visitors' book in mute signification that I had discharged my socio-official obligation.

I was also initiated into the rites at the Cafe de Luxe, a conveniently situated pub nearby, whose habitués included the "Empress Place" crowd, a motley collection of the denizens of the Colonial Secretariat and the Supreme Court buildings, and some members of the bar. They were great elbow-benders. Those days were, indeed, spacious. When the building later was compulsorily acquired by the government under its urban renewal scheme, the oasis was moved to the old Adelphi Hotel, Coleman Street. When it, too, was closed in due time for the same purpose, the legal crowd dispersed to other watering holes in the fashionable uptown Tanglin area, finally to reconverge in Empress Place, in the historic Singapore Cricket Club. I had an invigorating six months of successful prosecutions at the assizes, as it was then called, when I was unexpectedly transferred as assistant official assignee to the official assignee's chambers, a department charged in law with overseeing bankrupts and bankruptcies of individuals and corporations, and generally considered by insiders as outside the main stream.

A week or two after I had moved over to the official assignee's chambers, an important looking envelope, impressed on the cover with the official seal of Government House, arrived for me. On opening, I saw within it an embossed, gilt-edged invitation card from the governor inviting my wife and me to lunch at Government House. It was a novel experience for a young law officer. On the appointed day, we drove up Government Hill in my car to the governor's residence, where, under the high porticos, liveried servants were waiting to open the doors of our car, and one of whom chauffeured it away. A young British *aide-de-camp*, wearing the white uniform of a naval officer, greeted us politely at the top of the steps. He seemed to know who we were, and, before ushering us into the great hall, stopped by a blackboard on which were pinned three separate sheets of paper indicating the seating arrangements. He told Marjatta, my wife, that she would later be escorted into the dining room by a certain gentleman, while I would be accompanied by some other lady. He mentioned their names which I have since forgotten. We were momentarily perturbed as we did not know the parties concerned; but, he said, *sotto voce*, that, during the cocktails, he would point them out to us. Reassured, we entered the great hall where there were already a number of guests. He took us to where the governor and his lady were receiving the guests and, with urbane polish, introduced us. The governor spoke to me as if he had known me, and surprised me further by his acute awareness of my recent transfer, when he asked whether I liked my present appointment. A few more brief words, and he turned to greet his other guests, marshalled in by other *aides-de-camp*, resplendent in the uniforms of their respective services. I marvelled to my wife at the splendid briefing the governor must have had on all his guests, most of whom, I gathered, he was meeting for the first time, and at his ability to keep them in mind, as evidenced by the ease with which he talked to us about ourselves and our background. The lunch itself was unspectacularly forgettable. The luncheon man-management, however, left an indelible impression upon us, as it demonstrated the smooth and seamless way of British officials and officialdom at their best.

I remember well the last criminal case that I prosecuted on behalf of the state before leaving the AG's chambers to take up my new appointment. It was a corruption case involving a fire officer, accused of having accepted bribes from building contractors to overlook certain fire rules and regulations in their construction of concrete storage petrol pits for service stations.

The trial took place in the Third Criminal District Court in the historic Criminal District and Magistrates' Courts Building at South Bridge Road, opposite the Central Police Station, both of which have since been demolished in the name of progress and modernity. The defence counsel was Harry Lee Kuan Yew, then a PAP assemblyman. The judge was Joshua Benjamin Jeyaretnam, who was to become the first opposition MP to break the PAP's parliamentary monopoly and, in the process, metamorphosed into the prime minister's political *bête noire*.

The accused was charged with receiving illegal gratifications from contractors over whose work he exercised supervision. A perfectionist, he insisted at the same time on compliance with the department's fire safety rules and regulations. That there was a grave contradiction in the impulsion behind the gift and its acceptance apparently did not strike him. Not unnaturally, it caused great unhappiness among the contractors concerned in general, and the complainant-contractors in particular, who failed to see the purpose of the payola. It would in the very nature of things be only a matter of time before the Corrupt Practices Investigation Bureau got wind of it. And so it did. The accused was found guilty and was convicted of the charges. He appealed against both convictions and sentences. Lee argued the appeal, which was heard before the late Justice Tan Ah Tah, a good but dilatory judge, but, by the time of the hearing of the appeal, I had been transferred to the official assignee's chambers. Another Crown Counsel and deputy public prosecutor took over the appeal and, through want of industry and legal research, lost it.

In accordance with British standard of fairness and justice, the fire officer's interdiction from service was duly lifted, and he resumed his interrupted employment. Through the effluxion of time and merit, he was promoted, and, in due course, reached the ultimate heights of chief fire officer. At one of the occasional government receptions for senior officials and their ladies, he turned up with his stunningly attractive wife, who was beautifully attired and bedecked with expensive jewellery. Her scintillating adornments caught the practiced eye of the prime minister, who, recalling his legal defence of the officer, swiftly concluded from the dazzling vision before him that his erstwhile client had not mended his errant ways, and promptly had him dismissed from service.

The acting head of the official assignee's chambers was Abdul Wahab Ghows, a casual Muslim of Indian and Chinese admixture, who was more concerned with maintaining the *status in quo* of his tranquil and uneventful official existence than any bankruptcy activism. Innately suspicious of every one's intentions, his swarthy face perpetually wreathed in worry frowns, he spoke English with an earthy pathos readily intelligible to any abecedarian of the language. My reputation as a legal activist had preceded me, and I was sternly lectured by him the very first day I stepped foot in the chambers, to leave things well alone. The official assignee's chambers was not the place nor was there the need, he cautioned, for any legal heroics. Well pleased with himself after having delivered his halting homily, he nodded repeatedly to himself in seeming self-congratulation. And so, I rusticated for two years in idle existence, occasionally out of sheer boredom venturing into some fraudulent bankruptcy investigations to his ever expressive consternation. He did everything possible to discourage me from pursuing crooked bankrupts for fear I might expose him to personal monetary penalties, should any investigation fail. The official assignee is, in law, personally liable for the costs of any unsuccessful legal action undertaken by him on behalf of a bankrupt's estate. In a way, it was an understandable fear, considering that one of his predecessors in office was held personally responsible for the costs of an unsuccessful legal suit. Had the government of the day not bailed him out, he would have had to pay the costs. From that time onwards, successive official assignees adopted a conservative approach in administering the affairs of bankrupt persons and corporations.

As the official assignee's chambers were then housed on the top floor of the Supreme Court building, I almost daily ran into the court *peons* or the assize court clerk, who, long in the tooth of the law, would relate to me the latest prosecution case biting the dust of acquittal before judge and jury. In one unprecedented assize, save for those accused persons who had pleaded guilty at the outset, all the rest had been acquitted and discharged of the criminal charges preferred against them. It was said that if they had not prematurely pleaded guilty they, too, would have been acquitted.

In April 1959, I was sent for by Ernest P. Shanks, Q.C., who had succeeded C.H. Butterfield as attorney general. Shanks was disliked intensely by Lee for his single-minded prosecution of the student editors of the Socialist Club of the University of Malaya in Singapore, for publishing an allegedly seditious article in its journal, *Fajar (Dawn)* in which Lee had acted as junior defence counsel to D.N. Pritt, Q.C.. The students were all acquitted. The assize record of acquittals had assumed unparalleled proportions. I had a fair idea why Shanks had sent for me and, when he said that he wanted me to "jump straight into the deep end, *tomorrow*," I was not unduly surprised. I was quite thrilled. I had been loathe to leave the AG's chambers and had evinced during my sojourn in the barren wilderness of the official assignee's chambers a longing to return to them. Shanks's instructions to report for instant duty sent an exhilarating feeling through me at the sheer thought of returning to my chosen field of interest. I was returning to my natural domain. I re-entered the forensic fray. My prosecutor's lance, freshly reburnished, was bloodied in many a forensic battle with resounding victories. I acquired a reputation as a formidable and feared adversary.

In the May 1959 general election for full internal self-government, the left-wing People's Action Party vanquished the Labour Front government and other opposition parties into nonentities. Before Harry Lee Kuan Yew, the leader of the party, took over the reins of government, he insisted, as has been noted, on the release of his political comrades, who had been detained under the Preservation of Public Security Ordinance (PPSO) by the outgoing Labour Front government. But this was not before he and his immediate supporters had first savoured the fruits of victory and seen to their firm entrenchment in the party constitution.

During the election campaign, the English-educated and the civil service had been singled out by him and his followers as targets for political baiting and denigration. With a sense of dread, the civil service awaited the triumphal entry of the PAP into government. The expatriate as well as some local staff had long ago wisely *malayanized* themselves, collected their gratuities or pensions, left the civil service and the country so as to avoid any political harassment.

As many PAP MPs then were drawn from the ranks of the proletariat, they had to be initiated into the functional mysteries of the respective ministries of government. Accompanying the PAP MPs on their familiarization tours were the newly-released detainees, several of whom were dignified with the dubious title of "political secretary." Senior civil servants were given secret instructions prior to these visits to remove all confidential files from sight and, save for paying them their due as the elected representatives of the people and answering formal questions, not to respond to questions on any sensitive matters. So much for the trust and cohesive comradeship of the PAP! The mistrust was congenital, and it did not surprise many PAP watchers when the party soon split asunder.

Within months of taking office, the PAP government suddenly slashed the cost-of-living allowance of civil servants, which caused many good men and true to resign in droves. Although it was purportedly slashed in the name of economy, many felt it was an act of political appeasement to the Chinese-educated supporters of the party. My own brother, George, threw in an instant letter of resignation and walked out. He has never regretted his act. I decided to wait it out to see what would happen. The brain drain on the public sector could not long be sustained if an efficient standard of service was to be maintained. When the situation did not seem to improve, I decided to quit the Singapore Legal Service; but the attorney general, now renamed state advocate general, as a purely psychological ploy, persuaded me to remain, holding out the prospects of an imminent restoration of the pay cuts. Instead, a face-saving device called an upper-time salary scale was introduced. Together with a number of officers, I was promoted to the newly-created salary scale, which in effect meant the restoration of our cost-of-living allowance under a new name. This restoration began with the legal and the medical services and gradually was extended across the entire civil service.

Today, however, the PAP government sings a different tune. The civil service is more than amply rewarded and ministers are paid a salary that is the envy of their ministerial foreign counterparts in many an established government, while Harry Lee Kuan Yew, as prime minister, is paid a salary higher even than that received by the president of United States of America. "You cannot get a good government on the cheap" is now the enticingly, ringing credo. There is a lot to be said for the logic of his argument. His political packaging of this and other issues is worthy of study and emulation by other politicians.

In the initial, giddy flush of the electoral victory, the government introduced some hare-brained schemes to drive home the concept of the dignity of manual labour among members of the civil service. Senior civil servants were not exempted. All civil servants were ordered to report early one Sunday morning at Nicoll Highway, (which was then the principal highway connecting the eastern suburbs with downtown Singapore) to erect concrete railings along the highway, which runs for several miles along the newly-reclaimed sea front. I was not an artisan. I had no special skills to contribute to physical nation-building. Fearful of jeopardizing their jobs and pensions, hundreds of government servants turned up, to work under a blistering midday sun, under the instructions of overseers from the Public Works Department. It seemed to me not only demeaning but absolutely ridiculous for a white-collared civil service gentry to labour in this way, when we had a Public Works Department *par excellence* designed to do this very kind of job. Moreover, God had, in his infinite wisdom, decreed Sunday as a day of rest. I decided not to go. The following day, I was quietly pleased to learn that a number of similar-minded persons had also not turned up.

The following Sunday was another work day. In order to improve upon the last attendance record and to identify the recalcitrants, civil servants were told that an attendance roster would be taken. This prodded the faint-hearted to go. After the third or the fourth Sunday, work was abandoned, or rather PWD artisans, craftsmen, and skilled labourers were called in to take over and complete it.

The abundance of unskilled and aimless raw workers, albeit well-educated and highly-qualified, was probably more trouble than they were worth; and, certainly, to my mind, they constituted the most irrationally expensive labour force in the world. Cost effectiveness was nil. The propaganda value was doubtful. The public relations benefits were negative, at least where the civil service was concerned.

Still brisk and giddy-paced, the PAP government next ordered civil servants *en masse* to report on another Sunday to sweep the squalid, littered streets and drains of Chinatown. Surely, the argument ran, government servants could perform this simple chore with greater application and skill than they had displayed along Nicoll Highway some Sundays ago. Knowing that I had not attended the previous Sundays' labour, some well-meaning souls in my chambers guardedly told me in confidence that the prime minister, his cohort of ministers, and all the PAP MPs would also be turning up to sweep the streets. I was never cut out for that mission in life and, once more, neglected to attend. And, true enough, the next day, I saw a snap-shot of the proletariat prime minister in the newspapers sweeping the streets, or, rather, frozen in the timely pose of sweeping them. I do not recall the news report recounting his dexterity at sprucing up the streets of Chinatown that day. Well, I guess it was all right, if he enjoyed that sort of Sunday activity, and, in any event, that was a price of politics which he had to pay. This absurd political play-acting and posturing fortunately did not last for long and, at last, we could buckle down without further interruption to the task of administering the service.

The annual garden party in honour of H.M. the Queen's birthday was the high mark in the social whirl of colonial Singapore. Here, captains of industry, banking, and commerce, the diplomatic corps, senior civil servants and high ranking members of Her Majesty's armed forces, the social élite, beautiful and not so beautiful ladies but expensively draped, costumed in their colourful national or cultural raiment, and elegantly coiffured, some escorted by their uniformed husbands or *beaux* from the army, navy, or the air force, religious leaders and leaders of the local communities, representatives of organizations and associations, and persons with pretensions to honour and distinction saw and were seen, rubbed shoulders, and exchanged small conversations with one another.

Singapore's National Day supplanted the Queen's birthday garden party as the social event of the year. The first garden party under the PAP government was a memorable social disaster. Eager to demonstrate its egalitarian features, thank-you invitations were sent to members and supporters of PAP branches and grassroots organizations, which had helped the party to steamroller its way into Parliament. They turned up by the hundreds, indifferently or casually attired, seated crammed together on long timber planks placed athwart the rear of open haulage lorries, which, upon arrival, were parked haphazardly along the wide driveways of the *Istana*, choking access to other vehicular traffic. The plebeians and proletariats were more than punctual. They arrived early and, like a swarm of locusts, advanced upon and made short shrift of the food lavishly laid out, even before the *Yang di-Pertuan Negara* (the Head of State) and the first lady had appeared on the immaculately groomed lawns to welcome their first distinguished guests.

Unfortunately, their eyes, as the saying goes, were bigger than their stomachs and, unaccustomed to free and easy flow of the amber draught, they left impolite signs telling tales of unrestrained excesses on the manicured lawns. Additional liquor was hurriedly brought out from the cellar, but it was difficult to replenish food at short notice. The *Istana* liveried-staff, unused to such conduct and behaviour, looked upon the rude invasion by this horde of important political riff-raff with discreet patience and disdain. One such experience was apparently sufficient for the prime minister, for the following years saw a gradual whittling down in the list of rustic guests. I soon lost interest in attendance. My absence was, curiously enough, noticed and commented upon. My attorney general, Tan Boon Teik, thought that my absence might be taken amiss by the political élite and counselled prudence; he, for his part, dutifully attended each and every royal command performance, whilst I chose to attend select official functions.

Soon afterwards, the PAP started a political study centre, where senior civil servants were required to attend a re-orientation or, more accurately, political indoctrination courses. The calibre of speakers was uneven, several of whom were PAP sympathizers or apologists drawn from within the civil service. There was, however, one quality which was ever constant—they were politically correct and, therefore, reliable! The occasional sessions at which the prime minister spoke were more interesting, usually after a trip overseas. I made it a point to attend them. Often holding up those countries which he had recently visited as pitfalls to avoid for Singapore and its administration, he would make pungent observations on their leaders, the government, the people, and the country. The underlying theme of all these homilies was to exhort Singaporeans to excel in their endeavours. In due course, some indelicate observations leaked out to the political leaders across the causeway sparking unnecessary resentment against Singapore and Singaporeans.

During the annual National Day rally, the prime minister would characteristically deliver meandering speeches of Castro-length proportions, sermonizing while he spoke and blustering with the confidence of a man who was accustomed to a captive audience of cabinet ministers, members of Parliament, party members and supporters, senior members of grassroots organizations, the judiciary and members of the civil service, amongst many others. The docile media loyally serialized the speech over successive days. On one occasion, he spoke for as long as three hours. Lee's prepared speeches, on the other hand, were relatively short and often of more than passing interest.

In 1960, Ong Eng Guan was suspended as minister for national development and expelled from the party after issuing a sixteen-point resolution challenging the prime minister's leadership of the party. He assailed the integrity of the prime minister and the minister for law. In a commission, which was set up to inquire into Ong's allegations of corruption and nepotism against Lee and the law minister, I played only a peripheral part as junior counsel to the state advocate general assisting the commissioner. The commission was distinguished by the prime minister taking the low road of politics in an attempt to destroy an erstwhile political comrade. Gutter politics, however, were to prove to be one of his more unsavoury hallmarks. The conclusions of the commissioner were unfavourable to Ong, who, in an act of political bravado, resigned his parliamentary seat. But he contested the resulting by-election and was returned to Parliament after handsomely trouncing the PAP candidate, thereby amply demonstrating to the prime minister that the Hong Lim constituency was not only his political stronghold but his stamping ground as well. Ong formed his own political party, the United People's Party, which contested subsequent general elections; but, in 1965, he dramatically resigned his parliamentary seat and, inexplicably, renounced politics "forever."

In 1961, I was transferred to the Criminal District and Magistrates' Courts, then situated at Hong Lim Green, where I spent nine rewarding months as a district judge and magistrate. The old courthouse has since been torn down to make way for a recreational green for the people of "Chinatown." Lawyers at first avoided appearing as counsel in my court, as they mistakenly perceived me as a pro-prosecution judge. But those who had perforce to appear were pleasantly surprised to encounter, at the risk of trumpeting my own judicial attributes, a scrupulously fair but strict judge.

In those more spacious days, save for the district judge and first magistrate, district judges and magistrates acted as relief magistrate in turns during public holidays to deal with arrest cases, as arrestees might not be kept in detention for longer than twenty-four hours—since changed to forty-eight hours—without being produced before a court. On Deepavali Day, a public holiday celebrated mainly among the Indian population, that year it was my lot to act as the relief magistrate. Early that morning, some seven or eight sad-eyed, daily-rated, Indian labourers were produced before me. Upon due inquiry as to the nature of their offence, the usher of the court informed me that they were charged with being drunk and disorderly. Some of them had been found lying in drunken stupor in the middle of Dunearn Road, a main thoroughfare, a short distance away from the government-owned toddy shop, which was licenced to sell the intoxicating liquid (a fermented coco-palm juice) to Indians only, a paternalistic anachronism of British colonial legacy.

They pleaded guilty. It was not their first experience in the dock, if their demeanour was anything to go by. After lecturing them on the proper way to celebrate Deepavali without danger to themselves and other road users, I let them off with a stern caution. Eight astounded and delighted Indians left the dock with alacrity. My usher, all aghast, immediately stood up from his table below, "But, what will the Treasury say, when there is no revenue today?" It was so grotesque that the courts were being looked upon as primarily revenue productive. Recovering from my surprise, I instructed him to tell the Treasury that it could not look to the courts as a source of revenue. This perverse mind-set has not, unfortunately, changed. Indeed, if at all, it has degenerated into a legal pantomime. Justice today has taken a back seat for the courts have become an important source of revenue gathering, as a visit to the Subordinate Courts building will readily show.

I had been barely nine months there, when I was once more recalled to the AG's chambers. The records showed an unacceptable debit balance of acquittals in the assize lists, which was demoralizing the police force and, in particular, its criminal investigation division. It is a matter of record that members of the police force, as well as the other investigative branches of government, were genuinely relieved at my return. Notwithstanding, the present practice of interchanging officers between the legal and the judicial branches of the Singapore Legal Service should be vigorously discouraged, as it tends to create in the mind of the public a doubt regarding judicial independence. A sudden transfer of a judicial officer may be perceived by the public that he is wanting in his judicial performance in the eyes of the government.

My recall was the opening curtain to the tumultuous events which threatened to engulf the nation. There was students' unrest. Labour was restive. The communists, the pro-communists with their fellow travellers and supporters were active in the trade unions, the Chinese guilds, the Chinese schools, Chinese students' and old boys' associations and alumnae, and many other affiliated organizations. And, significantly, they were tied to the rumblings of disaffection within the PAP portending the inevitable crackup. On July 20, 1961, the PAP government split. The dissidents crossed the floor. On August 13, 1961, the *Barisan Sosialis* party was born. The government was on the defensive.

Sometime in October 1962, I was instructed by the state advocate general to go over to City Hall to see the prime minister over a matter of a criminal prosecution. As it turned out, it concerned the prosecution of Jamit Singh, the general secretary of a powerful dockyard trade union, the Singapore Harbour Board Staff Association (SHBSA), who was alleged to have committed a criminal breach of trust of the union funds. In addition to his trade union activities, the tall, handsome, turbanless Sikh was an amateur thespian with a fine resonant voice, which he used to work the crowds at public rallies. Besides being the proud possessor of considerable demagogic talents, he had undoubted leadership ability and skill, which could be seen from this random example: in concert with other militant factory and transport workers, he had brought his association members out in a sympathy strike with the dismissed workers of the Hock Lee Bus Company, while at the same time skillfully hitching their stoppage of work to grievances for more pay and better working conditions. The strike later degenerated into bloodshed and carnage, and is known to history as the infamous Hock Lee riots.

The left-wing SHBSA constituted a not insignificant segment of the trade union movement in the uneven political tapestry of Singapore. But what was particularly galling to the sorely vexed prime minister was that, after he had chosen Jamit Singh from among the student members of the University of Malaya Socialist Club as the paid secretary of the Association, to mind the store as it were, his conceited and charismatic protégé had instead sold the Association lock, stock and barrel to the opposition *Barisan Sosialis*. Fired with more than the usual consideration of justice, the prime minister was eager for a critical assessment of the case for the prosecution. His target was the fiery Sikh. But the prospects of the prosecution, however, depended upon the Association's elected treasurer, Yeow Fook Yuen, being charged with aiding and abetting the offence; for the alleged breaches of trust could not have occurred without Yeow's consent or connivance. Yeow was, in a way, inconsequential to the political dénouement, but was unfortunately in the line of fire and had to be sacrificed for the greater good of the state, a fate he meekly accepted with an equanimity bordering on fatalism.

Although the prime minister did not specifically articulate his hidden agenda, enough was said at our meetings to make me realize that the trial leading to a conviction was crucial to him and his government in several particulars: Jamit Singh should be kept preoccupied with his defence at the trial so as to lessen his capacity for political mischief and thwart his efficiency in organizing opposition to merger, as well as to discredit him as a union leader and diminish his stature with the workers; and, finally, to destroy his power base in the dockyards and docklands of Singapore. The prime minister's endgame of winkling him out of the trade union movement in general and the powerful SHBSA in particular, which was to be followed by the inevitable deregistration of the SHBSA, was left largely unsaid.

This was the year when Singapore was in a state of great sociopolitical flux over merger with Malaya. There was great opposition to it as there was support for it involving, as it did, every political persuasion. But, as the government saw it, merger was the only way to Singapore's independence and, indeed, given the political climate, its very survival. The national referendum for merger with Malaya and the Borneo territories was to be held on September 1, 1963, a date known only to the prime minister!

Upon my assurance that I was quite comfortable with the prosecution, he seemed satisfied; but nevertheless I had to walk him through the evidence of the main witnesses and indicate briefly my strategy at the trial. He kept in touch with me at various stages of the trial by telephone and by summonses to his office. During one of those telephone calls, he surprised me with a query as to whether I had a scrambler for my telephone, and instructed me to use it. But I told him that I did not have it. He was startled at that reply and, after a pregnant pause, advised that I should have it installed immediately to safeguard the confidentiality of our future telephone conversations. To mollify him, I said I would look into it, but, as he did not raise it again, I let the matter slip quietly into oblivion. One distasteful aside was his importunity that I should question Jamit Singh on his private life. The ISD had amassed ample information on his allegedly dissolute existence, and supplied it to the investigating officer. I tried to put it off but I was continually reminded of it. The prime minister's reason for this intrusive form of interrogation was that, in order for Jamit Singh to sustain his genre of life style, he had perforce to resort to the union funds.

The trial took place in the historic Criminal District and Magistrates' Courts Building at Hong Lim Green before the First Criminal District Judge, Choor Singh, who, unlike the defendant, was turbanned in the traditional Sikh fashion. A conscientious judge, he was not unaware that he stood at the crossroads of his judicial career and that the trial could prove to be his watershed.[2] The trial was protracted, enlivened by frequent outbursts from the defendant or his equally temperamental defence counsel, whose prodigious industry sadly did not often match his noisy presentation. The judge was hard put to maintain a semblance of judicial decorum in his courtroom; and security was heightened when one morning tell-tale signs of a ritual were discovered indicating that a sympathizer or sympathizers had in the night invoked the intercession of some unnamed gods at the rear private staircase leading to the door of his judicial chambers.

The trial was suddenly interrupted by a security operation called *Cold Store*. On February 2, 1963, the Internal Security Council—comprising representatives of the governments of Singapore, Malaya, and the United Kingdom—ordered Jamit Singh's detention under the Preservation of Public Security Ordinance. But, pending the outcome of the trial, the order of detention was suspended and replaced by an order of restrictive residence in Singapore "in the interests of Malayan security." The prime minister could not afford to take any chances with a popular and mercurial opponent.

On March 1, 1963, Jamit Singh was found guilty, convicted, and sentenced to 18 months' imprisonment and Yeow Fook Yuen to 9 months' imprisonment but, pending appeals against the decision, both were freed on bail. On March 9, 1963, at 3 a.m., Singh was arrested at the home of a friend and taken under escort of the Federation Special Branch to Kuala Lumpur, Malaya to serve his detention.

The following year, the Singapore Harbour Board Staff Association was deregistered. From out of its ashes the Singapore Port Workers' Union rose to take its place, a pale imitation of its former robust self. The prime minister had successfully managed to remove a political thorn from his side.

---

2. He was later elevated as a justice of the Supreme Court.

Before leaving this topic, it may be convenient here to leap over the vale of years to record another tale of another opposition politician, R.Vetrivelu, whose claim to political fame was an exaggerated and droll notion of himself as a giant slayer. He was a genial feature in general elections, where he would campaign under the banner of the opposition political party of the moment, and he was at the relevant time the secretary general of the United National Front. Although he was dismissed by the electorate as a seasonal provider of incidental comic relief in political campaigns, he was nonetheless of nuisance value.

The day after nomination day for the 1972 general election, on August 24, 1972, Vetrivelu was served with a writ for alleged defamation and a claim for damages and costs by the solicitors for the recently-retired Assistant Commissioner of Police, C.I.D. (Crime Investigation Division), Ong Kian Tong, arising out of a press statement made by him more than a year before. Like the egregious case of PAP MP Tay Boon Woo, who was suddenly inspired after more than six years to revive a statute-barred claim for costs of a failed action against him by the opposition Workers' Party, Ong Kian Tong was also well behind the times. But Ong had received timely trickled-down advice from officialdom that he should commence an action for defamation against R.Vetrivelu. As the advice was the advice of absolute power, he sought me out at the chambers for counsel and assistance. After listening to the reluctant litigant, I decided it best to provide him with a road map to legal firms and the Supreme Court. The writ of summons was the result. Thus, another political opponent, admittedly a political jester, faded from the political scene, unwept and unsung. There were other instances of intervention; but they do not however directly concern me, and, belong therefore to a separate and different narrative.

To return to 1963. The prime minister and his government were passionately pursuing a merger with the Federation of Malaya, which was opposed by a large section within the ruling party itself, as well as the communists and other segments of the population. The matter of merger was compounded by a boycott of the Chinese secondary IV examinations[3] by the students, who, together with

---

3. The government introduced in 1961 a change in Chinese education from three

political opportunists and other mischief-makers, accused the government of trying to eradicate Chinese language and culture. It was a highly emotive political issue, which rapidly involved every stratum of Chinese society, irrespective of political hues. These included such disparate groups as the Nanyang University alumni and teachers; shopkeepers and customers; merchants and traders; trishaw riders. Also involved were organizations such as the Chinese Chamber of Commerce, an ethnic mercantile association of millionaire merchants, businessmen, and traders; the Singapore Country People's Association and the Singapore Rural Residents' Association, both heavily penetrated by radical left-wing elements; trade unions and workers, and many others.

Before merger with Malaya could be pressed with *élan*, the government had to resolve the boycott of the secondary IV examinations and convince students, teachers, and parents alike of the superiority of the new Chinese secondary school system, its syllabi over the old, and the continued vitality and vigour of Chinese education. In order to placate genuine concern among parents and the public, the prime minister announced the government's intention to set up a commission to inquire into the soundness and the manipulation by the communists of the new Chinese education issue. I was sent for by him, after the state advocate general recommended me as the best counsel for the task in hand. Wherefore, I trotted over to City Hall, where the prime minister, in an open-necked shirt and summery light-blue jacket, was ensconced, unlike now, in a tiny office. He explained the strategic purpose of the commission and asked me whether I felt I was up to it. The only person he feared was the former chief minister and lawyer-politician, David S. Marshall, who understandably might try to fish in the troubled waters of Chinese education and culture. He wanted to know whether I could handle him should he be briefed by one or more of those Chinese associations. I told him I had previously crossed swords with him in court, and I was not unduly concerned if that eventuality should come to pass. He seemed satisfied with the reply. I was told

---

years of junior middle and three of senior middle to four years and two years of higher school certificate to bring it into line with the English educational stream.

to pick my team. I selected a Crown Counsel, Tan Wee Kian, now in private law practice, as my assistant. To complete the team, the prime minister detailed a lawyer crony, Chua Sian Chin, from his old law firm of Lee and Lee, as "political consultant," because civil servants "do not have a feel for politically sensitive things." The Special Branch would advise me on communism and the Communist Party of Malaya (CPM), and how Chinese schools and students and graduates were being used to create unrest to perpetuate the communist cause. After having studied the relevant Special Branch files compiled over the years, I was to advise him when I would be ready so that a commission of inquiry could be constituted under the chairmanship of a judge of the Supreme Court.

As already noted, the Special Branch, an internal security unit within the Singapore police force, was originally established by the British colonial government largely for security reasons. It monitored both the covert activities of the CPM, which was proscribed in June 1948, and its open front organizations. As a result of covert infiltration by the communists and their sympathisers into civic and political organizations, the Special Branch extended its area of interest to political parties, trade unions, schools and students, university and undergraduates. Its interest also extended to other political radicals and organizations committed to the violent subversion of the colonial government. Considering the multiracial character of Singapore, it was divided into English, Chinese, Indian, and Malay sections. Investigation results were referred to a collation unit, whose duty it was to try to fit the mosaic bits of information into a composite portrait of activity or intention of a targeted person or organization.

Investigations were carried out by a field section assisted by a technical section sometimes called the "dirty tricks" unit. Apart from the employment of ISD professionals and the ample use of electronic equipment and instruments, there were, then as now, paid informers in schools, universities, colleges and polytechnics, trade unions and industries. Besides the ISD infiltration into all political parties, their party headquarters, also, are key targets for electronic surveillance. For years, the conference room of the *Barisan Sosialis* headquarters was wiretapped without the leaders being aware of it. And the bugging of the residence of *Barisan Sosialis'* chairman, Dr. Lee Siew Choh, was only discovered when workmen accidentally found the bugging device above the ceiling of the dining room whilst making repairs in his home. Dr. Lee still retains it among his political souvenirs. The equipment and instruments used today are more sophisticated and difficult to detect.

The Special Branch had safe houses, maintained its own holding centres, such as the former top floor of the old Central Police Station, Moon Crescent Centre, and Whitley Detention Centre, which were gazetted as prisons for purposes of the Prisons Act. The headman was then known as "director." It was changed to "head," but has since reverted to its old familiar title. Because of the clandestine nature of its work, almost everything is classified secret or top secret, and disclosure, generally, is "on a need to know basis." The obsessive preoccupation with secrecy so typical of Singapore's bureaucracy sometimes led to ludicrous lengths, as even "miscellaneous" files were classified "secret." Save for the director and the sectional heads, the standard of education among the rank and file was not very high. Today, the staff status is completely transformed. Most senior personnel have at least had a tertiary education. The Special Branch, renamed the Internal Security Department (ISD), is now housed in superior premises at Phoenix Park, Tanglin Road. Millions of dollars have been poured into its technical section to obtain and install the latest equipment, gimmickry and gadgets for electronic surveillance of subjects. Computers are now the order of the day.

I spent almost a year at the Special Branch, then located at the old CID building, Robinson Road, poring over voluminous files, extracting bits and pieces of information, and collating them in preparation for the commission. It was tedious work. The political consultant stopped by in the late evenings, whenever his mood or fancy led him there, and, then, more often than not, was more curious about the existence and perusal of his own personal dossier and the dossiers of opposition personalities wholly unconnected with the work in hand. He was tactfully told by a senior Special Branch officer that no dossier was kept on him as he had not acquired such status as to merit attention. He was visibly disappointed, but wholly unconvinced. After a preliminary discussion with the political consultant, we decided that we would probably make better progress and sense without him. He was paid $100 per day—a princely sum in those days—per attendance, whereas we were limited to our relatively meagre civil service pay. Every now and again, the prime minister summoned me to his office at City Hall to inquire about our progress and the state of preparedness. At the end of one such summons, I hinted broadly at his choice of a mediocre political consultant, which he gruffly dismissed: "Then, ignore him." Wherefore, when he was later recruited as minister for home affairs—a position which he was to hold for many years—we were amazed beyond measure, as well as those officers at the Special Branch who had occasion to remember him. Notwithstanding, the intervening years have given me no reason to alter our initial assessment of him.

Throughout the early stages of the commission, the prime minister was in constant touch with me. He wanted to be kept informed on the identity of witnesses, the order of their call on a particular day, and the proposed line of examination. Later, well pleased at the way I presented the matter, he left me more to myself. I learnt many things at the feet of the political maestro, and had a rare insight into the devious thinking of this remarkable man. One important witness was the late Ko Teck Kin, a multimillionaire and rubber baron, who held the powerful position of president of the Chinese Chambers of Commerce. He was taller and larger in physique than the average Chinese. He was held in high esteem and regard by the world of business and commerce. A man of great pride, he radiated a powerful influence and authority over the Chinese populace. But Ko Teck Kin was, however, dabbling in national politics and, in the naïve belief that he was helping to man the ramparts of Chinese language and culture, had lent his name and prestige to the agitation against the new education system. It was obvious he was not *au courant* in the merits or otherwise of the new educational system; but, nonetheless, he had signed a number of public statements prepared for him by Chinese student activists, or agreed to their release under his name.

His standing with the communists was equally good. They also valued his socioeconomic achievements. According to captured communist underground literature, he had, unknown to him, been singled out as a potential minister of finance in any future pro-communist government. The government wanted to retain his goodwill because of his status with the Chinese commonalty but, at the same time, wanted to neutralize him, using the word in its best sense. I was caught in a dilemma. I asked the minister of education, Yong Nguk Lin, who is, incidentally, a brother-in-law of the prime minister, for instructions as to how I should deal with him in the commission. He himself was unsure, and suggested that I speak to the prime minister for instructions. The prime minister was keen that Ko should be exposed for dabbling in matters out of his depths; but was simultaneously anxious that he should not be so treated as to antagonize the Chinese community, for, to quote his words to me, "He is worth at least 50,000 votes." Given the size of the electorate and the prevailing political situation, the prime minister could not afford to squander this vote potential. No Chinese business leader acquires that pre-eminent position of power without merit and the support of his peers, who themselves were powerful and influential members of the Chinese community. After anxious deliberation, I was finally given a discretion to deal with him as I thought best, depending upon his performance in the witness box.

Supremely aware of his wealth, position, and power, Ko Teck Kin was a difficult witness. A man used to command, it was very difficult for him to admit publicly that he did not know what he had been signing or doing. It would be a severe loss of face. Ultimately, and not without great reluctance, I had to expose that he had been used by pro-communist elements to discredit the government via the medium of Chinese secondary school education. The increasingly tense examination was abruptly adjourned to accede to his pathetic plea for a glass of water and to allow him time to recover his composure. The Chinese interpreter opined that Ko was not accustomed to being treated in this brutal fashion. On the next morning, *The Straits Times* dramatically bannered the incident on its front page, "Ko's Jaw Dropped." I had made a lifelong enemy.

Following Singapore's involuntary independence on August 9, 1965, in a magnanimous gesture of high statecraft, the prime minister shrewdly appointed Ko Teck Kin Singapore's high commissioner to Malaysia. But Ko Teck Kin never forgave me for that public humiliation and, when our paths finally crossed again in the more congenial surroundings of an *Istana* garden party some years later, he refused my proffered hand of friendship, curtly turned his back, and, without a word, walked away from me.

The proceedings were given saturation press and radio coverage, and the sinister hand of the communists and their sympathisers was exposed in working and manipulating the Chinese school students and teachers, the undergraduates and alumnae, the faculty and staff of Nanyang University, various Chinese associations and organizations. The commission was an unqualified political success. It lasted almost one whole year, presided over by Justice Wee Chong Jin, who handled the inquiry with commendable political acumen and skill. Knowing the commission had achieved the immediate purpose of government, Justice Wee did not consider it necessary to produce a report. As a result, none was produced. He was later promoted to chief justice over a sorely disappointed and urbane Justice Tan Ah Tah, who, in order of seniority, was next in line for elevation to the highest judicial office in the land. Ah Tah had all the requisite erudition and judicial attributes and would have made a distinguished chief justice, but for an egregious propensity for procrastinating his judgments. The salutary influence of an extreme *exemplum* of non-promotion on judges was only momentary, as this endemic, highly-resistant, judicial virus soon reasserted itself as virulently as ever before on the bench of the Supreme Court. None of them, it seems, have heard of, or, if they had, obviously forgotten the axiom, "A judge who reserves a judgment saddles a burden on his back." An example of the resurgence of judicial procrastination may hereafter be seen in the case of Mei Siah.

The PAP government, a minority government of 25 members as compared to the 26-member opposition, then walked a political tightrope across a yawning gulf of conceivable defeat, where, at the bottom of abyss, the watchful communists and their supporters waited to finish off the survivors. My spirited performance at the commission of inquiry had put my professional career, not to mention personal safety, on the line. I was a red target. After its successful conclusion, I remembered a beaming, grateful prime minister congratulating me on a job well done, and saying that, had I failed the assignment,

> "Your head would have been among the first to be chopped off by them."

It was a forensic achievement for me, but a political triumph for him, a shrewd political strategist, who had used the commission to advance his objectives. More than his colleagues or any other persons, he appreciated its significance and consequences and how perilously close to defeat the government then stood. Throughout my entire service career and even thereafter, on more than one occasion, he recalled it with genuine appreciation.

At the commencement of and during the commission of inquiry, the Special Branch, concerned over my well-being, recommended a personal bodyguard, but I had refused, as I was unaccustomed to the restricting presence of a hovering secret paladin. But I however accepted the suggestions of using false vehicle licence plates, varying my daily movements and travel routes, and the carrying of a sidearm. With the commission of inquiry behind it, the government confidently planned for the exciting days of merger with Malaya.

In recognition of a difficult work well done, I was accorded the honour of leading a Singapore delegation to Canberra, ACT, Australia, for the seminar on the role of the police in the protection of human rights, auspicated by the United Nations' Organization. As they say, a change is as good as a rest. The Malayan High Commissioner, Datuk Suleiman bin Abdul Rahman, the elder brother of Tun Dr. Ismail and future Malaysian minister for home affairs, on whom I paid a courtesy call in Canberra, warmly congratulated me on my performance in the commission of inquiry, and entertained us to an excellent home-cooked Malayan curry lunch at the High Commission. He was a sterling character, a shrewd but gentle soul, whose untimely death robbed Malaysia of one of her finest sons.

After the seminar, I took extended leave to visit as guest of the several state police forces in the Commonwealth. Whilst I was in Melbourne, Victoria, I learnt that I had been awarded the Public Administration (Gold) Medal. I was disappointed at the award, which did not, in my view, truly reflect the nature and extent of work I had put in or the dangers that I had run. On my return to

Singapore, I told the state advocate general that I did not want it, thinking that he had recommended it. But he told me that it had been personally recommended by the prime minister. So, with some reluctance, I let the matter drop.

Upon my return to the chambers, detective officers from the élite Special Investigation Section, CID, came to see me about a case of a bar waitress, who was reported "missing" in a scuba-diving outing with her boy friend in the treacherous waters off the Sisters Islands, some few miles south of Singapore. Her body was never recovered. There were no means whereby the cause of her death, if death it was, could be established with certitude, save for the palpable assumption of drowning. Without making even a token rescue effort, her rather flamboyant and callous boy friend, Sunny Ang, had reported her as "missing, believed drowned" at the old Marine Police Station, which was situated close to the site where, according to tradition, Sir Thomas Stamford Raffles was said to have first stepped foot on Singapore island. She had been heavily insured against accidents, the entire benefits under those policies were willed to his mother, whom she hardly knew. The police suspected foul play.

The matter had already been dealt with by Senior Crown Counsel, Tan Boon Teik, as he then was, who had instructed them to take "no further action." The investigating officers were disheartened at this instruction, and, welling dissatisfaction within the the Special Investigations Section (SIS), made them to approach me with the object of taking another look at it, "with fresh eyes." After perusing the investigation papers, I agreed with them that it was a case of murder, but the dilemma was, without the *corpus delicti*, how to prove it beyond a reasonable doubt before a jury in a court of law. Because of the relative novelty of scuba diving as a sport in Singapore, the significance of Ang's narrative of the scuba-diving incident eluded the police in their investigations. In fairness, the police were also partially misled by the Royal Navy underwater demolition team, then stationed at the Sumbawang Royal Naval Base, who were at the time the only available experts on scuba diving. They had erroneously advised the police investigators that it was virtually impossible to prove any wrongful doings from Ang's statements, as they were consistent with accepted scuba-diving procedure.

Notwithstanding this powerful discouragement, I directed the police to reopen the investigations. The answer, I suspected, lay wrapped up in Ang's several statements to the police. I combed through his statements with an eye to any contradiction or inconsistency. The Royal Navy experts had not been of much help. They agreed with Ang's statement that it was very dangerous, nay, impossible, to attach a breathing regulator to an oxygen tank, (whose original washer, oddly enough, had conveniently "dropped off") with an improvised washer, as it would trigger off an "explosion," when the tank was turned on. I began to read up on scuba diving from all the books that the police could lay their hands on in the Singapore book shops, which were not many. But I still needed the aid of an expert with whom I could discuss and test out certain possible theories. M.Bertrand, a civilian scuba-diving enthusiast—a *rara avis* in Singapore in those days—was found, and, whilst he did not entirely pour cold water on my hypothesis of murder most foul via scuba diving, he was, fortunately, not totally negative in attitude. He agreed generally with the views of the Royal Navy experts. But he was ready to go along with me, within reason. As there were no other experts available in Singapore, I had to be careful not to upset him. At my urgent prompting, he reluctantly agreed to carry out, but not without first betraying traces of skepticism on their purpose or usefulness, certain simple experiments on breathing regulators attached to oxygen tanks with improvised washers. The unqualified success of the experiments vindicated my persistence. The results proved that Ang had been telling lies about the tank washers. From these experiments, we were able to show that he had lied on significant aspects, amongst other things, on his inability to dive into the sea in search of his beloved fiancé, owing to a missing oxygen tank washer.

Emboldened by this success, I requested Bertrand, who was by now as keen as a jar of English mustard, to carry out certain diving experiments with the selfsame scuba equipment initially used by the missing girl at the very same spot at sea where she had last disappeared after exchanging it for a second tank. The experiments were another unqualified success. They proved that her first scuba-diving equipment was not defective or short of oxygen, as Ang had claimed, and could have been used by him, if only he had the will, to go in search of her when she failed to surface from her second dive. I was thus able to prove conclusively that his narrative of the defective scuba-diving equipment and the incident was nothing but a tissue of lies. From there, I was able to build up a strong chain of circumstantial evidence which bound him tightly in its coils.

Notwithstanding the absence of a *corpus delicti*—her body was never found—he was unanimously found guilty by a jury, convicted, and sentenced to death. The uniqueness of the case caught the imagination of the public. There were endless queues outside the courthouse long before the courthouse opened its doors. His appeal to the Court of Criminal Appeal was dismissed, as was his subsequent appeal to the Privy Council, Singapore's last appeal court, in London. He was, subsequently, hanged. This case, coming close on the heels of the commission of inquiry, made my name a household word.

I was involved in the prosecution of almost all the important cases, the *causes célèbres* of the period. I had by this time acquired a formidable reputation as a prosecutor and was flattered to discover that I had become a legal paradigm who had unknowingly inspired a number of persons to pursue the profession of law. After the Sunny Ang case ended, I was pleasantly surprised to receive a letter from David Marshall, the foremost criminal defence lawyer of the day and my frequent forensic adversary. He generously congratulated me on the successful prosecution and the attainment of a reputation desired by many in the profession but seldom achieved, which made many an accused person to change a plea of innocence to one of guilty and mitigation, when I appeared in a case.

Sometime in 1967, I was suddenly informed the prime minister wanted to see me. It was always considered ominous by many within the government to be a subject of a sudden summons by him. Senior civil servants and even cabinet ministers were known to have become insomniacs overnight upon receiving a summons from him. I tossed it over in my mind as to what the summons could possibly portend. And, hard as I tried, could not relate it to any official acts of omission or commission. Thus when I appeared before him at his office at City Hall, I was still as blissfully ignorant as ever.

His secretary showed me into his small office. He sat with his back to the tall window overlooking the *padang*. No sooner had I sat down when he spoke, prefacing his remarks with a curious reference to the commission of inquiry into the secondary IV examinations boycott, on which he complimented me again, as "a very good job done" for which he was most appreciative, and recalled, almost nostalgically, that it was "a close call for the government." I was perplexed at this preface. And waited expectantly for what he was really trying to tell me. He then mentioned the names of the chief justice and the chairman of the public service commission. The latter, Dr. Phay Seng Huat, enjoyed at the time his unquestioned confidence, a claim which both he and his wife did not shy from letting all and sundry know. I should understand, the prime minister continued, that they were "devout Christians," who did not necessarily see things the same way that he or I saw them. Their outlook on life was different; but we had to respect that. He then dropped the bombshell that, in the forthcoming promotion exercise, the Legal Service Commission was not in favour of my appointment as solicitor general and, pausing for effect, added,

"Had it not been for me, and your minister for law, you would have been passed over." I was taken aback.

"You have been seen," he continued, "walking across High Street, [where the AG's chambers were then located] hand in hand, with a woman who is not your wife."

He paused again. To me, my private life was my concern, and it was irrelevant to considerations of meritocracy; and I interjected,

"If I am passed over, I would resign."

"That's not the point why I have sent for you, here," he shot back, visibly displeased at the interruption and the combative reply.

Knowing that the main ambition of career law officers as well as of many lawyers in private law practice, then as now, was ultimately ascension to the Supreme Court bench, he tantalized me with the prospects before me:

"Wouldn't you like to be a high court judge one day?"

As I had never seriously considered being a High Court judge, I replied,

"No, I would rather be on my feet than on my bottom."

I did not think he liked the reply. It was not a reply he had expected. Nonplussed, he persevered on a different tack and held out the ultimate jewel in the crown:

"Do you not wish to be chief justice one day?"

"Prime Minister, that's a different proposition altogether."

Again, the answer was not what he had expected, and he brushed it off.

Accentuating every syllable, he would have me know that he had identified for me my "enemies," repeating for effect that, "But for my intervention and the intervention of your minister for law, you would not be appointed solicitor general." He warned me to avoid the pitfalls that had besetted a predecessor in office, whose romantic involvements with a named lady eventually made his legal opinions "not worth the paper they were written on." I assured him that I was not that kind of man, and thanked him for his support and trust in me. He then asked me whether I could work with Tan Boon Teik, director of legal aid, who was then away on a Rockefeller Fellowship in the United Kingdom. I told him that I could. And he revealed that he would be appointed as attorney general. We were both promoted at the same time. I have sometimes wondered what his reaction would have been, if I had replied that I could not work with Boon Teik. In any event, it was an illuminatingly instructive introduction into Singapore's byzantine politics.

I left the meeting buoyantly jubilant and grateful that I was, in the parlance of the horse-racing world, wearing his colours. I was duly promoted to act as solicitor general and, in due course, confirmed as substantive solicitor general. I had vaulted over the heads of some ten or more law officers senior to me in service. It was no mean Olympian feat of achievement, which signalled loud and clear to all and sundry my most favoured standing in the eyes of my prime minister, Harry Lee Kuan Yew. Although the word *beholden* did not once cross his lips that fateful day, I was left in no doubt whatsoever as to the underlying purpose of that august summons.

My iconoclastic style and behavior in the service had not marred my meteoric rise. And, as a dear friend, George E. Bogaars, the head of the civil service, once put it to me in a car-lift ride back to my chambers, "Francis, you are the envy of the civil service." Indeed, I was. I enjoyed his confidence and, on many an occasion, he sought my views and opinions over the attorney general, which drove the latter into frenzied outbursts of insecurity. He was in continual dread of facing the prime minister and often sought from me the purpose of his summons and spent many a sleepless night over it, which I, not being psychic, could not divine for him. Poor man, he was in continual dread that our opinions and views would diverge. Eventually, in order to preserve a peaceful working atmosphere in the chambers, I gave him full liberty to quote me to the prime minister that he had already discussed whatever the matter with me, and that our views thereon were the same. In retrospect, it was a monumental error of incalculable proportions.

I was prosecuting one Freddy Tan for the murder of Gene Koh, a spoilt and wayward son of a multimillionaire road contractor and housing developer, Koh Bok Thye, before Justice Choor Singh and a jury. It had all the traditional ingredients of a sensational case given the plot and personalities involved, and the media gave the trial wide coverage. The defence claimed that Freddy was a psychopath, and set up a plea of diminished responsibility. It called as its main medical witness, Dr. Wong Yip Chong, a former deputy medical superintendent of Woodbridge Mental Hospital, whose suasive powers were such that he was able to prevail upon every mendicant psychiatrist passing through Singapore to interrupt his holidays to give supportive evidence in court for the accused. It was an astonishing achievement and an extraordinary spectacle.

Whilst Yip was giving his evidence in chief, I received a note from the cabinet secretary that the prime minister wanted to see me during the luncheon adjournment. I was musing to myself what serious breach of law and order could have occurred on which he wanted to see me in the middle of a murder trial, because he was not the kind of person given to idle chatter. When the court rose for the luncheon adjournment, I went to the Crown Counsel's room, changed into my street clothes, and walked across the street to see him at City Hall. He was waiting for me. He had read the morning's papers reporting the evidence of Dr. Wong Yip Chong. Expressing robust views about the man and his evidence in court, which the law of defamation inhibits me from repetition, he wanted me to discredit Yip in the witness box. To say I was shocked would probably be an understatement. This was the last subject I had suspected was on his mind, believing he would have been more preoccupied with weightier matters of state. I told him I was about to begin my cross-examination. Hewing to usual courtcraft, I had already planned to challenge his expert evidence rather than make an *ad hominem* attack on him. However that might be, unlike previous forensic encounters, the upshot of it was that Yip did not thereafter speak to me for many months. But, more significantly, it became the catalyst for the abolition of the vestigial remains of the jury system, of trials by a seven-man jury in capital cases, against which I was but a lone dissenter.

Freddy Tan was found guilty and convicted of manslaughter and sentenced to life imprisonment.

The passage of years, far from mellowing the prime minister, has made him more imperiously intolerant of the common man. His abrasive, intrusive style of governance has not changed, and is best exemplified by this statement, brimming with his customary, boastful insensibility:

> I am often accused of interfering in the private lives of citizens. Yes, if I did not, had I not done that, we wouldn't be here today. And I say without the slightest remorse, that we wouldn't be here, we would not have made economic progress, if we had not intervened on very personal matters—who your neighbour is, how you live, the noise you make, how you spit, or what language you use. We decide what is right. Never mind what the people think.[4]

Before I left the service, prior to resignation, I did a tour of Changi Prison with the director of prisons, in the course of which an inmate in the printing section greeted me by name. Seeing my quizzical look, he introduced himself as Freddy Tan. I could hardly recognise him. The handsome youth, whose good looks brought giddy and impressionable school girls out in numbers to queue up

---

4. *The Straits Times*, April 20, 1987.

for a glimpse of him in court, was prematurely bald and bloated. His slim, athletic figure had given way to podginess. We had a short talk on matters inconsequential. He has since been released from prison with time off for good behaviour.

Some years after I was in private law practice, the investigating officer of the case, who had retired from the police force, met me in a chance encounter and, in a casually bold manner, offered me his services. He revealed that counsel for the defence had a complete set of the prosecution's investigating papers on the Freddy Tan's case at the time of trial, as a result of which the defence was able to anticipate and block my every forensic move. I was totally dumbfounded at the revelation. Without batting an eyelid, he offered me similar services for a consideration, which I pointedly declined, and showed him to the door.

In 1969, I was given the unique opportunity of representing Singapore at the prestigious United Nations' conference on the Law of Treaties in Vienna, Austria. It was also one of the happiest and most nostalgic six weeks I had ever spent in a European capital city. It was an interesting education. For one idealistic moment, I had dreams of becoming an ambassador. I observed at first hand the stratagems of international politicians and experienced the cold-blooded blandishments of the representatives of Communist and Third World countries to secure my vote on specific resolutions.

Not long after my return to Singapore, I began to feel restless and, perceiving the wisdom of the Chinese saying that "a mountain cannot have two tigers," decided to quit the service. I had by then spent sixteen of the best years of my life in the service of my country and government, for which then I had nothing but the greatest respect and admiration. It was time to carve out for myself a new niche of life.

Concerned that I did not leave a bitter taste in the mouth of the powers that be, I first discussed my intention to resign the service with the attorney general, who made a symbolic resistance to my plan for departure. I saw my minister for law, Eddie W. Barker, with whom I had a long and relaxing meeting and who, finally, conceding the axiom that no man is indispensable, gave me his blessings. He was one of the nicest and most approachable ministers of government, well-liked by the Legal Service, including the Civil Service, and the public. I was particularly keen to receive his ministerial approval to take my service leave, accumulated up to almost a year, and be gainfully employed at the same time, prior to the effective official date of resignation. He ungrudgingly approved it. After my departure from service, government's standing orders were changed, reportedly at the instigation of the attorney general, to discourage officers from accumulating service leave.

I told Eddie that I wanted to see the prime minister to bid him farewell, but he did not think it necessary.

"Don't bother the old bugger. I'll tell him about it."

As I was not particularly enamoured of seeing him myself, I was grateful that Eddie had offered to do it for me. Characteristically, Eddie inquired whether I would be receiving any pensions or gratuities, and was genuinely surprised to be told in the negative.

"Nothing!" he echoed, incredulously. "After all these years!

And for what you have done for the state."

Besides the prime minister himself, Eddie was the other minister of government who knew the perils I had run and truly appreciated the quality and quantum of service I had rendered the state those many years, without a break, on important prosecutions or appearances on sensitive issues in all the courts of the country. Recalling an amendment to the Pensions Act, which he had moved in Parliament only a few months before, permitting the retirement of a civil servant from the service after a fifteen-year stint at half-pension, he said:

"Leave it to me. I shall talk to that bugger." And, after a momentary pause, continued, "But, first, I shall have to catch him in a good mood."

I did not really think I fitted into the scheme of things, but I was touched by the spontaneous gesture. A week or so later, I was back at his office. After the usual pleasantries, he told me of his discussion with the prime minister, and the disappointing response,

"That chappie said, 'Francis would be insulted if he were to be retired under the new pensions scheme. It is intended for civil servants, who are considered to be 'u.b.e.'—unlikely to become efficient. It was not meant for persons like him.'"

I assured Eddie that I was not easily insulted, and had been brought up in the belief that "half a loaf of bread is better than no bread at all." The prime minister's response was what I had expected, and I was, therefore, not surprised or disappointed.

I made an appointment to see Dr. Goh Keng Swee, the minister for defence, the most powerful man after the prime minister, with whom I had worked more closely than with any other ministers, save my own law minister. I acquainted him of my decision. It was a congenial meeting. The leave-takings, concluded in an atmosphere of seeming cordiality and sweet reasonableness, assured me that all my bridges were well secured behind me. At least that was what I thought.

Shortly before I was due to leave the service, a Geoffrey Fernandez, the secretary and legal adviser to the Malaysian Singapore Airlines (MSA), a two-nation air carrier, whose head office and main operating station were based in Singapore, was brought back to Singapore, after lengthy extradition proceedings in England, charged with the offence of criminal breach of trust of a paltry sum of $5,000. His more heinous offence, which was carefully muted, was that he had translated national airline company politics into a dangerous game of international politics by pitting the two governments against one another. Banking heavily on his presumed friendship with Tungku Abdul Rahman Putra al-Haj, the prime minister of Malaysia, Malaysian cabinet ministers, and other high Malaysian dignitaries, he had waged an indiscreet campaign of malignity against the prime minister himself and impugned the integrity of his bosom friend, the MSA's chairman and now Chief Justice of Singapore, Yong Pung How.

J.B. Jeyaretnam, now in private law practice, was retained as his legal counsel and saw me regarding bail for his client. My immediate reaction was that it was an impudent request. For, when he was released in Malaysia on a personal cognisance as a member of the Malaysian bar, he had jumped bail, skipped out of the country using his brother's passport to boot, and fled to Ireland. While on an ill-advised sojourn to England, he was arrested. The offence was ordinarily bailable, but, for the antecedents and the prime minister's personal interest in the matter, it would take more than a manful judge to grant him bail. In all the circumstances, it was difficult to accede to such a request for bail unless there were compelling grounds.

I perused the investigation papers, and noted that the case against him was not as strong as I had thought. It turned on a single witness whose evidence, if successfully impugned, would leave the prosecution without a leg to stand on. Upon due consideration and notwithstanding the minus factors of his having jumped bail, I thought it was a case where bail could be offered if the amount of the bail bond was sufficiently large enough to ensure his attendance at the trial. I sounded the request for bail with Yoong Siew Wah, Director, Corrupt Practices Investigation Bureau (CPIB), whose bureau had investigated the offence. Yoong was quite sanguine, provided it was underwritten by substantial bail money. After protracted negotiations regarding the amount of the bail bond, I agreed to give instructions to the deputy public prosecutor not to oppose the application for bail. The next day, *The Straits Times* emblazoned the front page with the news that Fernandez had been released on bail.

All hell broke loose that morning. A wild-eyed and ashen-faced deputy public prosecutor, K.S. Rajah, who had not opposed bail application on my instructions, burst into my room, stammering out that the minister for law had demanded to know why bail had been offered in the circumstances. Observing his distraught state, I suddenly felt sorry for him, as I could see that he beheld his whole future legal career crumbling into dust before him. Before I could respond, the normally imperturbable First Legal Assistant, P. Ramoo, came panting into my room, breathlessly saying that the minister was on the phone asking for the attorney general. Although not formally trained in the law, Ramoo is a valued member of the drafting section, whose rich fund of drafting legalese and knowledge of legislation straddles a period of service under no less than six attorney generals reaching back into the colonial era. Indeed, he knows more of the laws of Singapore than the average lawyer.

I was covering the duties of the attorney general while he was away in Japan. I told K.S. Rajah not to worry, as I would explain it to the minister, and instructed the telephone call be routed to me. Skipping all pleasantries, the minister immediately protested that a junior prosecutor had blundered in acceding to bail, but I quickly disabused him of it in the presence of my deputy; it had been done on my specific instructions. I could hear an audible sigh of relief from my deputy, signalling the great weight of ministerial suspicion had been lifted from his inadequate shoulders.

Surprised, the minister reminded me that Fernandez had been brought back to Singapore at great public expense, and that he could easily skip bail again. I told him that I had given instructions to the CPIB to issue an all-points bulletin for any such eventuality; but the minister retorted—facetiously, to my mind—that Fernandez could "easily escape by rowing a boat across the Straits of Johore" to Malaysia. I replied, if he did that, it was the best thing he could have done for us. The minister sounded aghast and must have thought I was being facetious. But I was serious. I did not think, I said, we had such a great case against him. Anyway, we had adequate bail bond from him.

I was inundated that day with phone calls from the minister and the prime minister. I had hardly relaxed in my chair, when the minister came back on the line to say that I should check carefully the conditions of the bail bond. Some minutes later, he was on the phone again to ask me about the progress of the bond. He came back a couple more times and, finally, spoke to me again seeking assurance that all was well and that the matter was under my *personal* control and supervision and not any other deputy public prosecutor! I reassured him once again; and then, he disclosed that *he* would be calling me and that I should explain to him *exactly* what I had just said to him.

Ten minutes had not ticked away when I received a call from the cabinet secretary saying the prime minister wanted to speak to me. In a sharp no-nonsense voice, he demanded to know why bail had been granted. And so, once again, I explained the rationale of my action. The case was widely believed to be politically motivated and, if Fernandez jumped bail again, the prime minister would be vindicated and the state would be richer by the amount of bail bond forfeited. In any event, the case was not as watertight as many had originally thought. I did not think he appreciated the insouciant manner of my approach; but he seemed satisfied with my reply.

A few moments later, I received another call from him regarding the bail bond and how secure it was. I reassured him that it was very safe. Peace reigned for a while. Then he called again to say that he wanted me to prosecute the case personally, but I told him that I would be on leave prior to resignation.

> "Your leave is hereby cancelled. Your resignation is approved, subject to your completing the case," was the peremptory reply.

I told him that there were other prosecutors who could do the work just as well, but he countered that he was holding me responsible for the results. And thus, the case of the public prosecutor versus Fernandez became my parthian contribution to the legal service and the cause of justice, as prosecutor. But my last act as a civil servant was the execution of a solemn written undertaking that I would not work with or for or be employed by a foreign government for at least five years from the date of my resignation—a new requirement introduced to deny the services of past senior civil servants to foreign governments. Although loosely termed as governments, its focus was on the Federation of Malaysia whose relationship with Singapore was then far from ideal.

As David Marshall was interested in taking on an additional partner in his law firm, I decided, after much thought, to join him. I had told my minister of law of my plans. When the prime minister heard about it, he sent for me. By then, he had moved to more palatial surroundings in the *Istana Annexe*, adjacent to the official abode and office of the president of Singapore. After negotiating my way through several security checkpoints and the ubiquitous Gurkha guards, I was ushered into his presence.

Waiving all niceties aside, he plunged straight to the point of the summons and a monologue, the gist of which was this. Saying that he respected my wish to leave the service, and, knowing me well enough, that I would not be so foolish as to do or disclose anything inimical to the interests of the state, he had decided not stand in my way; otherwise he would be forced to post me out as an ambassador before I was allowed to resign the service. Because of "our past cooperation and relationship" in the commission of inquiry, he "owed it to me to warn me that Marshall and he were on a collision course." Marshall was a politician, still an opposition politician. By joining Marshall, I was in the way, in the line of fire, and that he did not wish me to be hurt in that inevitable collision.

Marshall was at the time a sharp, vocal critic of the PAP government and enjoyed taking political pot shots at the prime minister, a practice which the latter did not appreciate. There was "no future in going with Marshall, who will shrivel on the vine" and, as he spat out those words, he clenched his right fist and stabbed the air with it for added emphasis in case I missed the point. He droned on in this tenor for a good twenty minutes, threatening repeatedly to send me out as an ambassador for three "debriefing" years. I listened quietly to him. "Why cannot you start out on your own? If you are any good, you should have no difficulty. Go out on your own!" It was the advice of absolute power. With this pregnant advice still ringing in my ears, I rose to leave but not before he had seriously warned me that this was a "non-meeting." Until then, I must confess I had not heard of this rather quaint expression. His power had grown so prodigiously that he could now will the non-existence of creation.

Back in my chambers, I pondered over how and what to say to David Marshall. What was there to tell or say anyway, when it was supposed to be a non-meeting? David, however, knew that I was having a "farewell" meeting with the prime minister that day. I had told him. I decided to ring him up to say that I could not join his law firm. Period. And left it as vague as I could. I felt bad, very bad about it. He pressed me for explicit answers to specific questions. I hemmed and hawed. It was difficult to tell him because it was supposedly a non-meeting.

Sensing that my sudden coolness in joining him was directly traceable to my visit to the prime minister, which could portend ominous tidings for him, David, his native cunning a-bristling, sought an appointment to see the prime minister. Whether the prime minister saw him or not, and, if so, what transpired between them, I do not know. I did not speak to him. Nor did I try to find out. I felt wretched that I had let him down without being able to tell him the reason why.

In October 1970, I started my law firm. Lest it be unkindly accused that a conflict of interest arose in the cases I was briefed by clients, I refrained from taking on legal cases where the investigation papers predated my resignation, even though I had not personally dealt with them in the AG's chambers. News of my resignation having preceded me, the very first morning I walked into my law office, still under renovation, clients were already waiting. Business was brisk. Unfortunately, I took on a former Crown Counsel and deputy public prosecutor, who had previously served under me as junior partner. Not very long thereafter, he did my law practice untold damage.

He had tried to join David's law firm in partnership, but David's partner had cannily objected, and his firm was thus spared the misfortune that was about to befall my firm. Unbeknown to me, he had illegally assisted in or attempted to dispose of his clients' properties, which were the subject matter of police investigations. Foolishly relying on his word as a partner, I gave an undertaking over the telephone to the attorney general, who had earlier refused to accept his undertaking that certain books of account belonging to his clients, which the police were searching for, were not on the firm's premises, when, in fact, they were in his room. The attorney general filed a complaint with the Law Society for breach of the undertaking to him. Sadly enough, my relationship with the hypersensitive attorney general had by then undergone a professional strain, although not of my own making or choosing.

I spoke to my dear friend, George Bogaars, to acquaint the prime minister with the facts of the matter. But George brought back this dismissive reply:

> "I did not ask him to leave the service. He had left it of his own accord. He knew who his enemies were. But he chose to leave the safety of my protective umbrella. There is nothing now that I can do to assist him."

The honeymoon was over. I was suspended from law practice for twelve months by the Chief Justice Wee Chong Jin. At about the same time, on a separate but similar breach of undertaking to the attorney general, he also suspended David Marshall, however for only six months. It was a revealing demonstration of even-handed justice. After the period of suspension, I resumed my law practice. Start-up was slow. It was not as spectacularly brisk as when I had first begun. Clients tended to conclude that I was now in bad odour with the government and, whilst they appreciated my legal ability and skill, felt their case might suffer as a consequence if they were to retain me. This was an understandable sentiment and it took a lot to convince them otherwise. In between my law practice, I travelled overseas on clients' behalf, especially in the region.

In 1976, I was elected a member of the Council of the Law Society, in which capacity I served uneventfully for a year. No threats to the stability of his government by my election were perceived by the prime minister. Wherefore no amendments to the law were considered necessary, as I had not assumed a high profile to cast a shadow on him and his government.

In October 1986, I was relaxing in the Subordinate Courts' bar room during an adjournment, when I was approached by Noor Mohamed Marican, a young, Indian Muslim lawyer, with the nickname of Sammy Davis, Jr., as he bore a striking resemblance to the late actor. He asked me in a rather bashful manner whether I had thought of standing for the presidency of the Law Society. The nominations to the annual council elections were closing shortly. Many lawyers were unhappy at the usual slate of PAP and pro-establishment lawyers seeking re-election. I would stand, I replied, provided I could muster sufficient support from members of the bar. He said that he and his friends would canvass support for me. I thought no more about it, as I was busy on a marathon case defending a medical doctor accused of cheating six patients in his treatment of them, but whose offences appeared to me to be more ethical than criminal. He was not greatly liked by members of his own medical fraternity, who resented, not without some cause, his professional hubris. Sometimes, on such marginal considerations a person's whole future can turn, for better or, more often, for the worse.

Sammy and his lawyer friends were true to their word. They ensured that my nomination papers were properly filled in, duly proposed and seconded, and filed before the deadline with the Law Society. When it was noised abroad that I was standing as a candidate, two young lawyers, whom I later knew as Miss Teo Soh Lung and Patrick Seong, sought me out in the Subordinate Courts' bar room to know my platform, as it were, for election. I explained my philosophy and agenda for a more active bar. Satisfied, they promised to campaign for me. I was elected to the Council of the Law Society with the largest majority of votes. And, on the basis of that resounding endorsement from the bar, elected president of the Law Society.

My robust speech at the ritualistic opening of the legal year in January 1987, before a full bench of judges of the Supreme Court, ceremonially attired in their scarlet robes and full-bottomed wigs, presided over by Chief Justice Wee, was roundly received by an overflowing throng of advocates and solicitors. In each previous legal year, we were treated to an obsequious exchange of congratulatory messages and pious platitudes between bench and bar. That year, I served notice of a sea change, that the bar demanded more respect from the bench, which, together with the attorney general and his chambers, had been treating it in shoddy fashion. I had plans for a more assertive and caring bar, that the Law Society should be consulted on the selection and appointment of Supreme Court judges, and be heard on the appointments, promotions, and transfers of subordinate judicial and legal officers by the Legal Service Commission. Taken aback by the unprecedented boisterous ovation, the Chief Justice, greatly mortified, set aside his prepared text, and chided me for demanding that the bar be given the respect as its due; but the signal had been sent. It had to be said. Someone had to say it. The lot had fallen on me. The die was cast. The signal was, however, picked up at Government Hill.

In the meantime, what was particularly gratifying to me were the personal acknowledgements by some judges, but who felt that those barbs could have been better directed at the attorney general and his chambers of deputies, whilst some other judges felt the subordinate courts should have been spared, as the High Court judges were the chief culprits. In the main, they all agreed privately it was time that it was said. *The Sunday Times* heralded, "The new champion at the bar." The bar was on the move.

In early 1986, the government set up a commission of inquiry, presided over by Justice Sinnathuray, an ambitious and egregiously conservative judge, to hear allegations by opposition MP for Anson J.B. Jeyaretnam of executive interference in the subordinate judiciary. There were four terms of reference. The first three terms dealt with the truth or otherwise of the allegations and, if the commissioner found them proven, he should "receive proposals" as to how to improve the system of appointments and transfer of the subordinate judiciary. The Law Society was however interested only in the fourth term of reference. I was deputed by the Council to represent it together with Soh Lung and Patrick. Not surprisingly, the commissioner never got round to the last term of reference, as he held that all Jeyaretnam's allegations were not proven.

The Leader of the House, S. Dhanabalan, thereafter lodged a memorandum of complaint in Parliament against Jeyaretnam. On September 8, 1986, a Committee of Privileges was constituted under the Speaker of Parliament to consider the complaint. The proceedings were televised. With the committee packed with PAP cronies plus a lone opposition Member of Parliament, Jeyaretnam did not have a ghost of a chance against the prime minister, who blatantly usurped the functions of the chair and speechified in characteristic fashion between and during the interrogation of witnesses.

Considering that the Law Society's interest was limited to the fourth term of reference only, the prime minister's insistence on my presence before the Committee, "as he is beyond question, the most prominent member of the Council [of the Law Society]" raised many eyebrows within the legal profession and the public at large, and heightened excitement when he had the Speaker adjourn the hearing to secure my attendance. The prime minister's total disinterest in the testimony of other council members, who could have provided the same evidence as I, was telling. I happened to be out of town and, owing to the uncertainty of the date of my return to Singapore, the Committee reluctantly concluded its deliberations without me. Jeyaretnam was, predictably, found guilty of "abuse of [parliamentary] privilege," and fined. The Speaker of Parliament subsequently declared Jeyaretnam's seat in Parliament vacated because of a fine imposed on him in another matter.

As I envisaged it, the Law Society could, under its constitution, play a more meaningful role than it had hitherto been doing in articulating the profession's views and promoting public awareness of the implications of the spate of legislation and amending legislation to existing Acts, which the legislature was churning out with bewildering rapidity. This viewpoint was shared by almost every lawyer, except that they had neither the time nor the energy for a conscientious scrutiny of the laws. To my mind, no other professional body of persons was as ideally endowed for this enterprise as the lawyers themselves, trained in the law.

In early 1986, the Council agreed to consider the Newspaper and Printing Presses (Amendment) bill, which would enable the government to restrict the circulation of foreign publications if the relevant minister deemed that they were interfering in the domestic politics of Singapore. The Special Assignments (Civil Legislation) Subcommittee, under the chairmanship of Soh Lung, was delegated this task. Its critical report was duly discussed by the Council, which approved the issuance of an equally critical press statement under the president's hand. The prime minister later made the scandalous allegations that the Council's decision had been influenced by Marxist lawyer-conspirators, and its president by the pocketbook of the CIA.

Soh Lung was subsequently arrested and detained under the ISA. A letter of the Council of the Law Society to the chairman of the advisory board, supportive of Soh Lung's representation against her detention, is a telling rejoinder to the prime minister's bizarre allegations. It might be mentioned here that every professional society and association in Singapore has government appointees or nominees on its governing or management board, who act not only as the eyes and ears but also the mouthpiece of government. Insofar as government-appointed lawyers were concerned in my year of office as president, they were more professional and independent than sneakily political.

The Law Society was widely attacked by the government for acting as a political pressure group, and roundly told off that it had no business to be commenting on such legislative matters. The upshot of all this was that the prime minister introduced amendments to the Legal Profession Act ostensibly to tighten disciplinary procedures, to disqualify errant lawyers from standing for election to the Council of the Law Society, and to prohibit the Law Society from commenting on existing or proposed legislation, unless its views were specifically sought by government. It was apparent to the most obtuse observer that the main thrust of the amendments was directed towards my ouster as president of the Law Society and to still the voices of dissent.

Sixty-two lawyers, including Soh Lung and Miss Tang Fong Har, requisitioned an extraordinary general meeting of the Law Society to deplore the introduction of the Legal Profession (Amendment) bill which, after an animated debate, was passed by an almost unanimous vote. The meeting confined only to lawyers was strictly confidential; but the ISD had managed to wire it for sound. To Soh Lung's somewhat naïve inquiry at the subsequent Select Committee hearing on the amendments to the Legal Profession Act as to how the prime minister possessed a transcript of her speech made from the floor, he scornfully replied, "in the age of the tape recorder, you want to know how I am able to get a transcript of what you said?"

At about this time, I began to experience unusual pressure from my bankers, especially my Malaysian-based bankers, with whom I had a long and cordial banking relationship. The bank pressed for an immediate and full repayment of overdrafts on both my personal and my law firm's accounts, and, to my anxious inquiry, reluctantly explained it was on "instructions from its head office" in Kuala Lumpur (KL). It would not hear of any schemes or further schemes of repayments. But a friendly bank officer within pulled me aside and suggested that my only hope was to speak personally to the chairman of the bank in KL, who alone could countermand the "instructions." I made a trunk call to his secretary for an urgent appointment.

The next day, I flew up to KL with Mei, of whom I shall relate more shortly, to meet him. He was a lawyer by profession, and had heard of my legal reputation. He seemed genuinely ignorant of the action taken on my accounts by his Singapore branch. He checked with his staff, who indicated that no recall instructions had emanated from the KL office. It was intriguingly significant. Anyway, he appeared sympathetic to my predicament, and suggested that I should see again the general manager in Singapore with fresh proposals whilst he looked further into the matter. On my return, I immediately went with Mei to see the general manager with new proposals, but he told me that he had not heard anything from his head office. I telephoned KL and was startled to be informed by the chairman's secretary that it was "strictly a Singapore affair" and that, much as the chairman would like to help me, there was nothing more he could do. I was told in effect to sort it out with the Singapore branch, which I attempted to do, only to discover that Singapore would not, or could not do anything without specific instructions from KL. It was an absurd situation. Overnight, the situation had undergone a dramatic change. Every which way you lose!

I suspected the hidden hand of the Singapore government. I had known the bank's general manager for many years. To my pointed inquiry as to the part the Singapore authorities had played in this loan recall, he became acutely uncomfortable and greatly agitated. He tried to exonerate them from any involvement saying that it was a banking decision *simpliciter*; but the more he tried to defend the so-called bank's action the more his body language betrayed him. He left Mei and me with no doubt whatsoever from where or from whom those instructions had come. Fear of the authorities had paralysed the bank and its officers.

Some years later, as a Visiting Fellow at Harvard Law School in Cambridge, Massachusetts, I met with two former Malaysian government ministers, one of whom was doing a sabbatical at the same university. In the course of our meeting, he recounted a surprise telephone call he had received from the prime minister in Singapore regarding my bank accounts and Mei. This fortuitous encounter confirmed vividly my earlier suspicions concerning the sudden recall of those bank overdrafts.

In the meanwhile, it was painfully evident that I could not take this matter up any further and that, unless I produced the money within the next few days, my position as the president of the Law Society would be seriously compromised. As time was of the essence, Mei kindly offered to lend me the money to pay off the bank on the understanding that I would repay her as soon as I could get my finances in order. The loan was afterwards regularized by an agreement secured against my insurance policy and assets of my law firm. Less than a fortnight later, on September 5, 1986, the good Samaritan was served with a ministerial order revoking her permanent residence status and ordered to leave Singapore.

Coincidentally with these events, the Inland Revenue Department served me with a request for a statement of my assets and liabilities for the last twelve years, a fishing expedition normally embarked by the Inland Revenue Department to trace the source of unexplained wealth of businessmen or traders. This device is rarely used on professionals. To underline the point that I was in bad odour of government, I was also served with additional assessments to tax. I referred the request to my law firm's accountants, who were also my tax agents, to respond to the Inland Revenue Department. But it was not long before they pleaded with me to be discharged from handling this matter.

Members of their staff had attended on the Inland Revenue Department's officials and were given the treatment of "the long wait." They were repeatedly kept waiting all day or the best part of a day at the Inland Revenue Department without being able to see the tax officials concerned, who would either be too busy to see them at the appointed time or saw them only for a few minutes and told them to return on the next or another day. A few times of this treatment were sufficient to drive the message home. They were being deliberately inconvenienced resulting in sheer wastage of valuable time and energy. And when the officials finally condescended to see them, they dropped broad hints that I was *persona non grata* with the government and that it would not be in their interests to represent me. I could not blame my accountants for backing out, as they pointed out that they are a small firm and could not spare members of their staff idling in the waiting room and corridors of the Inland Revenue Department waiting endlessly to see the officials. They had to consider the interests of their other clients too, the resolution of whose tax problems could be made more difficult because of their representation of me. To overcome this problem, my accountants suggested that they would prepare all letters and queries on my own firm's letterheads for my signature and, wherever necessary, brief a member of my staff before she went to see the tax officials. I found this arrangement wholly unsatisfactory. I decided to approach a more intrepid firm of accountants to take over, but even it agreed only after much persuasion. They, too, begged to be let off eventually for very much the same reasons.

In the hands of a vindictive government, the Inland Revenue Department can be a powerful instrument of oppression against its political adversaries. Consider the case of Ong Eng Guan, the former quixotic PAP mayor and minister for national development. He was a public accountant whose accountancy firm, when he held mayoral and ministerial reins of local and national government, retained an enviable portfolio of accounts of major corporate clients and wealthy Singaporeans. But, soon after he fell out with the government, he lost this lucrative business, and, according to the story circulating the professional rounds at the time, endured constant audit by the Inland Revenue department. At that time I had dismissed it as apocryphal, but now that I am a target of official displeasure, it seems to have a familiar ring.

To counter adverse public reaction, in a gesture of seeming magnanimity, the government appointed a Select Committee to hear and receive evidence on the proposed amendments to the Legal Profession Act. The Council discussed the representations it intended to make before the Select Committee and, in an honest but ingenuous belief that there was going to be a professional exchange of viewpoints on the relative merits and demerits of the bill, appointed two Council members to present the Society's views thereon, when every Council member suddenly found himself served with a subpoena. Surprise was further enhanced when members of the Special Assignments (Civil Legislation) Subcommittee reported that they had been subpoenaed too.

We discussed this unexpected turn of events. We agreed that, notwithstanding, the two members who had been delegated this responsibility would present the case for the Law Society as originally resolved, whilst the rest of us would attend to provide moral support. We duly turned up *en masse*. Parliamentary Select Committee proceedings are usually confidential and any unauthorized coverage of the proceedings could end up in a contempt action against the reporter. But, in this instance, they were televised; the script and screenplay for what can only be described as parliamentary burlesque were written, presented, produced, and directed by a versatile prime minister, with the virtuoso himself stealing the show as its consummate political actor. His genius so completely dominated the theatrical performance that the Speaker of Parliament as chairman and the other members of the Select Committee seemed as relevant to the proceedings as flies on a wall.

The attorney general, ill-at-ease in the witness box, even though having been well-primed beforehand, intoned self-consciously by rote a litany of disciplinary actions, which the Society was said to have been remiss in energetic prosecution. It was a sad performance. Upon cross-examination, he ingenuously claimed that the amendments were directed at no one,[5] an answer which was plain to all that he himself did not believe in. The prime minister then called as the first Council witness, Harry Elias, the immediate past president of the Law Society. Cross-examining Council member Mirza Namazie next, the prime minister referred to his postgraduate practical law course many years ago, accusing him of having cheated at tests. We were taken aback by the vengeful personal thrust of his examination. Caught totally off guard, Namazie gamely tried to defend himself by explaining that, during that period, no law graduate really took the practical law course seriously and, for that very reason, the so-called cheating was rampant among law graduates. But, to score his point regarding errant lawyers, the prime minister resurrected ancient ghosts of alleged misdemeanours past, utterly disregarding whether the personal and professional harm done would far outweigh their evidential relevance or value.

The next Council member witness called by him to the stand was Jernail Singh Khosa, a former senior police officer, who had resigned the police force to read for the bar. The prime minister insinuated that Khosa had left the force under a cloud and been involved in some past corruption in the force. He wondered aloud whether he would have been admitted as "a fit and proper person" to the bar, had the attorney general's sieve of approval been as fine as it should have been. Dreading the prime minister's egregious proclivities for wallowing in the gutter, his confidence torn into shreds, Khosa meekly agreed to everything put to him. Asked later why he had assumed such an obsequious posture, he replied dejectedly, he feared not so much the so-called corruption allegations as the public disclosures by the prime minister of past extramarital activities, which would have threatened his home. He brooded long

---

5. See Report of the Select Committee on the Legal Profession (Amendment) Bill, October 16, 1986, at pp. B-11 and B-19, and Hansard, May 31, 1988, col. 288.

over the public humiliation, withdrew into himself, and drank more than was good for him into an early grave.

Listening to the line and nature of questioning and the order of witnesses called by the prime minister, I perceived that this crucifixion of Council members was being performed for my edification, if I should prove recalcitrant in the witness box. It had little to do with the merits of the proposed amendments. By this time, it was abundantly clear the amendments were aimed principally at my deposal as president of the Law Society. I was appalled and incensed at the reprehensible character assassination of two Council members from the dastardly safety of the parliamentary dais. And I firmly resolved to disappoint him.

Alluding briefly to my prowess in commissions of inquiry and courage in discharging my duties in difficult situations, he slyly offered me a way out with a rhetoric of sweet sensibility. But I resolutely refused to yield to his blandishments. Seeing my obduracy, he tried to discredit me. But I decided to forestall him by declaring that I was not bashful about discussing details of my private life, chronologically if he so desired. He deflected it, however, by pretending that he was not interested in my private life but in my public life. I had to be careful that I said or did nothing which might prove detrimental or injurious to the interests of the Council and the bar, and restrained myself in my answers. I had constantly to remind myself to be presidential. Notwithstanding, it was the first time in decades that anyone had stood up to him.

He barely touched upon the relative merits of the bill and, with his face contorted in livid red, made no bones about the fact that the amendments were introduced with me in mind, because I was not fit, in his view, to be the president of the Law Society. That he had unwittingly exposed his attorney general's patent ingenuousness did not trouble him at all. I roundly told him off that it was not for him, but for my peers to decide whether or not I was a fit and proper person to be the president, and they had thought otherwise. He recalled me to the witness box the next day for another session of questioning, feigning that I had taken unfair advantage of him the previous day. He did not emerge from our lively exchange under the merciless glare of the television cameras in the way he had planned, even though it was afterwards heavily edited before transmission, and technicians reportedly had to be brought in to tone down his rubescent face in the TV film. Public reaction was decidedly negative. Thanks to him, overnight a TV star had been born. It is inconceivable that he could perceive in me such a grave threat to the political stability of his government as to justify the awesome exercise of the powers of the apparatus of state.

Two other lawyers who were the subject of his political venom were University of Singapore graduates, Misses Teo Soh Lung and Tang Fong Har, two petite, bright-eyed and idealistic members of the Special Assignments (Civil Legislation) Subcommittee. He tried to browbeat them but they held their ground. They bested him. That was *lèse-majesté*. For this offence they were arrested eight months later, labelled as Marxists, subjected to indignities and repentance at leisure in the grim, solitary confines of Whitley Detention Centre!

A perplexed Lim Chor Pee, a law graduate of Cambridge University, was summarily summoned by him to give evidence, to catch me out in a lie. But he failed for, as the Latin maxim says, *magna est veritas et praevalebit*—truth is great and will prevail. However, in a shabby attempt to show up Soh Lung, the prime minister prefaced his examination:

"Mr. Lim, unlike Miss Teo, you come from a reputable university, ..."

That it was a horrible slur on the reputation of the National University of Singapore did not worry him as long as he could score a point, nor did it evoke any demurral from the graduate-professor of that same disreputable university, S.Jayakumar, the minister for law, or the other members, all of whom sat dumbfounded and vacuous on the Select Committee. Several Council members squirmed in their seats in acute embarrassment or shyness for the prime minister and, more particularly, his mute professor of law.

With no warning, the hearings ended. The official feedback unit had apparently reported unfavourable public reaction to the prime minister's stellar bullying performance. Still smarting from that encounter, in a subsequent rambling speech in Parliament on dark conspiracies and foreign interference in Singapore's domestic politics, he said:

When I met the young lady, Miss Teo Soh Lung, and the other young lady, Tang Fong Har, all they needed were two pig-tails, and we go back to 1950s, 1960s, because they've got determination, they want to change the world.

They do not want to change the world. This "pig-tail" allusion to radical schoolgirls of that epoch, spartanly dressed with severely braided hair, was an unfair aspersion, which thoughtful Singaporeans reject. Like so many other Singaporeans, they want only to see a Singapore changed to a less repressive society, a society not only with a human face but a heart as well, or, as Goh Chok Tong, his successor in office, put it, borrowing the language of U.S. President George Bush, "a kinder, gentler Singapore."

Unlike previous Select Committee hearings, it was highly doubtful whether the prime minister derived any benefit from this political theatre. Thus began my *affaire* with national politics. In the aftermath of those proceedings, I was courted by political parties; Chiam See Tong, secretary-general of the Singapore Democratic Party, approached me, and so did J.B. Jeyaretnam, secretary-general of the Workers' Party. On the other hand, there were suggestions that I should form my own party. Later, the newly-formed National Solidarity Party asked me to lead it. I still remained undecided as to the wisdom of engagement in national politics. Friends and acquaintances and even strangers tried to talk me into entering the political arena. Not since the heady days of David Marshall and Harry Lee, who frequently locked horns in Parliament, had they witnessed anything quite like it. And everywhere I turned, there were endless complimentary references to that TV encounter, pleas and persuasion to provide a lead for an opposition. The people were tiring of a one-party government.

The televised Select Committee hearings on the Legal Profession (Amendment) bill had a most salutary effect in quickening the interests of the people, especially young and idealistic professionals, in opposition elective politics.

4

May 21, 1987

> If it is not totalitarian to arrest a man and detain him, when you cannot charge him with any offence against any written law—if that is not what we have always cried out against in Fascist states—then what is it?
>
> —Lee Kuan Yew[1]
>
> Alas, what poor Marxists they were!
>
> —Lee Kuan Yew[2]

On Thursday, May 21, Singapore was shaken by an official announcement of the arrest by the Internal Security Department (ISD) of sixteen young men and women, amongst whom was Soh Lung, "in connection with a clandestine communist network." In a follow-up exercise in June, another six persons were arrested, including K.C. Chew, a Harvard Business School graduate. Many of the arrestees were associated with Roman Catholic (RC) social and welfare organizations.

With communism *passé*, Marxism, Marxist, or Marxist-inclined became the fashionable buzz words in Singapore's official lexicon. News of the arrest of dangerous Marxist plotters was greeted with profound skepticism by a shocked public. In a world where the winds of change were pounding hard at communist dogma rattling its very institutions throughout the Soviet Union and Eastern

---

1. Legislative Assembly Debates, September 21, 1955.
2. Legislative Assembly Debates, July 30, 1963.

Europe, it boggled the mind that anyone in an economically vibrant modern Singapore and, more especially, Roman Catholic Singaporeans would knowingly subscribe to communism or mix with communists and their ilk to subvert the government violently and replace it with a Marxist state. Against the prevailing currents of history, these hapless young men and women were swept up and labelled Marxists or Marxist-inclined.

They were detained at the Whitley Detention Centre under the Internal Security Act (ISA), which had been introduced by the colonial administration to deal with the communist insurgency in Malaya. The ISA enables the government to arrest and detain a person without trial, two years at a time. By renewing the order of detention, a person can be detained indefinitely, as in the case of opposition *Barisan Sosialis* MP, Chia Thye Poh, who had been detained since 1966.

Although the British colonial administration authored this draconian legislation, it was applied only when the administration was satisfied that a suspect posed a security risk to the nation. The power of arrest and detention was not indiscriminately invoked as an aid to, but as the culmination of careful investigation into the suspect's involvement in subversion, civil disorder, or labour unrest. Furthermore, political detainees were treated differently from convicted prisoners. The ISA was never employed, as now seems to be the trend, to nip in the bud serious political opposition to PAP rule. The PAP approach of shooting first and asking questions afterwards, is rather reminiscent of the grotesque trial, which a bewildered Alice witnessed in her adventures in a bizarre world, wherein the Queen of Hearts insisted upon, "Sentence first, verdict afterwards."[3] If, after arrest, a person turns out to be innocent of any complicity, he is quietly released. Such was the plight of the unfortunate two guests of the president of Singapore and the first lady. He is made to feel that he is exceedingly lucky to be freed without more ado, but never with so much as a word of apology or compensation, for that would be considered inappropriate and bad for public relations, exposing as it would be, the fallibility of the internal security apparatus, which

---

3. Lewis Carroll, *Alice's Adventures in Wonderland*, Penguin Books, 1960.

would be absolutely unthinkable. Or, in the more succinct words of *The Straits Times*, it would "confuse the people."

On May 26, the Ministry for Home Affairs (MHA) issued a statement detailing the ISD discovery of "a Marxist conspiracy to subvert the existing social and political system in Singapore through communist united front tactics to establish a communist state."[4] The dark conspiracy, it narrated, was being masterminded by Tan Wah Piow, a second-year law student at Balliol College, Oxford University, some 8,000 miles away. Wah Piow's Marxist network, as depicted in the statement, showed him ensconced, strangely enough, not in the customary centre but at the periphery of an amorphous spidery web. A "local ringleader," Vincent Cheng, a former seminarian and full-time Catholic lay worker, occupied instead the focal point of the web, whose gossamer threads stretched awkwardly outwards to the fifteen detainees, former student agitators turned social activists infiltrating two main fronts—RC groups and student organizations for political agitation. "Their subversive activities are prejudicial to the security of Singapore and, if left unchecked, would lead to unmanageable political instability and chaos,"[5] the statement said.

The unprecedented detention of so many church and voluntary workers in the RC social welfare centres, such as the Geylang Catholic Welfare Centre for foreign workers and related organizations, created an impression among the public of a church under siege. This impression was lent credence when some Catholic priests intervened on behalf of the faithful detained, thereby precipitating a crisis in the making with the government. In the process, it laid bare longtime ISD surveillance of the church, its priests, and their activities.

The prime minister perceived the clerical intervention as a threat to the stability of the government, which could assume seismic proportions. On June 2, 1987, he met at the *Istana* at a private meeting with Gregory Yong, the Roman Catholic archbishop of the archdiocese of Singapore, eight priests, and lay leaders after they had first been screened by the ISD for political correctness. The

---

4. Ministry of Home Affairs statement.
5. *Ibid*.

meeting was intended to dispel the common perception that the arrest of the faithful was directed at the church. Present, too, were the minister for home affairs, the permanent secretary to the Ministry for Home Affairs and the director, ISD, none of whom appeared to have participated meaningfully in the ensuing discussions.

According to the secret minutes recorded at the several meetings that day, the prime minister was "not worried" about nor "interested in" Vincent Cheng and his group, because they were "*novices;*" and he contemptuously dismissed Tan Wah Piow as "stupid," "a simpleton," who did not have a "sufficiently good mind," and one whom he "could not believe was in control." It was only a "little problem," the prime minister haughtily told the Reverend Giovanni D'Aniello, chargé d'affaires to the Apostolic Nunciature, (who had at his request come down from Bangkok) and, with equal disdain, said the so-called conspirators were actually *"do-gooders, who wanted to help the poor and the dispossessed*, getting perverted along the way to Marxism," but who, "given sufficient time, would eventually become like the communists in the Philippines." It was a significant judgment. But, according to the MHA statement, it was a dangerous Marxist conspiracy, waged by dangerous Marxists!

But he was, however, more concerned about the sociopolitical activities and involvement of several priests, specifically Frs. Edgar D'Souza, Patrick Goh, Joseph Ho, and Guillaume Arotcarena, in their defence of the faithful detained than in the sixteen detainees because they, he said, and not the detainees, were going to bring the Church onto "a collision course with the government," a course which he was trying to avoid.

It was a momentous assessment of the prevailing security situation and of the detainees' relationship *vis-à-vis* the activist priests by a prime minister, whose experience of, and egregious collaboration with dangerous, full-blooded communists was legendary, and who had never ceased to brag how he had outwitted them. There was a divergence of views amongst his ministerial colleagues; but he had the "power of override." This crucial evaluation of the so-called Marxist conspiracy and conspirators was classified *secret*. It was not known to the general public or to counsel representing the detainees, until the *Far Eastern Economic Review* on December 17, 1987, reported an interview with Fr. Edgar D'Souza in Australia captioned, "New Light on Detentions," which the prime minister claimed had libelled him. In early June, Fr. D'Souza prudently had left for Australia, where he has remained ever since. It was only on September 25, 1989, that the secret minutes of the meetings entered the public domain at the libel trial against the weekly magazine in the Singapore High Court.

Immediately after the *Istana* meetings, the prime minister and Archbishop Yong met with the domestic media, which had been alerted by the prime minister's secretary for the occasion. The press conference was as brief as it was instructive. The archbishop, who, understandably in the circumstances, appeared far from convinced that Vincent Cheng and the others were involved in clandestine communist activities, asked for proof. When the prime minister interjected with a sharp disclaimer, "I have never said that I was going to prove anything in a court of law," he left his audience stunned. He continued: "It is not the practice nor will I allow subversives to get away by insisting that I [have] got to prove everything against them in a court of law or evidence that will stand up to the strict rules of evidence of a court of law."

This represented a 180-degree shift in principle, a right-aboutturn from his previous position on preventive detention, on which he had heaped righteous indignation and for which he had denounced the government of the day as "totalitarian" and "fascist." In the egregious 1956 civil unrest in Singapore, he demanded the Labour Front government release his political colleague, PAP assemblyman, Lim Chin Siong, or hold an open trial or a public inquiry "if the government wants to retain the slightest pretensions to democracy. If it cannot, then it must release him. And that goes for all the other persons who have been detained."[6] He was then speaking as an opposition PAP assemblyman in the legislature on his motion deploring the arrest and detention of Lim Chin Siong and others under the Preservation of Public Security Ordinance[7] by the government "without producing any evidence to justify its action."

---

6. Legislative Assembly Debates, November 5–6, 1956.
7. The precursor of the Internal Security Act, Cap. 143.

The bloody evidence however lay in the civil strife that wracked Singapore where the Singapore police force, reinforced by units of the Royal Federation of Malaya police force and the British army, sought for several days to prevent the spread of arson, riots, and mayhem. Some thirteen persons were killed, and as many as a hundred or more persons were injured or hospitalized. The imposition of an island-wide, round-the-clock curfew finally restored law and order. If, notwithstanding such bloody, murderous circumstances, he could still be motivated to deplore the arbitrary detention of his colleague and the others, how much the more deplorable was the detention of sixteen young men and women who, in his own words, were only "novices" and "do-gooders?" And who, far from instigating or inciting foreign maids or workers to mutiny and rage, were advising and counselling them on their legal rights and remedies against exploitation by unscrupulous employers! But, weirdly, he had to deal with those do-gooders "in a way that would make it less likely for others to follow in their wake," underscoring his statement with his favorite Chinese adage, *sha ji xia hou*—slaughter the chicken to teach the monkey—by drawing the back of his hand across his throat.[8]

On June 20, four detainees were released; but six other persons were arrested as "follow-up" action, amongst whom was Fong Har. They were released one month later after interrogation.

Formal orders of detention were issued against twelve detainees. The relatives of four detainees retained me as counsel to secure their release: Miss Wong Souk Yee, a 28-year old research executive and amateur dramatist; Miss Teresa Lim Li Kok, a 32-year old publisher; William Yap, a 40-year old, subtitling editor with the government-owned Singapore Broadcasting Corporation, and Vincent Cheng, a 40-year old full-time church worker, who, as noted, was alleged to be the local arch-conspirator of the nebulous Marxist plot. They denied they were Marxists or had any Marxist connection. I represented Vincent for just about twenty-four hours. The next day, I received a letter from his father apologising for the sudden termination of the retainer. He had been dissuaded from retaining me as

---

8. To Colin Smith, *London Sunday Observer*, December 10, 1989.

counsel by his ISD captors. Within a fortnight or so after I had interviewed him at the Centre, William Yap also decided to dispense with my services.

Among the detainees were three women lawyers and a young law graduate, Kevin De Souza. De Souza's conduct in "forsaking a well-paid legal career for a lowly-paid job of a helper at S$500.00 per month with the Singapore Polytechnic Catholic Students' Union" was interpreted by a materialistic government as heinous confirmation of a Marxist inclination.

Soh Lung was, at the time of her arrest, a Council member of the Law Society. Her steely courage in travail won her the respect of her peers and the admiration of many Singaporeans and people around the world. In 1990, she and Vincent Cheng were recommended by U.S. human rights organizations for the distinguished Jimmy Carter Human Rights Award; but they lost out to two other human rights monitors from Guatemala and Sri Lanka. Yielding to powerful ISD persuasion, Souk Yee and Teresa decided to abandon their representations on their detention to the advisory board.[9] That left Soh Lung, who had retained me for that purpose.

The MHA reasons for her arrest were totally and utterly absurd:
(1) she had arranged the entry of Marxist conspirators, including Teresa, into the opposition Workers' Party[10] to make use of the Party for the group's cause;
(2) she was an activist in the Geylang Catholic Welfare Centre and legal adviser to radicals in the Singapore Polytechnic Students' Union;
(3) she was a legal assistant to one G. Raman when Raman was legal adviser to the University of Singapore Students' Union then headed by Tan Wah Piow; and
(4) in 1986, she had been engaged by Tan Wah Piow to ascertain his citizenship status.

The Workers' Party (WP) was and is a lawful political organization, registered with the Registrar of Societies. Notwithstanding

---

9. See section 2 of the ISA, and Article 151(2) of the Constitution of the Republic of Singapore.
10. It is a legally registered political party whose manifesto is not dissimilar to that of the British Labour Party.

its history of having had a fair share of radicals, it was never de-registered. It was formed in 1957 by the former Chief Minister, David Marshall, who served as its head. After his 1966 electoral defeat, it lay dormant until it was resurrected by former senior district judge and lawyer, Joshua Benjamin Jeyaretnam, who campaigned unsuccessfully in several elections under the WP's banner. But the year 1981 marked a watershed in Singapore's national politics when Jeyaretnam won the Anson constituency by-election which had been caused by the National Trade Unions Congress (NTUC) secretary general and PAP MP, C.V. Devan Nair's ill-starred elevation to the presidency of the Republic of Singapore. That victory owed in no small measure to the assistance given by those so-called Marxists who were, at their request, introduced to Jeyaretnam by Soh Lung.

The Geylang Catholic Welfare Centre, a worthwhile social organization of the archdiocese, provided an important outlet for women and girls—mainly Filipinas—far from their home and friends (having been imported from the Philippines for domestic duties). It furnished sociolegal counselling and advice by volunteers like Soh Lung, a lawyer with fine social sensibilities and a founder-member of the Law Society's Criminal Legal Aid Scheme.

G. Raman, a human rights lawyer, was arrested under the ISA on February 10, 1977, for alleged communist united front activities. The allegation against him was his association with Dr. Malcolm Caldwell, an acerbic PAP critic and eccentric left-wing lecturer in Southeast Asian history in the renowned London School of Oriental and African Studies, who was subsequently found shot dead in mysterious circumstances in Cambodia. In a ritualistic television appearance, Raman "confessed" he was a communist before he was conditionally released on February 25, 1978. Raman was stripped of his Singapore citizenship, and he travels now on a certificate of identity. He was not charged or tried in a court of law.

Tan Wah Piow, as noted, was at the material time a law student at Balliol College, Oxford University. Prior to being labelled a Marxist, he had been a student in architecture at the National University of Singapore, when he was charged, together with two others, with the offence of rioting at the premises of the Singapore Pioneer Industries Employees' Union. He was found guilty, convicted, and sentenced to one year's imprisonment by senior district court judge, S. Sinnathuray, who shortly afterwards was promoted to the Supreme Court bench.

Conventional wisdom has it that Wah Piow was framed for the offence by a rising PAP MP and trade unionist, Phey Yew Kok,[11] who was himself some time later charged with criminal breach of trust of union funds and, while on bail, absconded from Singapore. (He is still at large, and the apparent lack of drive and energy displayed by the government to locate his whereabouts is a continual source of political speculation.) Immediately after his release from prison, Wah Piow was ordered to report for national service, but he left Singapore suddenly without any deferment leave from the army unit to which he had been ordered to report. He later surfaced in England, with, so the government claimed, a false Singapore international passport.

Irked by his acceptance as a student into Oxford University and the Honourable Society of the Middle Temple Inn, the government sought in vain to have Wah Piow disbarred from both institutions of learning, as not being "a fit and proper person" to read law by virtue of his conviction and sentence, but, was soundly rebuffed by both institutions. With Wah Piow and other displaced dissidents like him targeted in its cross-hairs, the government amended the Constitution providing for the deprivation of citizenship of Singaporeans, notwithstanding they are natural-born, who remain out of Singapore for ten continuous years. After approaching several lawyers to take up the cudgels on his behalf, without success, Wah Piow asked me to represent him in the matter of the deprivation of his citizenship; but, because of a then possible conflict of interest, I declined. I suggested, however, some names to him. He contacted Soh Lung to act for him. In the best traditions of the bar, she accepted his brief and, incredibly, this was used as a ground for her arrest. I have often wondered if I had accepted his brief and espoused his grievance whether I, too, might not have been tarred with the brush of Marxism.

A formal order of detention for one year was issued against her. The grounds and allegations accompanying the order narrowed

---

11. A nephew of Dr. Phay Seng Huat, Chairman, Public Services Commission.

down to two main bases. They were just as mystifying and bizarre, declaring that "between 1984 and May 1987, ... she had acted in a manner prejudicial to the security of Singapore by being involved in a Marxist conspiracy to subvert the existing social and political system in Singapore, using communist united front tactics with the view to establishing a Marxist state" in that—
(1) she had facilitated the infiltration of the Workers' Party in 1984 by a group of Marxists after discussions with Paul Lim Huat Chye, Tan Wah Piow's fellow Marxist, and other activists and had actively assisted them in their efforts to make use of the Workers' Party as a vehicle to further the Marxist cause; and
(2) she and Tang Fong Har made use of the Law Society of Singapore as a political group at the suggestion of Paul Lim Huat Chye.

I was then president of the Law Society. The Council of the Law Society consisted of, amongst other elected lawyers, three die-hard, government-appointed representatives, who, as stated, were the eyes and ears of the government. Soh Lung and Fong Har were relatively junior women lawyers and not even members of the Council of the Law Society. Considering the Council's structure and makeup, the procedure and conduct of its meetings, it can only be described as Kafkaesque even to suggest that they had manipulated the staid Council for pernicious Marxist ends. The accusation left Council members, including even pro-establishment members, dumbfounded and bereft of words. Government credibility dropped to an all-time low.

Council proceedings including dissenting views, if any, are duly recorded in the minutes of the meetings and properly kept by an executive lawyer-secretary. Decisions are decided by a majority vote. Copies of Council minutes, notwithstanding their confidentiality, regularly find their way on to the desks of the law ministers and government, including the ISD. The MHA was particularly miffed, when the Council initially refused its official request for a copy of a confidential research survey of foreign publications circulating in Singapore on the Newspaper and Printing Presses bill by its Special Assignments Committee (Civil). The Council was unhappily assailed as being hostile to government. Confidentiality has practically no meaning vis-à-vis the government, even though it is expressly spelled out in the law.

On August 15, 1987, together with lawyer, Subhas Anandan,[12] I appeared for Soh Lung to argue her representation before the advisory board chaired by Justice Sinnathuray, a judge of the Supreme Court, and two lay members. Because of a promise made, Soh Lung instructed me not to make any reference to the assault on her by ISD officers. She had given in to the anxious pleas of the case officer who feared for his future career and family—an excellent demonstration of the Stockholm syndrome!

The advisory board has no overriding powers under the ISA, but can only make recommendations to the president of the Republic of Singapore regarding detention; he is not bound to accept them. Nevertheless, the advisory board is not particularly known for courageous decisions, headed as it is by an ultraconservative judge. Realizing the almost insuperable odds against us and that Soh Lung could not be in any worse position than she was already in, I felt we should vigorously pursue with the representation, notwithstanding—for miracles were still known to happen in this cynical age, even in a repressively materialistic Singapore!

On September 26, 1987, seven detainees, including Soh Lung and Souk Yee, were conditionally released from detention on suspension orders by a direction of the minister for home affairs. But not before they were made to appear before the television cameras to mouth contrite confessions scripted by the ISD.

Some detainees, like Souk Yee, had written, produced or directed plays on the tragi-comic plight of Filipina maid-servants or satirical skits or farce on or about Singapore and Singaporeans for an amateur drama group called the Third Stage. The government alleged this was a communist open front organization trying to "reach out to and radicalize the public."

But any organization in Singapore, be it the Third Stage or another, could not exist without its promoters and office-bearers having first been given security clearance by the ISD and several other

---

12. For more on Subhas Anandan, see chap. 5.

government departments. Thereafter, each and every public stage performance requires official sanction or approval. Scripts of plays, including the names of the organizers and promoters, players, and other myriad details, have to be submitted for review by the censor and approval of government departments without which they could not be staged.

Divisional plainclothes police officers attend each performance to ensure that the conditions of the written permit are complied with and that there are no moral or political deviations from the approved script. ISD officers often mix and mingle with the audience. Classified reports are thereafter submitted to the relevant departments of government.

Since its founding, the Third Stage has invariably had the requisite official *imprimatur* to stage its experimental theatre. It was, ironically enough, subsidised by the Ministry for Community Development as part of its efforts to encourage local talents in the arts. The minister himself attended as an official guest on one occasion, and, by most accounts, enjoyed immensely the satire. Its plays were generally well-reviewed and received by the local press and the public. There was not the slightest whisper of Marx or Marxism echoing through the auditorium; nor were there any hints that Singapore and its quality of life were being lampooned by these Marxists for evil political ends!

In August 1989, the Traverse Theatre, Edinburgh, Scotland, put on a series of plays, which were banned in a playwright's own country, under the title, CENSORED, as a part of the Festival Fringe activities. A play by the Third Stage drama group, *Oh Singapore!* was performed, to which the Singapore government had taken objection. In a preview of the series in *Scotland Sunday*, a member of the International Committee for Artists' Freedom commented:

> There's no political ideology in *Oh Singapore!* It's like a student revue. Astonishing that it should be banned.[13]

A review in *The Scotsman* stated:

> The eloquence of *Oh Singapore!* ... lies not in the play itself but that the Singaporean authorities should find inoffensive material worthy

---

13. August 13, 1989.

of banning .... As a play it is insubstantial, as satire tremulously weak. Yet it was still enough to have members of the Third Stage arrested and detained.[14]

The plain unvarnished truth was that the prime minister had marked this group of sixteen young professionals, augmented by the later arrest of another six persons, for retributive action because of their effective assistance to opposition MP J.B. Jeyaretnam and the Workers' Party in snatching victory in the 1981 by-election and the 1984 general election. They helped him to print and distribute WP pamphlets during the elections. They also helped to brighten the editorial contents and pages of *The Hammer*, the WP's stodgy official publication, an important source of the party's news and funds. But the MHA luridly described their presence in the WP as an "infiltration," and the editorial assistance rendered at *The Hammer* as a "capture of control" of the publication alleging that they saw it was a "useful medium to disseminate antigovernment propaganda and influence public opinion against the government."

They were a group of young, intelligent, and idealistic graduates who, if they were to enroll as members in the WP, could give it credibility and status in electoral ratings. And provide in due course a serious alternative to the PAP. But, before the flowers could bloom and contend, it was crucial, using officialdom's favourite metaphor, to "nip them in the bud," to frighten them and other similar-minded persons away from the WP and other opposition parties. With the general election around the corner, the mass arrests of the "novices" and "do-gooders" had served the prime minister's hidden purpose of striking a serious blow at the heart of a budding credible political opposition. Therein lay one of the verities behind the arrest and detention.[15]

Although the prime minister had managed to exercise damage control over the clerical intervention, his vaunted "over-the-horizon radar" vision warned of a real possibility of organized future threats to the stability of his government, not necessarily from the Roman

---

14. August 23, 1989.
15. For a notable analysis of the arrest and detention, see "The Politics of Singapore in the 1980s" by Dr. Michael Haas, *Journal of Contemporary Asia*, vol. 19, no. 1 (1989).

Catholic Church, but from more militant religious quarters which might not be so easily contained. But, in characteristic fashion, he delayed action until the dust of the present conflict had settled. Then he introduced legislation euphemistically packaged as the Maintenance of Religious Harmony bill, where, under the pretext of maintaining religious harmony, religious and related organizations, associations, or societies could be controlled effectively by his government. For who could be so base or unruly as to oppose so lofty and cosmic an ideal as the maintenance of religious harmony in multireligious and multiracial Singapore?

5

Pavilion Intercontinental Hotel

> What's past is prologue.
> —William Shakespeare, *The Tempest*, Act II, sc. 1

On Thursday afternoon, April 14, 1988, I received a telephone call from Subhas Anandan, a stocky and jocose Indian lawyer with a shock of wavy black hair. He reminded me of his invitation to dinner with Soh Lung that night at the Summer Palace Chinese restaurant in the luxurious Pavilion Intercontinental Hotel. Subhas was reputed to be well-in with the ISD; and his jocosity, it was rumoured, cloaked his true ISD role and lowered the barrier of caution erected by suspicious and wary lawyers. He, however, volunteered to me one day in the course of a convivial conversation the information that he was friendly with a number of ISD officers, but the relationship was more social than professional. I had no reason to gainsay his statement. But others among the profession were, however, not so sanguine.

Be that as it may, he appeared to be genuinely fond of Soh Lung and had assured her that he would "climb the slope [of Whitley Detention Centre] when [sic] the necessity arises" for her. Meanwhile, her spirits, he said, had lately been in the doldrums and needed to be lifted up. I thought it odd that she should be feeling in this way; and promised to turn up after I had seen a client that evening.

Arriving sometime past eight, I found the two of them were well into the dinner. There were not many guests about the restaurant.

Despite the flowing support of an almost empty bottle of Johnny Walker Black Label Scotch whisky beside him, Subhas did not somehow have his customary impish ebullience. There was none of the usual wit and persiflage. Soh Lung did appear rather dispirited and resigned. Trying to cheer her up, I inquired what was troubling her. Before she could answer, Subhas explained she had premonitions of an imminent rearrest by the ISD. It struck me as preposterous, and I told her so, that the ISD would not be so foolish as to do that and, in any event, what had she done to deserve rearrest?

"You don't know; but, I hope, you are right," she replied cryptically.

"I can't see how the authorities can be so insensitive to public reaction in making another arrest."

She did not answer.

I complimented Subhas on his excellent dinner selection. He rejoined that, if she were incarcerated again, it would be a long time before she could savour such culinary delights, which would provide her with the necessary vital nourishment. It was a good choice of tasty yet wholesome dishes, but I felt he could have been less gloomy, nonetheless. His words were to prove uncomfortably prescient. I emptied the remains of the bottle into a glass. He ordered a replacement bottle of Johnny Walker Black Label. Soh Lung however stuck to her cup of Chinese tea. She disclosed that she would be meeting ISD Deputy Director, Sim Poh Heng, for lunch on Saturday. I remarked, half in jest, that if it was at his invitation, she should select an expensive restaurant. She returned a weak smile. Subhas left the table. The whisky had begun to exact its toll and he went in search of natural relief.

While he was away, Soh Lung took out a brown envelope from her valise and, looking around her, handed it across the table to me with the injunction I should read it at home. She did not want to tell me what it was. I was mystified by all the drama. In deference to her wishes, I put it away in my brief case. Subhas returned. We had a few more drinks. The atmosphere was suddenly invested with dark foreboding. The conversation began to pall, interspersed between silence and liberal libations of Scotch and soda. Soh Lung cautioned Subhas against imbibing any more as he had to drive home. In his state of inebriation he would be vulnerable to any ISD-contrived accident to his undoubted detriment. I agreed. Deep in thought, we left the restaurant. Before Soh Lung drove off in her car, she whispered confidentially to me that she sensed that we were under surveillance. I reassured her and bade her a fond good night. Subhas offered to send me home. On the way back, he was strangely silent.

I reached home past midnight. I emptied my brief case of its documents and files and left them on the dining table. I did not notice her letter. I was tired. I had had a long day. I had also quaffed a generous potion of that amber liquid, and the sandman was beckoning seductively to me.

On the morning of Friday, April 15, 1988, I went to the office. After attending to urgent matters, I took the afternoon shuttle flight to Kuala Lumpur to spend the weekend with Mei, then my *fiancée*, who stands trim and tall, of fair mien and an alabaster-smooth complexion. She has a personal magnetism and an attractive rhetoric which can captivate her audience. She belongs to that dwindling breed of idealists whose impassionate sense of justice is often etched by impetuous directness, disconcerting to persons who do not know her well. Her presence in Kuala Lumpur calls for some explanation.

A citizen of Malaysia, she had lived and worked for some thirteen years in Singapore in several executive positions. Her administrative talents and managerial skills were recognised by a government in search of skilled and talented individuals to make Singapore their home. She received in September 1985 an unsolicited invitation from the Registrar of Citizens to submit her personal particulars and relevant papers to enable him to evaluate her eligibility for *accelerated* Singapore citizenship. Although flattered by this unsought honour, she replied that she needed time to consider it. One does not renounce one's birthrights at the drop of a hat, even though it might belong to the Singapore government. In late January 1986, the Registrar reminded her by letter that he had not heard from her; but before she could respond, extraneous occurrences, independent of them both, were already underway.

Shortly afterwards and, on a tight, little island like Singapore, news of our friendship gained wide currency. It is, alas, an inevitable price of fame or notoriety or what you will, or, as Shakespeare put it more tersely, "what the great ones do the less will prattle of." But, more importantly, our movements and close companionship became the focus of more than passing interest to the authorities.

Suddenly and without the slightest forewarning, she was declared a prohibited immigrant by the immigration department, and her permanent resident status was cancelled without explanation. Given the unsolicited invitation, she could not conceivably have posed a security threat to the government of Singapore. Ignoring her repeated requests for the reason, she was unceremoniously ordered to leave Singapore. We searched long and deep for the possible reasons that could have brought about this reversal of her fortune. The only reasonable explanation for this sudden official change of heart was her financial assistance to me, which had thwarted at a crucial moment the government's game plan for my political annihilation. There could be no other plausible reason.

Mei challenged the immigration orders by way of *certiorari* proceedings in the High Court.[1] It was heard by none other than Justice Sinnathuray, whose judicial specialty appears to be the handling of sensitive cases. Pending delivery of the judgment, she took up residence in Kuala Lumpur, the federal capital of Malaysia, some two hundred and fifty miles away. Because I had to commute between Singapore and Malaysia over the weekends, I left Singapore on Friday afternoon for Kuala Lumpur. On Tuesday morning, April 19, 1988, she tried to persuade me to delay my return to Singapore by another day. It was always a heartrending moment for me, torn between a desire to tarry a little longer and the call of office. My indecision was interrupted by the harsh ringing of the telephone. It was my secretary, who said that Soh Lung wanted to see me urgently as she was about to be arrested by the ISD, and that Patrick Seong, a lawyer, and some others unknown had already been arrested. My secretary did not know the reason for the arrest. I was shocked and

---

1. See Originating Motion No. 60 of 1986. After a long delay, Justice Sinnathuray dismissed her application on September 12, 1988. The appeal against the judgment was eventually dismissed by the Court of Appeal.

puzzled at Soh Lung's rearrest. I told Mei of the call, and we explored the possible reasons, but could find no satisfactory explanation. We knew she was neither a Marxist nor was she Marxist-inclined, notwithstanding the government's allegation the year before. So, what could it possibly be?

The reason, which was subsequently revealed by the ISD officers during my own detention, was, as we had originally suspected, neither Marxism nor Marxist-inclination, but "more to do with the old man." The prime minister had instigated the arrest. For, absurdly as it may seem, Soh Lung and her performance at the Select Committee hearing on the proposed amendments to the Legal Profession Act were still rankling "the old man"! In the televised bruising public encounter, the prime minister was perceived as a common bully, browbeating a diminutive young woman lawyer who had won the sympathy of Singaporeans by her cool and measured response. Soh Lung, thereafter, walked tall among the people, particularly among members of the legal profession.

Mei had met Soh Lung at a social gathering at Beverly Mai. She knew her as a courageous and principled lawyer and admired her sense of purpose and direction. She appreciated the efforts put in the Council election campaign by Soh Lung and Patrick in galvanizing the lawyers to vote for me and the presidency of the Law Society. I owed it to her to return to Singapore immediately.

At Subang International Airport, Kuala Lumpur, while waiting in the CIP—Commercially Important Persons—lounge for the plane, my eyes lighted on the headline of a Malaysian morning newspaper: "Ex-detainees allege they were tortured." Soh Lung and eight other ex-detainees had the day before issued a joint press statement in response to the cruel taunts made by or on behalf of government ministers regarding their arrest and detention and treatment in custody by the ISD. I was unaware at the time of the joint press statement. It was the cause of her depression at dinner which she was at pains to keep back from me. Whilst in custody, I learnt from Sim Poh Heng, Deputy Head, ISD that the ISD had espied the plan. He had warned her against signing it, and the Saturday meeting was his last futile attempt to talk her out of it.

A preface to the joint press statement explained in crystal-clear language the reasons for the issuance. It read in parts:

... While we had always kept a rueful and fearful silence on the unjust treatment we were subjected to, and would have been inclined to keep our silence, the Government has since repeatedly raised the issue of our arrests and detentions and made false and damaging statements about us.

... We make this statement now because of this constant barrage of Government taunts and its public invitation to speak the truth on the conditions we were subjected to under arrest and detention.

... Following our sudden arrests, we were subjected to harsh and intensive interrogation, deprived of sleep and rest, some of us for as long as 70 hours in freezing cold rooms. All of us were stripped of our personal clothing, including spectacles, footwear and underwear, and made to change into prisoners' uniforms.

Most of us were made to stand continually during interrogation, some of us for over 20 hours and under the full blast of air-conditioning turned to a very low temperature.

Under these conditions, one of us was repeatedly doused with water during interrogation. Most of us were hit hard in the face, some of us not less than 50 times, while others were assaulted on other parts of the body, during the first three days of interrogation.

... We were threatened with the arrests, assault and battery of our spouses, loved ones and friends. ...

We were actively discouraged from engaging legal counsel and advised to discharge our lawyers so as not to jeopardize our chances of release.

We were compelled to appear on television and warned that our release would depend on our performances. We were coerced to make statements such as "I am Marxist-inclined," "My ideal society is a classless society," "So-and-so is my mentor" and "I was made use of by so-and-so" in order to incriminate ourselves and other detainees.

What we said on television was grossly distorted and misrepresented by editing and commentaries, which attributed highly sinister motives to our actions and associations. ..."[2]

Ex-ISA detainee K.C. Chew, a Harvard Business School graduate, helped them to edit, print, and distribute the joint press statement; but he had refused to sign it because his wife apparently could not stand the emotional trauma of another detention. His refusal to sign it did not however save him from rearrest. He had offended the

---

2. See Appendix 1 for full statement.

authorities. So, it was the *sha ji, xia hou* treatment again—punishment had to be meted out as a warning to deter other similarly-minded persons.

I telephoned Mei from the CIP lounge and read out the news report and told her that I thought the joint press statement was probably the reason for the rearrest. The arrest of Patrick Seong, who was not a cosignatory, was however puzzling, as it did not fit into the general pattern of arrests. Deputy Prime Minister Goh Chok Tong, at a subsequent ministerial press conference, explained in mixed metaphor that the rearrest was "to get to the bottom of the whole picture." He promised the government would set up a commission of inquiry to show that the detainees' allegations were all untrue! I welcomed the setting up of a commission of inquiry, but stipulated that it should be headed by an eminent Queen's counsel. The government accused me of "misusing [my] status as a legal counsel as a cover for political propaganda and agitation," and distorted my call for a Queen's counsel, as implying that "no Singaporean, not even a High Court judge" was fit to head the inquiry.

Upon my return to Singapore, as I was clearing entry formalities at the Changi International Airport immigration checkpoint, I noticed a momentary hesitation by an immigration officer in returning my passport. I dismissed the incident from my mind. I took an airport taxi and went straight to my office, where I learned that, shortly after Soh Lung's telephone call to my secretary, the doors to her law office had been forcibly broken down by ISD officers, who arrested her.

I found on my desk an envelope addressed to me, hand-delivered early that morning by Souk Yee[3] before she, too, was rearrested. I opened it. It was a copy of the joint press statement together with a note from Soh Lung:

> Enclosed is a press release [on the joint statement.] You will now know why I saw you last week ....

This note confirms that I did not know then of the joint press statement let alone its contents.[4] Accordingly, I could not have

---

3. She was later released at the same time as Kevin De Souza.
4. *Cf.* Patrick's statutory declaration dated April 23, 1988.

done what was alleged against me by the government. The ISD had "persuaded" Patrick, a captive, to say that I knew of the existence of the joint press statement and had urged its release to coincide with the prime minister's visit to America to embarrass him. I suddenly recalled the brown manila envelope from Soh Lung, which, in my haste to get to my office last Friday morning, I had left behind unopened back in the apartment.

I telephoned several usually knowledgeable lawyers and persons regarding the rearrest, but none could throw any light on it. Until the situation became clearer, there was really nothing that I could originate to secure her release. In the meantime, I tried to immerse myself in the business of the office.

That evening, when I returned home I picked up the brown manila cover and opened it. It contained her diary and a gloomy handwritten note, imparting her fear of a rearrest with instructions to act for her in that eventuality, and to do all things necessary in connection therewith, including initiating *habeas corpus* proceedings and using the enclosed diary in whatever way I thought fit. The diary related to her detention the year before, written after her release in the relative liberty and safety of her home. She had noted down her recollections on and of persons and events, the assaults, the threats, and the sleep deprivation, the ISD promises made and broken with equal callousness, its Machiavellian manipulation and maneuvering, all designed to achieve its nefarious purpose—an abject confession.

My law firm set about preparing an application for a writ of *habeas corpus ad subjiciendum* ordering her immediate release from detention. Her brother, Teo Eng Seng, a renowned artist, who had recently returned from the United Kingdom after a successful art exhibition appropriately entitled: "On the Other Side of Silence," affirmed an affidavit in support of that application. I advised him to make a police report of the assault on his sister during her previous detention. I had considered the rearrest as a negation of her earlier instructions not to raise this issue. The police sent him on a merry-go-round of the island's several police stations. According to convention and good sense, it does not really matter at which police station a report of an offence is made, as it will automatically be referred to the appropriate police station for necessary action. This was, however, no ordinary police report. The complainant was no ordinary person. It was no ordinary case of assault. There are, indeed, many ways to test the perseverance of a perceived apostate.

Sometime on the morning of Tuesday, April 19, 1988, John Hoog of the U.S. embassy, stopped by my office, but I was not in. He left a note requesting me to call him. I phoned him, and we agreed to meet for drinks at the lobby bar of the Century Park Sheraton Hotel at eight that evening. I brought my son Ashleigh along with me. John was covering for Hank Hendrickson, who was away on holiday in Thailand. He wanted to know more about the rearrest of the ex-detainees, as he had to send a report to Washington. I gave him my views. Since he had spoken to me earlier that morning, he was relieved to learn that Hank would be back from leave the following week. He was also quite pleased when I told him that Eric Schwartz of Asia Watch had called me from Washington, D.C., and that I had briefed him on the latest situation. We then chatted on other mundane matters against a musical background provided by a visiting Filipino pianist. Subhas, whom I had informed about the meeting, joined us later for drinks; but he was unusually subdued during the conversation.

On Thursday, April 21, 1988, Jocelyn Seong, the lawyer-wife of Patrick Seong, came to seek my services. She had originally approached the doyen of the bar, C.C. Tan, a senior partner of the law firm, Tan, Rajah, and Cheah, but he was in delicate health and had recommended me instead. There were, and are, very, very few lawyers of stature, competence and ability, who would willingly act in ISA cases, notwithstanding the government's claim to the contrary. This is a hard fact of life in Singapore. Lawyers who accept such cases are pricked in the lists of one or more of the investigative agencies of government, in particular, the Income Tax Department. Notwithstanding, I agreed to represent him.

Together with Soh Lung and other like-minded lawyers, Patrick shared my view that the Law Society should play a more active role in examining the reams of legislation that were being churned out without much debate by an obsequious Parliament and lauded by a tame press. What was so disgraceful was that the Constitution of Singapore, such as it was, was being equated to and treated, in the words of the prime minister, as "old shoes" which could be "stretched, softened, re-soled or repaired" at will to suit the expediency of the moment by the prime minister, who once claimed to have a "vested interest in constitutionalism," and seriously vowed: "We will work out a Constitution that will prevent constitutional changes in three readings."[5] The use of the word "shoe" or "old shoes" is a metaphor of serious disparagement of a person or thing in Asian tradition and culture, and to be struck with a shoe is considered the highest possible form of insult. Is such an elastic, elusive Constitution, derisively valued at no better than old shoes, really worth a solemn pledge to preserve, protect, and defend it?

During the 1987 arrest of the alleged Marxist conspirators, Patrick, using the electronic facilities of his law office, had kept Amnesty International, Asia Watch, Echris,[6] and other human rights groups, regional and international bar associations, and concerned organizations closely informed on their plight. He was so effective in disseminating the information that a piqued ISD, which had been monitoring this news traffic, warned him through his client-detainees that, if he did not cease forthwith, he would also be "pulled in" under the ISA. To underscore its threat, it mounted a round-the-clock hostile surveillance on him.

The government accused him of providing information to foreign correspondents in order "to generate hostile publicity that would pressure the government into releasing the detainees early;" and of being an "instigator, organizer and propagandist," who regarded the joint press statement as an "opportunity to discredit the government and embarrass it externally, especially while Prime Minister Lee Kuan Yew was in the United States." Assuming all this to be true, were they really good and sufficient grounds for arresting him under the ISA? Where was the offence in law of alerting the world to acts of repression? For this, one has to go back to Stalinist Russia during its worst excesses, or to Communist China, where a

---

5. Fullerton Square rally, August 29, 1972.
6. Emergency Committee for Human Rights in Singapore, a New Zealand-based organization.

prominent Chinese dissident, Liu Qing, a leader of the 1978-79 Democracy Wall movement, was jailed "for passing information about injustices [in China] to the outside world."

On Friday, April 22, 1988, the U.S. embassy issued a statement expressing its concern over the rearrest of the eight former detainees and the arrest of Patrick Seong.

In the ensuing days, Jocelyn was a veritable tower of strength, an indefatigable source of energy, earning for herself the sobriquet of lady of steel. Indeed, her singular dedication to secure not only the release of her husband but the other detainees as well had to be restrained, lest she land herself into unnecessary trouble with the authorities. Roslina binte Baba, Soh Lung's legal assistant, a pleasant, round-faced cherubim, was also a tower of strength. She did not shirk any task assigned to her to secure the release of her employer and friend, rendering sterling service.

An accused person is entitled in law to access to counsel within a reasonable time from the time of arrest; and to be produced before a magistrate within twenty-four (since changed to forty-eight hours) of arrest. Save for production before a magistrate, the law applies to ISA cases as well. Despite repeated requests and in violation of their constitutional rights, we were denied access to Soh Lung and Patrick. We initiated *mandamus* proceedings in the High Court to compel the ISD to allow us, as counsel, to interview Patrick. Success in one would *ipso facto* lead to similar access to Soh Lung. The proceedings were set down for hearing before Justice Lai Kew Chai, on Wednesday, May 4, 1988. Events however overtook us. The ISD suddenly informed us that we could interview them. We then withdrew the *mandamus* proceedings. It turned out to be a wicked lure to draw me into the snare in Whitley Detention Centre, as well as to delay the interviews with Patrick and Soh Lung.

Soon after he resumed work, Hank Hendrickson gave me a call from the U.S. embassy. We arranged to meet at 9 a.m. the next day for breakfast at the coffee shop of the Pavilion Intercontinental Hotel. Our conversations were listened to as my office and home telephones were being tapped by the ISD. On Wednesday morning, April 27, 1989, I was there at the appointed hour. Hank was accompanied by two ladies. He introduced one of them as his wife, Anne, whom I had not met before, and the other as his new assistant, whose name now escapes me. Hank asked me for an update on the events, and more particularly, what I was doing for Soh Lung and Patrick. I filled him in on the *habeas corpus* applications, in which his lady assistant, a lawyer by training, showed keen interest. I thought it did not differ greatly from the U.S. law and practice. And so, we discussed it briefly. There was nothing in our conversations that morning which could have alarmed the most sensitive of governments. But this is Singapore, where everything is taken seriously, where every word, every motion, and movement are milled for hidden meanings!

During the buffet breakfast, I began to notice a scruffy, young, Chinese male, accompanied by an indifferently dressed, plain-looking Chinese lass, trying to occupy a table close by us. There was something about them, which struck me as just not right. Somehow, they did not seem to belong there, as if they had strayed outside their normal milieu and drifted into a place completely out of their social depth. The man held a clutch bag in his hand, and his female companion fidgeted with her handbag, which was not responding to her efforts to arrange it in a desired position on a divider-ledge opposite us. I watched this curious spectacle for a while, and casually remarked to Hank that I thought we had a tail. We observed them momentarily, which made them more uncomfortable. As there was nothing conspiratorial about our rendezvous, we were not overly anxious or concerned about their presence. After a while, we lost all interest in them.

Back at my office, it suddenly dawned on me that they *were* ISD field officers, who were covertly trying to photograph us and tape our conversations with concealed gadgets. I could not resist the devilish urge to send Hank an instant fax saying that we were on "candid camera." In the course of their search of my office, a copy of the fax was found by ISD officers. During my interrogation, they indicated that they were not amused that I had blown their agents' cover to Hank. Indeed, I was seriously accused of not being sufficiently "loyal" to Singapore. I could only smile at the convoluted logic.

In the meantime, on Thursday, April 28, 1988, the government released a statutory declaration purportedly made by Patrick, while in custody, stating, *inter alia*, that:

> ... In early April 1988, ... I had lunch with Francis Seow in which he indicated his intention to stand as an independent candidate in the forthcoming General Election. When I informed him of the intention of some ex-detainees to release the [joint] statement, he said it would be useful as it would keep the issue alive in view of the General Election as it could be used to discredit the Prime Minister and the second-generation leaders. He suggested timing the release when the Prime Minister was in the United States.[7]

As explained, I was not consulted on the joint press statement, nor did I know of its existence. My initial reaction was that Patrick was probably confused or had a faulty recollection of the luncheon meeting. I had not allowed for the ISD's vaunted powers of persuasion. Our luncheon meeting had taken place at the Singapore Town Club on Thursday, March 17, 1988. Over a leisurely lunch, we discussed the on-going hostile surveillance of him by ISD officers, who earlier that day had made no effort to disguise their movements in following him to the luncheon rendezvous. They tailed him daily in cars and on motorcycles, sometimes in a combination of both, from his apartment to his office and back and wherever he went. Dismounting from their surveillance vehicles, they made it a point to ride up the lift together with him, stake him out, and again ride the lift down with him. If it was intended as an espial exercise in intimidation, it failed dismally in its objective, for we had a most relaxing and pleasant lunch.

We compared notes on our respective client-detainees. We discussed the forthcoming general election. I told him that I was planning to contest the election and was trying to gather a group of professionals to stand as independents together with me. I explained why in the context of Singapore politics I thought a group of independent professionals stood a better chance of success at the polls. We discussed a list of possible candidates. He disclosed that Soh Lung had expressed interest before her arrest, but he did not know whether she was still of the same mind. I asked him to join me, but he declined saying that he was not cut out for politics. Besides, public speaking was not his forte. I tried to persuade him that

---

7. See Patrick's statutory declaration dated April 23, 1988.

public speaking was a matter of getting used to it and knowing the subject matter beforehand. We discussed the latest gerrymandering scheme; the Group Representation Constituencies (GRC), where the electorate had to vote for a slate of three candidates, one of whom had to be a Malay or a member of a racial minority; and the problem of procuring viable ethnic representatives, and I requested him to keep his eyes open for any one credible. After lunch, he returned to his office from where he called to say, rather impishly, his shadow had reappeared. We did not meet again until after we were both released from detention. It would appear that he had conveyed the gist of our luncheon conversation to Hank at one of their meetings.

On Saturday, March 26, 1988, I was in Hongkong and, whilst there, I heard for the first time on the media grapevine of the prime minister's proposed visit to Washington, D.C. The official announcement of this visit[8] appeared in *The Straits Times* only on Saturday, April 9, 1988—almost a month after our luncheon meeting!

Jocelyn was extremely cross with him for those and other remarks and repeatedly apologised for him. But they were words which had been put into his mouth, so that the government could discredit me and justify my arrest. After my release, Jocelyn saw me on a couple of occasions and she profusely apologised for him. She was acutely embarrassed and wanted to know how he could make it up to me. Seeing her distress, I told her gently that I knew of the torturous conditions under which her husband's inquisitors had coerced the statements out of him. Very much later after my release, I learnt the signatories had discussed among themselves whether to retain me as counsel to oversee the dissemination of their joint press statement, but decided against it and to do it themselves.

I accidentally ran into Patrick much later. He nervously apologised for his unwarranted remarks. He had tried to undo the harm, he said, by offering to swear an affidavit for use before the advisory board to the effect that he had been coerced into stating those untruths and reinforcing it with an oral testimony on oath. But before he could approach my counsel, Howard Cashin, he was

---

8. The visit ended officially on April 19.

overjoyed at the news of my release. As I myself had gone through that harrowing experience, I told him that no apology was needed for I fully appreciated the infernal circumstances under which he had made them. He was grateful for my understanding.

On Friday, April 29, 1988, in a bizarre twist, the government released an extraordinary statement that it would not set up the independent commission to investigate the public allegations by Soh Lung and the eight ex-detainees that they had been physically and psychologically abused into making false confessions while in detention last year, as it was no longer necessary. Miraculously, it seemed, while they were in custody, Soh Lung and the eight ex-detainees suddenly saw the light and underwent a complete conversion. They recanted their recantation, in *sworn* statements, to boot, that their allegations were only "a political propaganda ploy to discredit the government." Patrick, too, underwent the same conversion. The only remaining apostate, Fong Har, whose name appeared as a cosignatory, fortuitously was out of the country, and, in a BBC World Service interview in London, challenged the government's statement, maintaining the truth of the joint press statement.[9]

To bolster the government's case, the ISD corralled five former detainees from the group arrested last year, including K.C. Chew, and subjected them to days of intensive interrogation and threats of indefinite detention. They made declarations on oath that they had not been subjected to the illegal use of force. After they were released, K.C. revealed to Jocelyn, Tan Kheng Sun, the husband of Souk Yee, and several others, the ordeal through which he had just gone. He had been held for intensive questioning for fourteen hours in all over two days by the ISD, whose officers had threatened him with rearrest if he did not sign a statement saying that he had *not* been assaulted during the detention last year. And, as a kind of sop to him, the ISD promised that Soh Lung and his other detainee-friends would be released in June or July, at the latest. But, two days after my own arrest, and for all his cooperation and the ISD's solemn promises, K.C. Chew was rearrested.

---

9. There is a warrant for her arrest for being a cosignatory to the joint press statement.

In an attempt to get the former detainees to perjure themselves, the government and the ISD had, however, overlooked one salient fact—that many detainees, immediately after their release last year, had already exchanged gruesome tales and experiences of their detention with one another, their husbands or wives and other family members, and close friends in the relatively safe privacy of their homes. To overcome any similar future predicament, a condition of release now stipulates that detainees are no longer allowed to associate with one another after their release.

Given this important information, my law firm prepared statutory declarations for Jocelyn and Kheng Sun—the others were much too frightened to do so—challenging the voluntariness, veracity, and validity of those so-called corroborating statutory declarations. We challenged especially the statutory declaration which we knew the ISD had impressed K.C. Chew to make. We were set then to release them to the foreign media. The domestic media was impotent. I was spearheading the escalating offensive against the government. It was so much easier for the government to relieve the pressure by arresting me. But on what grounds? An arrest would certainly blunt that offensive.

The government accused the foreign press of waging an "hysterical campaign against the Singapore government" and warned "overseas interest groups, the foreign press, and foreign powers to stay out of Singapore's affairs." It threatened it "will use the Internal Security Act to detain without trial subversive elements. ... Singaporeans, who allow themselves to be used as proxies by foreign groups, or become agents of foreign powers, should remember the government's warning, made in 1971, ... that subversion means acting for foreign powers, whether communist or Western."

In amongst the prime minister's black bag of political tricks is the subversion ploy by foreign interests, a ploy to which Singaporeans are long inured. He has conjured it up with varying degrees of success against the U.S. and other foreign governments and interests. It is useful to note its origin in his psyche, as it has coloured many a time his political outlook and evaluation. In late March 1959, when the PAP was in opposition, a civil servant—a closet PAP member—in breach of government standing orders and the Official

Secrets Ordinance, leaked to the prime minister and his political cronies confidential information concerning the receipt by the minister for education of half a million dollars from American sources for the party's campaign war chest. Investigations into the funds deposited with an American bank in Singapore were inexplicably suspended. Primed with this illicit intelligence, Harry Lee Kuan Yew raised it in the legislature, squeezing maximum political capital out of it. Before an inquiry commission was constituted, the minister resigned. The scandal shattered all the electoral hopes of the outgoing Labour Front government. In the wake of the PAP's ascension to political power, the loyalty of the civil servant concerned was noted, and, in due course, he enjoyed the perks of leakage as a senior official in government.

For a long time afterwards, the prime minister characterized Americans as cultural boors and political dilettanti. Coloured by this perception, he tended to view their actions with suspicion, if not downright distrust. Specifying two examples in support of this viewpoint, he disclosed on television in 1965, first, that a CIA agent had been apprehended in Singapore in 1960 trying to bribe a Special Branch officer to furnish him with secret information and, following a protest, the Eisenhower administration had offered the prime minister and his party a "gift" of S$10 million for development purposes. Negotiations continued until the Kennedy administration withdrew the offer to hush up the matter. The U.S. State Department issued a denial, whereupon the prime minister released a letter of apology that he had received from Secretary of State Dean Rusk in April 1961.

Secondly, he was piqued at what he considered a slight to him and the former minister for finance, Dr. Goh Keng Swee, when the U.S. State Department had failed or neglected to make courtesy protocol arrangements for them at U.S. airports, when they had flown in to defend Singapore's merger with Malaya before the United Nations General Assembly in New York. And, for good measure, he cited a personal incident. He described the "impudence and impertinence" of an eminent U.S. gynecologist, who was not free to go to Singapore, but who had suggested that his wife fly to Switzerland or the U.S. instead, when he had specially requested the assistance of the U.S. ambassador to procure the doctor's services to see her in Singapore. The foreign subversion ploy had not been invoked against the United States for some time, because relations between the two countries had generally improved from about the time when President Lyndon B. Johnson wined and dined him at the White House and effusively lauded him on his stewardship of Singapore and as Southeast Asia's most dynamic leader.

On that same Friday, April 29, 1988, Goh Chok Tong held an important press conference to explain the rearrest of the former detainees. A journalist pointedly asked him why I had not been arrested, too, to which he replied that the ISD had not recommended it. At that critical moment, I was at the Changi International Airport. I had momentary glimpses of the press conference on the airport's public TV screens, as I traversed the airport to board my plane for Kuala Lumpur, blissfully unaware of that momentous reply.

On Saturday, April 30, 1988, Roslina binte Baba, accompanied by Subhas in a supernumerary role, went to interview Soh Lung at the Whitley Detention Centre. Later, Roslina alone saw Patrick to discuss the *habeas corpus* applications. I was away in Kuala Lumpur.

After the respective interviews, Roslina made a beeline for my office, anxious to give me an immediate note of her colloquy with Patrick. Expecting that the ISD would arrest him as a Marxist as it had several times threatened to do so in the previous year, Patrick was confounded when the ISD suddenly abandoned the line of questioning regarding the "Marxist conspiracy" and seemed no longer interested to link him to it. Instead, it was endeavouring to establish the existence of an "American plot." Alarmed at this new line, Patrick wanted Roslina to note and to alert me (before he was forced to incriminate himself later) that he had met Hank, a first secretary (political) to the U.S. embassy whose full name is E. Mason Hendrickson, on only three occasions; once, in the company of an American named David Lambertson,[10] and that at no time did either of them offer him money. It was an incredible quantum leap from Marxism to American domestic interference! She gave the note to

---

10. A deputy assistant secretary for East Asian and Pacific Affairs, State Department, Washington, D.C.

Ashleigh who left it on my desk. I did not see the note or know of its contents until after my arrest and interrogation at the Centre.

To digress for a moment. It is, indeed, a weird, if not ungrateful, client who gratuitously denigrates his own counsel and, more especially, when he knows his counsel is doing his level best to gain access to him and secure his release from prison. But this was part of his "voluntary" statement:

> I was apprehensive that the government would also discredit me if I associated myself politically with Francis Seow. I heard about his affairs with women and that he was financially indebted. For example, there were talks in the Bar Room that his phone bills had been cut because he did not pay his phone bills.[11]

On Tuesday, May 3, 1988, I ran into Jocelyn at the lift lobby of the Straits Trading Building in downtown Singapore where my law office was located. She had come to see me and she was visibly concerned. She had visited her husband in detention. She pulled me aside and whispered urgently that I should leave Singapore and seek asylum overseas. Asylum! The very word was like an ill-tuned cymbal which was to resonate ominously in a small, squalid, ISD cell No. L-9. I could not appreciate her agitation. She voiced her fears that I was going to be arrested. She was quite agitated. I tried to calm her down. I did not believe her. It looked to me like the same old trick the ISD had employed last year to frighten Patrick into giving up representation of the detainees and to cease being the conduit of news and information for the foreign press. With hindsight, I fear I was too complacent. I could not envisage in my wildest dreams that the government would be mad enough to arrest me. I dismissed it out of hand. We rode the lift together up to my law office.

A day or two later, she repeated her fears and urged me to leave Singapore before it was too late. I assured her that I had done nothing wrong to warrant an arrest under the ISA or any other law and, in any event, I owed it to myself and the people who believed in me to remain in Singapore. Wanly, she smiled and, shaking her head, said: "You are brave, Mr. Seow." Bravery did not come into

---

11. See Patrick Seong's statutory declaration, dated May 3, 1988.

the picture at all. I did not realize the government was so politically insecure that it allowed its fears to cloud its better judgment and override the ISD's "professional" advice. Why, only less than a week ago, had not Deputy Prime Minister Goh Chok Tong publicly told a conference of local and foreign journalists that the ISD had recommended against my arrest?

On Thursday, May 5, 1988, the representatives of several international human rights organizations flew into Singapore to observe the *habeas corpus* applications on behalf of Soh Lung and the other detainees in the High Court the next day. That night, I had dinner at the Century Park Sheraton Hotel with Professor Jerome A. Cohen, former associate dean of Harvard Law School and director of its East Asian Legal Studies representing New York-based Asia Watch, the American human rights organization; Jill Spruce, an English barrister based in Hongkong representing the International Commission of Jurists, Geneva; and Udo Janz of Amnesty International, London, whom I had met on previous occasions.

By this time, in spite of myself, I was well in the forefront of human rights work and, given my previous positions in government and the Law Society, I had become better known not only to international human rights organizations but also to the foreign mass media. For them, it became a matter of stopping by a convenient oasis for any viewpoints or opinions on Singapore's domestic matters and policies. We were later joined by a German correspondent from the *Frankfurter Allgemeine*. I briefed them on the law, practice, and procedure on *habeas corpus* applications in Singapore, which were derived from English law and substantially not much different from *habeas corpus* applications in America or in the Commonwealth. Considering Singapore's political ambience and conservative judiciary, I was not unduly optimistic, I told them, about the prospects for success, but their presence was warmly welcome and indeed might well inspire rare judicial boldness.

Professor Cohen, no stranger to Singapore or its prime minister, disclosed that he had an appointment with him at the *Istana Annexe*, at about 4:00 p.m. the next day. They were to renew an acquaintanceship made during the latter's sabbatical at Harvard University some years before and discuss the ISD detentions, which were giving many human rights and related organizations much concern. Jim Anderton, a New Zealand Labour Party MP, representing about thirty concerned New Zealand members of parliament and the Emergency Committee for Human Rights in Singapore (Echris), was also in Singapore to observe the proceedings. There were also representatives of international law or bar associations, including William K. Coblentz, a representative of the American Bar Association. I did not, unfortunately, have an opportunity for any meaningful dialogues with many of them for the reasons that hereinafter appear!

6

May 6, 1988

> What he [the Chief Minister] is seeking to do in the name of democracy is to curtail a fundamental liberty, and the most fundamental of them all—freedom from arrest and punishment without having violated a specific provision of the law and being convicted for it. ...
>
> —Lee Kuan Yew[1]
>
> The bloody book of law
> You shall yourself read in the bitter letter
> After your own sense.
>
> —William Shakespeare, *Othello*,
> Act I, sc. 3, 67

The incarceration of the so-called Marxists a second time generated immense global interest, and the *habeas corpus* proceedings seeking their release attracted international observers to Singapore. On Friday, May 6, 1988, long before 10:30 a.m., Court No. 7 in the Supreme Court building, where the applications for *habeas corpus* were being made, overflowed with lawyers, human rights organizations' representatives, voice and print journalists, parents, husband and wives, relatives and friends of the detainees, and curious members of the public. No standing room was permitted in the well of the court, and many observers were locked out. ISD officers were very much in evidence in and out of the court room. Uniformed policemen, too, were much in evidence in the vestibule and along the corridors of

---

1. Legislative Assembly Debates, September 21, 1955, col. 722.

the court, whilst outside the courthouse, an anti-riot van with its full complement of anti-riot policemen stood a discreet distance away.

The prerequisite legal documents had been served on the attorney general representing the minister for home affairs and the director of Internal Security Department and on other government authorities concerned. I wanted to telescope the two stages of the proceedings, the *ex parte* stage and the second and main stage of the application, into one expeditious hearing. But the attorney general avoided a tactical appearance by not filing, as he was entitled to do, any affidavit in reply on behalf of the minister for home affairs and the director of Internal Security Department thereby making an adjournment an absolute certainty.

Adjournments, long adjournments, of legal proceedings usually tend to dampen or distract public interest and fervor in them. Our applications were further compounded because the court registry had allotted only one day for them which, together with several applications by other lawyers, was clearly not enough time. Depending upon the nature of the case, delay is among the first weapons in the arsenal of a lawyer, whose forensic skill and experience are often measured by the length and number of times he can procure adjournments for his client.

The morning's proceedings proved a disappointing anticlimax. We had perforce to settle for an adjournment to Wednesday, May 18, 1988—nearly a month after the rearrest of the detainees! For obvious reasons, *habeas corpus* applications are inherently matters of urgency—but Singapore judges have a regrettable tendency to take such applications in their stride.

A small group of lawyers, relatives of detainees, journalists, and human rights organizations' representatives adjourned for lunch to the coffee shop of the Goodwood Park Hotel. There, almost every one registered his or her disappointment at the morning's court proceedings. However, before long, the discussions became more animated as they converged on the confluence of two topics: one, the detainees, who had been visited by their loved ones, were observed to be "extremely tired, haggard, and ... thinner," and several had an unnaturally dark complexion; and, two, they had complained of the peculiar taste of the potable water at the Detention Centre. As they were forbidden to talk about their detention with their loved ones or inquire about the state of their health or conditions, imagination fed by suspicion ran riot. Several persons amongst them thought that drugs had been surreptitiously introduced into the food or the drinks of their loved ones. I opined it was unlikely and, before any such grave charges were made, they should first be verified. I told them that I would keep a sharp lookout for those signs and symptoms when I visit Soh Lung and Patrick later that afternoon. I was soon to learn at first hand that the extreme tiredness, haggardness, and thinness observed in the detainees were largely due to prolonged sleep deprivation, their dark or tanned complexion was caused by exposure to the powerful spotlights in the interrogation room. The disagreeably peculiar taste of the water probably owed its phenomenon to stagnation in conduit compounded by a high chlorine or fluoride content.

Earlier that morning, my law firm had received a facsimile letter from the ISD permitting a visit to Soh Lung and Patrick at 4:00 that afternoon. I informed Roslina and requested her to wait for me at my firm so that we could go there together.

As time was marching on, I excused myself to return to my firm to collect my files and the relevant papers. Roslina was already there waiting for me. Ashleigh drove us to the Whitley Detention Centre and left us at the foot of the hill. Roslina and I trudged up the steep slope to the iron gates of the Centre. I grabbed hold of the door-knocker and rapped smartly thrice on the heavy, dark blue iron gates. The sharp, metallic sounds echoed eerily through the Centre beyond the gates. A little while later, we could hear someone from within opening a peep-hole. It was a Gurkha guard. We explained the purpose of our visit. He already knew the purpose. He shut the peep-hole again. Then, one leaf of the heavy, iron gates creaked noisily as it swung slowly open, just wide enough to let Roslina and me in, in Indian file. We turned right onto a paved sidewalk, which skirted the perimeter fence of the Centre. As we walked, I remembered remarking, half in jest, to Roslina that we were entering the lion's den. Little did I realize then how prophetic my words would soon turn out to be!

The paved sidewalk (screened from the main building by a thick leafy fence) wound its way gently towards what the inmates called an outhouse, with which I was reasonably familiar having made several previous professional visits to it. The whole Centre had been alerted about our visit. There was an air of general expectancy. We entered the anteroom, where a young Chinese woman ISD officer, smiling deferentially, pointed wordlessly to a visitors' book on a small desk by the entrance. We were to sign in our names, addresses, and purpose of visit, after which another equally deferential and smiling Chinese male ISD officer, also wordlessly, ushered us into the interview room. Blissfully unaware that the trap had been sprung, we waited expectantly for Soh Lung and Patrick to be brought in to us in turn.

The air-conditioned interview room was small. There was an antique desk in the middle of the room and two equally old matching chairs on either side of the desk. A faded, baize, vinyl-covered, decrepit settee, which was conspicuously out of place in the room, was set below a window, whose heavy curtains were drawn shutting off the view of the paved sidewalk outside. The settee did not appear a government-issued. Whoever the original owner had been, his colour sense left much to be desired. At one corner of the room stood a forlorn, rusty, metal filing cabinet on the top of which an obsolescent-model, green-coloured telephone sat in ominous isolation. Although one knew that the room was bugged, nonetheless one was still uneasy, and the telephone was the prime suspect. Confidentiality of communications between counsel and client was a game of charade. We were allowed only a meagre half-hour interview each for Soh Lung and Patrick; but we could have requested for a longer period. We did not do so, as it was only a preliminary interview. An electric wall clock silently ticked all too swiftly the minutes away. Outside the room lolled the seemingly disinterested ISD officers and alert Gurkha guards.

Conversations between a detainee and members of his family are decidedly not confidential, because the ISD officers make it abundantly clear that their conversations are being monitored. The detainee is placed in a small, soundproof room separated from the family visitor by a thick, transparent, shatter-proof, perspex screen.

Conversation between them is through telephones. They can see one another but are cruelly deprived of any tactile opportunity. They are warned beforehand that they may not discuss matters relating to the detention or the Centre, save on family matters. ISD officers and Gurkha guards stand on either side of the perspex screen behind them within ear-shot of the conversation to enforce the rule. Infraction would result in immediate termination of the teleconversation, and the visit, and jeopardize all future visits. Visits are once a week only for thirty minutes. A story was told of a distraught detainee's brother who, frustrated by the restrictive nature of the conversation, in the overwhelming presence of ISD officers, flung the phone down in anger and cracked it. The matter was referred to the attorney general's chambers for advice on prosecution, which suggested a restriction of privileges for the detainee and family.

The trap sprung

On that late, sultry afternoon, Roslina and I settled ourselves down as comfortably as we could in that intimidating room and waited for Soh Lung. After a moment, a male Chinese ISD officer came in and said that a Mr. S.K. Tan wished to have a word with me. I excused myself from Roslina and followed him out into the compound of the Centre, a part of the Centre where I had hitherto not set foot. I noticed what turned out to be a posse of about fifteen or more plainclothesmen milling around several cars. I was brought before a tall, rough-hewn, lantern-jawed Chinese who, without a shadow of a smile, suddenly placed a heavy hand on my left shoulder and said:

"Mr. Seow, I am arresting you under the ISA."

I was shocked. I stood there in utter disbelief, rooted momentarily to the ground.

"What have I done to deserve arrest?" I asked recovering my composure, but he remained anvil-faced to this and further queries.

Save for the bald statement that I had been arrested under the ISA, he gave no further reason or explanation. Outraged, I tried again to ascertain the cause of my arrest, but I could have spoken to a wall of stone for all the response I got. He had suddenly become mute, a robot programmed to say those words and no more. He had accorded me the courtesy of addressing me as "Mister." Considering the disadvantage of numbers and the fact that I was in the lion's lair, any physical resistance on grounds of legal niceties was clearly ill-advised and certainly futile. There was no independent magisterial authority at hand to whom I could successfully appeal! In any event, it flashed through my mind that no judge of whatever status in Singapore would have the requisite judicial courage to uphold my appeal. And ever mindful that discretion is always the better part of valour, I yielded to overwhelming brute force. And so, for some weeks, I toiled in ignorance of whom or what I had so grievously offended in word or deed to deserve the incarceration.

The government meanwhile announced that I was arrested to determine my involvement and role in a scheme of "foreign interference in Singapore's internal affairs" initiated by U.S. officials. That was the ostensible ground for my arrest. That was the pretext. It was part of a diabolical scheme hatched by the prime minister whose true motive, however, was more malevolent.

While this dismal incident was taking place at Whitley Detention Centre, a different drama was unfolding itself at the *Istana Annexe*, where former Professor Jerome Cohen was meeting with the prime minister as scheduled. Professor Cohen raised with him the issue of the rearrest of the detainees during which he ventured the opinion that it would do no political good for persons like me or Patrick Seong to be arrested. The prime minister nodded. At about 4:20 p.m., an aide interrupted the colloquy and brought in a note to him. After reading it, he grunted approvingly and, shortly afterwards, indicated to Professor Cohen that he would have to terminate the meeting as "something had cropped up." He left Professor Cohen with the distinct impression that he agreed with those sentiments about me and Patrick. Later that same evening, Professor Cohen was distressed to hear from the TV news broadcasts of my arrest at the critical moment of his discussions with the prime minister.

Back at the Whitley Detention Centre, Tan said that they wanted to search my apartment. I was then living in my *fiancée's* apartment, pending her return to Singapore from banishment. His words brought me back to the awful realization that I was no longer a free man, but a prisoner of Lee Kuan Yew. Stunned at this outrageous turn of events, I took a couple of steps back, when a menacing voice behind me said:

"I hope you will not do anything foolish; otherwise we will have to handcuff you."

"I want to tell Roslina," I said, freezing in my track, "of my arrest and that she should not worry, but to carry on with the interview with Soh Lung and Patrick."

They refused to let me see her. Several of them moved to close in on me, at the same time saying that they would undertake to inform her. But they never did, for it was an undertaking they had not the slightest intention of fulfilling. Lies are, alas, part and parcel of their trade so that lying comes naturally to them. Unbeknown to me, they had lied to Soh Lung and Patrick that I had cancelled my respective appointments with them that afternoon. Their fiendish plan was to arrest me as soon as I entered the Centre, the letter purporting to grant me access to Soh Lung and Patrick was the lure to draw me into the lion's den. They had not, however, anticipated that I would turn up with Roslina; they had therefore to go through the motions of granting the interviews. Soh Lung was then told to change from her prison uniform into her street clothes for the interview, a meaningless ISD masquerade, which only an unforeseen event had made inevitable. Immediately after the interview, the detainee had to change back into prison uniform.

When I did not return after some time, Roslina and Soh Lung inquired from the omnipresent ISD officers about my prolonged absence. They wove an elaborate web of lies, telling her that I was in protracted conversation with the director and that I had left word that Roslina should carry on alone with the interview. But when I still failed to appear, her suspicions aroused, an angry Soh Lung demanded to see me, her lawyer. But they lied again, saying that I had to rush back to my office to get some important documents, which I had inadvertently left behind, and that I had left a message for Roslina to make her own way home. Both Soh Lung,[2] who was adopted by Amnesty International as a prisoner of conscience, and Roslina had by now suspected that something dreadfully untoward had happened to me. It was dusk when Roslina came down the hill, distraught and in tears. Ashleigh was nowhere to be found.

She went straight to my office and, as she had dreaded, discovered that I had not left any message for her and, worse still, I had not returned from the Centre. There, at the lift lobby of the Straits Trading Building, she ran into some council members of the Law Society (which fortuitously was due to meet in council that evening) who brought her to the Society's office at Colombo Court, where she tearfully related the tale of treachery and deceit to an awe-struck Council.

In the meantime, I was unceremoniously bundled into the back seat of an unmarked police car, hemmed in between two burly, granite-faced Chinese ISD officers. S.K. Tan, known among his subordinates as "Jaws," sat stolidly in the front passenger seat of the car driven by an Indian ISD officer. I was forced to remove my spectacles and wear a blindfold constructed from a cheap pair of glasses. The temple-arms of the glasses were secured to one another by an elastic band. On the inside of each glass piece were glued thick, grey, styrofoam cutouts. Pressed against the eyes, the styrofoam cutouts improvised as an effective blindfold. Blindfolded—it conjured up in my mind's eye visions of gangs of kidnappers and kidnappings, of those cases which I had prosecuted as solicitor general when the offence of kidnapping was so rife in Singapore that it necessitated a drastic change in the law to one of capital offence. Throughout the motor journey, I tried again to find out from them the reasons for my arrest. No one answered. I was met with a curtain of silence. I was bewildered and angry in turn at my arrest, clinging at the same time to the naïve belief that, once they had discovered the ghastly error of my arrest, I would be released. I should of course have known better—the ISD never makes a mistake. It is the arrestee who makes the mistake. This was repeatedly impressed upon me.

---

2. On June 17, 1989, she was served with a fresh order of detention for an additional one year.

Their conspiracy of silence forced an assortment of thoughts to run through my mind. I thought of Mei who was expecting me in KL that evening, of what she would say or think at my unexplained absence, whether my arrest would repercuss on her *certiorari* application, and in any other way. I thought of my dear wife, Marjatta, ill in an hospital in London with my daughter, Annalisa, to keep her company. I mused on her reaction to the misfortune which had overtaken me. I knew deep within me that it would distress her immeasurably, and prayed in my heart that she would not come to know of it. She was an intensely loyal wife, an unselfish and wonderful woman with an infinite capacity for love. I thought of my aged mother and wondered uneasily how she would take to the news of my arrest and reassured myself that my brothers and sisters would know how to comfort her. I was very glad that my father was no more because it would have broken his proud heart to see me thus. He was very proud of me; indeed, he was one of my most loyal fans, who never missed any of my prosecutions in court. My thoughts flitted the gamut of my life's experience, and dwelt on, amongst other things, my children and Ashleigh who, unaware of the grave danger ahead, had unknowingly driven me to the foot of the lair; my law office, its prospects and the vulnerability of legal sole-proprietorships in the circumstances.

Abruptly denied of any means of communication, my anxiety for Mei's safety and well-being greatly increased my sense of disquietude and helplessness. Indeed, Mei soon became aware of a number of strangers "hanging around" her apartment block, where she was then living alone. Being innately cautious, she took counsel of mutual friends who advised her to move out and stay with her brother and his family until the matter of my detention was resolved. The ISD, it transpired, had requested its counterpart in Malaysia, the Special Branch, for surveillance assistance under their mutual aid scheme.

7

The Search

> Man's inhumanity to man
> Makes countless thousands mourn.
>
> —Robert Burns, *Man Was
> Made to Mourn*, st. 7

Notwithstanding the blindfold, I could sense the direction in which we were going and, before long, we ended at Beverly Mai, a towering block of apartments in an elegant and conveniently situated part of suburban Singapore. Throughout the entire journey no one had uttered a word. There, before we alighted, they took off my blindfold and returned to me my own pair of glasses. As in a well-rehearsed pantomime, the ISD officers silently got out of their respective cars, followed Tan and me into the lift lobby of the apartment block and into the lift up to the floor of the apartment. I unlocked the door. They streamed in and, without so much as a word amongst them, immediately fanned out, each group to its predesignated place in the apartment. So well-rehearsed in their movements and destinations, it seemed as if they had been in the apartment before. Some ISD officers went upstairs to the bedroom. Others went to the kitchen at the rear, some to the sitting and dining room. They examined silently the various papers, documents, and files on the dining table, the books on the shelves, and my still unpacked suit cases from my recent travels lying on the floor.

Whilst they were rummaging the apartment, I was ordered to sit quietly in a corner by an ISD officer who stood guard over me. I watched them go laboriously through the search. It occurred to me that I should give Ashleigh or his wife a call, as he would have by then made his way home, to let him know what was happening. But Tan forbade me from doing so, saying that his officers would inform him of the situation. There was nothing that I could do except to take his word for it. They were in the apartment for an hour or more. They seized anything and everything that they conceived relevant to national security; but their concept of national security relevance regrettably did not coincide with mine or that of a reasonable man. Photographs of our holidays in the United States, England, Hongkong, Thailand, and elsewhere; hotel bills; used airline tickets; album upon albums of business name cards, including numerous loose name cards accumulated over the years; cassette tapes of several Shakespearean plays; video tapes; expired international passports; cheque butts; old Christmas cards, *et cetera*, were all seized and fed into the voracious maws of their oversize black trash bags. Save for my international and restricted passports, it was assuredly an indiscriminate and wanton seizure of property. They repeated it with even greater indiscriminate enthusiasm in the search and seizure of my personal and clients' files and property at my office premises. According to Ashleigh, who was requested to accompany them, a van-load of files, books, papers, and documents was carted away. They were far too numerous for any orderly registration.

I was suddenly told to go upstairs to observe the search in the master bedroom. The ostensible purpose of this was presumably to avoid any future allegations whatsoever of misconduct against them. My presence upstairs was intended to serve a cosmetic purpose, as I could not conceivably be in two places at one and the same time. Whilst I was upstairs, other ISD officers were going through the various files, papers, documents, books, *et cetera*, downstairs. They had, in fact, already ransacked the bedroom upstairs when they thought of summoning me there.

An ISD officer was examining an antique Korean chest of drawers, taking out each drawer in turn and running his forefinger lightly along its joints, as only an ISD officer could fantasize for secret hiding places, in spite of my assurances that there was absolutely nothing in them nor any secret compartments. I had not the slightest inkling what they were looking for. They were deafly silent. They only spoke to a purpose. There was a second, locked bedroom, used as a temporary storage for Mei's books, glasses and china, antiques, and other household items. I did not have the key. They threatened to break it down. None of my personal effects, I assured them, were kept in the room; but if it was considered absolutely vital to do so, I could contact her in Kuala Lumpur to arrange for the key to be sent down. Their sudden but brief volubility was astounding. With an overweening egoism and a superfluity that could only have been bred out of long unchallenged authority, they imperiously told me they had the powers to break it down or, indeed, anything open. As if I was not aware of that already! Fortunately, good sense prevailed; and the display of their powers of and prowess in destruction was rendered unnecessary.

The search was resumed in a mime of silence. Conversation was kept to the very minimum, and that to essentials. Upon my request, Tan began to write out a list of the individual items seized. It soon became apparent that it was impossibly time-consuming to register each and every item. Finally, we compromised by him giving me a general list of the items seized. I then locked the door to the apartment. After that, we all trooped silently downstairs with the trash bags in tow, now full with the spoils of their search.

We left Beverly Mai in the same cars in which we had come, watched by the startled and curious security guards. I was not blindfolded. Tan then said that they wanted to search Ashleigh's apartment. I did not reply. It was more in the nature of information than a request. We went along Stevens Road towards Bukit Timah Road and, as we turned right at the second set of traffic lights into Balmoral Road, I saw Ashleigh driving his car coming from the opposite direction of Stevens Road with an unknown male Chinese seated next to him. That male Chinese, I later discovered, was an ISD officer. Just then, an ISD officer in the car suddenly exclaimed aloud that he had left my international passport behind on the dining table at Beverly Mai. So, the procession of cars stopped. He got out of the car, taking my keys with him to return to Beverly Mai.

We proceeded on to 9 Chancery Lane where the other ISD officers who had gone on ahead were waiting. Not every one went up to the apartment. Some six or seven ISD officers began to search it. The rest waited below, and then returned to the Centre. I was afraid Ashleigh might resent the law's intrusion into his apartment; but he comported himself with dignity and good-humoured detachment to see these "funny little men" searching vainly for signs of conspiratorial subversion. His behaviour was unlike that of some detainees and their families who, understandably upset, vented their outraged feelings in screaming abuses and, in one instance, spitting at the ISD officers. I was proud of him. Indeed, long after the ordeal was over, they complimented him and me on the quiet and responsible bearing and manner with which we had accepted the unpleasant situation. They were interested in business name cards and also cheque butts and used bank passbooks, which they seized, including my 2-year old granddaughter, Francesca's savings account book into which her parents had deposited the contents of her *angpao*—red envelopes—(a delightful Chinese custom of venerable vintage where a sum of money is wrapped in a red packet or paper which is then given to the recipient on his or her birthday or other auspicious occasions by relatives and close friends). The answer to their singular interest in these items only became evident later on. They were in the apartment for about two and half hours.

Tan then said that they wanted to search my office premises. It was getting late. My office staff would have gone home. I did not have the keys to the office, whereupon they predictably threatened to break down the door and any locked drawers and cabinets. They reminded me of the omnipotence of the ISD—it could break open anything with impunity if I did not cooperate. As I did not think violence was necessary, or indeed the answer to the immediate problem, I told them calmly that all they had to do was to contact the officekeeper or my personal assistant at their home. Both of them had the keys to the office and, I was quite sure, would let them in.

They tried to contact the officekeeper several times by phone but he was not yet home; nor was my personal assistant. Eventually, as time was pressing on, they decided to return to the Centre, but requested Ashleigh to accompany some twenty or so ISD officers to the office. The search of my law office took about seven hours extending into the wee hours of the morning. Unlike the searches

The Search

made of, for example, Patrick's law office, this was thorough but patently unfocused. Despite their assertion that they were "looking for evidence of subversion," it was unquestionably a "fishing expedition." They did not know what they were looking for and seized a van-load of materials such as sale and purchase agreements and other legal precedents, and clients' files, *et cetera*, all of which had absolutely nothing to do with any sinister plot, American or otherwise. The true reason behind the arrest and search was inadvertently given away in this ominous remark by ISD officer Eric Tan to Ashleigh during the search :

"Remember that we don't just look for subversion, we prosecute as well."

We left Chancery Lane. Whitley Detention Centre is but a stone's throw away. But I was mindlessly blindfolded once more and driven back to the Centre *via* its rear entrance, off Mount Pleasant Road. I was taken to a room where I was told to remove my blindfold, given back my pair of spectacles for a photo session for the ISD's archives and posterity, after which my spectacles were taken away again. They took away all my personal belongings and effects, including the general list of items seized from Beverly Mai, laboriously listing them out in receipt form, and kept it. What was the purpose of it all, I wonder?

I was escorted to a spartanly-furnished room in the same block which, with an examination couch and a small medicine almeirah, passed for the medical room. When not otherwise employed as such, it is used as a detainees' changing room. I was ordered to remove all my clothes and shoes in exchange for a well-worn, unsized but ill-fitting unisex prison outfit, which consisted of a pair of off-white, Bermuda-length pyjama trousers with a drawstring and a matching, short-sleeved, pullover-style chemise. The cloth, the colour, and the style of cut were similar to the mourning clothes worn by Singapore's professional mourners on funereal occasions. I was given no footwear. I was forced to walk barefooted on unswept floors blackened with soot and slime. The periodic "Keep Singapore Clean" campaign had not yet penetrated beyond the forbidding iron gates of the Centre.

ISA detainees are not criminals convicted of crimes involving moral turpitude, but political prisoners and, as such, should be allowed to wear their own clothes. This proper attitude found in mature and civilized societies formed part of the recommendations of the 1960 Devan Nair Prisons Inquiry Commission, whose provisions on political detentions, although publicly accepted by the government, were not wholly implemented. No reasons, as far as I am aware, were given for its nonimplementation. It is in such little things as this that one appreciates the necessity for a strong political opposition to make a government accountable to the people for its deeds of commission or omission.

After changing into those horrid prison clothes, under the wary eyes of ISD officers and Gurkha guards, I was examined by a young bespectacled Chinese doctor surnamed Ngoh, who appeared somewhat overwrought by the occasion. He asked me in a quavering voice, his eyes blinking nervously through his thick horn-rimmed glasses, routine questions about my medical history and the state of my health. I answered him accordingly. I also told him of my heart problem and my diabetic condition.

After a rudimentary medical examination, I was escorted, barefooted, by two grim-faced Gurkha guards along the corridors to Block L at the far end of the Centre, where I was locked in cell No. L-9[1] and left there alone. It was well past eventide. I looked around me. The cell seemed to have been prepared to receive me. It was very small, six feet wide by twelve feet long and fifteen feet high. It is said to be standard American cell size, as if it were the ideal yardstick for prison accommodation. Be that as it may, it is still inhumane to coop a prisoner up for twenty-three hours in a day, every day, in a tiny, matchbox cell for months on end, and sometimes years. The walls, painted naval grey had, through age and long neglect, turned into dirty grey. A raised concrete platform on which was placed a wooden plank, with neither mattress nor pillow, served as a bed. There was not a single stick of furniture. It was mean and bare. It was windowless. Natural light could not penetrate into the cell because it was walled up to the ceiling. A bright, perpetual,

---

1. For Centre and cells layout, see Appendix 2.

fluorescent tube on the ceiling and a naked, ordinary light bulb, high up on one wall, replaced the natural illumination, which the ISD in its ingenuity has denied. There was no means of telling night from day.

The cell had not been cleaned or swept for a long time. Once in a while, a fat, male, Malay scavenger, clad in a dirty, sleeveless singlet and shorts, made a token appearance in the block and a pretence of sweeping the corridors. And, as suddenly as he appeared, he swiftly vanished. The cells appeared to be out-of-bounds to him. There were cobwebs in the corners presided over by their spidery guardians, and the tiny floor was stained with traces of food and drinks consumed by unknown detainees long ago.

It was warm and stuffy. I felt the walls with my hand. I could feel the heat of the day waning slowly away. Ventilation was poor. An electric, extractor fan, right at the top corner of one wall, whirred incessantly, trying valiantly to suck out the warm, stale, humid air in the cell. The switches to the lights and the fan were outside by the thick cell door.

The massive, flushed, handleless wooden door had a peephole about twelve inches long and six inches wide, secured from the outside by two small iron bolts. The door itself was similarly secured from the outside by a large metal bolt, and, whenever it was drawn in the eerie stillness of the night, occasioned a sharp discordant crack of impending doom, jarring a sleeper out of his wits. The resounding acoustic effect was nerve-wracking, and it took some time before one could drop off to sleep again. But it is amazing how swiftly a person develops aural hypersensitivity in such surroundings. In the quiet of the night, the changing of Gurkha guards with their muffled conversations or any unusual sound or noise would immediately awaken me. Oddly enough, I found I could intuit with reasonable accuracy whether or not they were coming to take me out of the cell for interrogation.

I had no wrist watch because it had been taken away from me. I did not know how long I had been in the cell, when the sharp clangour of the cell door opening shook me out of my grim reverie. A thickset, tousled-haired, bespectacled Chinese ISD officer came in and brought six pieces of cream cracker biscuits and a small paper cup of sweetened tea. He apologised that there was no dinner available, for by the time I had been brought in, dinner had already been served. Dinner was normally served between 5:00 p.m. and 5:30 p.m. Courtesy is still our way of life. With those few words of apparent remorse, he bowed his way out. The door slammed shut once again. I was in no mood to eat anyway and left his offering untouched.

I was still trying to work out in my mind the rationale for the arrest and detention, intertwined with thoughts and concern for my wife and Mei. Mei and I had been to Bangkok together, and I had left her there with the promise to rejoin her in Kuala Lumpur. I reviewed the state of affairs. It was a most unsatisfactory position. I did not know how long I would be detained or how soon I could get a message of my predicament across to her, my relatives, and friends. My position was much too pregnable. There were too many hostages given to the prime minister. My thoughts were again rudely interrupted by the clangorous opening of the cell door.

I was taken out and escorted barefooted by two Gurkha guards back to the same medical room where I was once more examined by the same doctor. Consequent upon the recent allegations of ill-treatment, the practice of medically examining a detainee before and after every interrogative session was revived to avoid any future allegations of torture or ill-treatment. The doctor is supposed to ask the detainee whether he has any complaints, look for signs of bruises or assault or other injuries, and record them. The detainee is, however, examined in the watchful presence and hearing of ISD officers and Gurkha guards. Now, even if a detainee has any such complaint, he would be extremely foolish, if not recklessly suicidal, to ventilate them in the hearing of his captors. Therein lies the flaw in an otherwise seemingly fair procedure. There are so many subtle ways wherein a detainee's life, unpleasant as it already is, could be made even more unpleasant for him in the Centre, and all well within the law. One is vividly reminded of the prisoners-of-war camps run by the Nazi *Reich* or Japan during the last World War where, prior to visits by International Red Cross officials, the camps were cleaned and spruced up, the inmates warned against making any complaints, and given steaming hot food, new bedding, blankets, *et cetera*, which were immediately taken away from them once the officials had left the camp—after which, it was back to the same old routine.

I looked at the doctor's wrist watch. It was 7:30 p.m. I was escorted to Block C, or to what is better known among the Gurkha guards as "the underground"—where the interrogation rooms are located in the maws of the Centre.

That same night, millionaire-businessman, Baey Lian Peck, threw a sumptuous banquet to celebrate his son's wedding at the grand Pavilion Intercontinental Hotel. Seated at the main table were Professor S. Jayakumar, minister for home affairs; C.V. Devan Nair, former president of Singapore; and Dr. Toh Chin Chye, former deputy prime minister. During dinner, Jayakumar leaned towards Devan and whispered to him:

"We had to arrest Francis Seow this evening."

"What on earth for?" Devan, startled, inquired.

"Because of his involvement with an American diplomat," was the laconic reply.

"I hope you have got your facts right."

Later, Devan went to the toilet and was joined by Dr. Toh. Suspicious of their movements, Jayakumar slyly signalled to an ISD officer. There, Devan told Dr. Toh aloud in the presence of the ISD officer and several senior civil servants who happened to be there about the information on my arrest.

"Whatever for?" Dr. Toh asked, surprised.

"For his American connection."

"What are we coming to?"

On his way back to the dinner table, Dr. Toh met Dr. Lee Chiaw Meng, a former minister for education, and walked with him towards the toilet where he related the news, whereupon Dr. Lee confirmed the stale information,

"Francis Seow has been arrested earlier this afternoon."

"I have lost my appetite," a disconsolate Dr. Toh was overheard to utter.

On August 21, 1988, at the National University of Singapore's forum, Singapore's omnicompetent prime minister, usurping the role of the ISD professionals, pronounced:

> ... If, this is a big IF—if on the day they arrested Patrick Seong, they had also arrested Francis Seow and not waited till the 6th of May—more than two weeks—*I believe* documentary evidence was possible ....[2] [Emphasis added]

Belief! I believe! Shades of Sherlock Holmes! There was no evidence—there never was—that I was ever involved in any conspiracy with the U.S. government or its agencies. His remarks presupposed that I was an American agent or one "beholden" to the Americans owing to filthy lucre, and the delay in my arrest had caused the destruction or disappearance of a treasure-trove of incriminating documents and evidence. The truth of the matter was that I had not thought arrest, let alone detention, at all possible. Recall the ministerial press conference,[3] on April 29, 1988, where Deputy Prime Minister Goh Chok Tong, in response to the question as to why I was not arrested, had replied that the ISD had not recommended my arrest. What, then, had caused the sudden change of heart? Who had instigated, urged, or masterminded my arrest? It is noteworthy that the situation had changed dramatically upon Harry Lee Kuan Yew's return to Singapore from overseas! It does not require a Sherlock Holmes to deduce the identity of the malevolent author of my arrest. It, also, speaks volumes for the ISD officers' endlessly defensive reference to the extraordinary nature of my case. Where was the ISD's touted professionalism, if it could be so easily overridden by the private feelings of one man, even though he may temporarily hold the exalted office of prime minister of the nation?

---

2. *The Straits Times*, August 22, 1988.
3. *The Straits Times*, April 30, 1988.

8

In the Eye of Harry—The Interrogation

> The air bites shrewdly; it is very cold.
> —William Shakespeare, *Hamlet*,
> Act I, sc. 4, 1

> A little touch of Harry[1] in the night.
> —William Shakespeare, *Henry V*,
> Act IV, chorus, 47

Block C serves a dual purpose. It is also the Whitley Detention Centre's administrative *omphalos*. I was conducted by the two Gurkha guards to interrogation room C-22,[2] a room with which I was to become all too familiar in the course of my stay as the reluctant guest of my dear prime minister. The dark corridors were illuminated at intervals by fluorescent tube lights, supplemented by two spotlights at either end of the narrow corridor. The powerful beams of light instinctively compelled a prisoner to avoid looking into them and to cast his eyes downwards as he walked, behind and around which all else was inky darkness. Above the lintels of the interrogation rooms outside the corridors, there were naked, coloured light bulbs, which were lit up to warn against intrusion whenever the rooms were in use. On that night, all the coloured light bulbs were on, radiating a surrealistic feeling that one had wrongly wandered into a weird, silent discotheque; the presence of grim-faced Gurkha

---

1. Lee Kuan Yew's English name to intimate friends.
2. See Appendix 2.

guards quickly dispelled such thoughts. I had read of police interrogation methods, but nonetheless was unprepared for the ugly raw side of the prime minister and his strong-armed minions.

The Gurkha escort left me outside the outer door in the charge of a waiting ISD officer, who ushered me into the room, a procedure which became a daily ritual thereafter. As I walked through the doors of the interrogation room, a freezing coldness immediately wrapped itself around me. Instinctively, I folded my arms tightly in front of me to preserve my precious body warmth. I was chilled further by the horrible realization that I really was under detention and it was not all a bad dream. The room was in total darkness, save for two powerful adjustable spotlights on either side of the walls with a third powerful spotlight, like a luminous third evil eye, centred high up on the far wall directly in front of me. On either corner of the far wall behind a desk were a pair of video or sound monitors. The room was painted in midnight blue. In the ensuing days, I made out the room to be soundproof, about ten feet wide by eighteen feet long by fifteen feet high, with double-doors diagonally separated by a narrow passageway the width of the room, so that a person standing at the first door could not see inside the interrogation room. (See Appendix 2.)

I was made to stand in the middle of the room. I could scarcely make out a desk behind which there was a chair. I became uncomfortably aware of an air-conditioner blower duct directly above me on the ceiling, which directed a continuous and powerful cascade of wintry cold air down at the spot where, barefooted, I was made to stand. The floor was like a slab of ice that rapidly drained away the body's heat. I could not see any one; but I could sense the presence of several persons sheltering behind the anonymity of darkness, whose silhouettes assumed bizarre forms as they moved. As I stood there, someone shouted out with mock civility:

"Oh, give him a chair to sit."

A chair was thrust forward into the spotlight. I sat down and was momentarily thrown off my poise. The chair was unexpectedly low and wobbled precariously. It stood on three legs. The legs had been perversely sawn off to shorten them and its fourth leg sawn shorter than the rest of them. A sudden shift in weight could throw a person

In the Eye of Harry—The Interrogation

off his balance. It was difficult to maintain a mental equilibrium of keeping the questions in mind simultaneously with one's sense of balance. I recalled Soh Lung telling me of her unpleasant experience on it. So, she, too, had been interrogated in this very room! I wanted to avoid a repetition of her experience of being suddenly tipped over backwards by someone behind me. I gripped the seat of the chair with both hands, steadied myself in it, and adopted a leaning forward posture. I had not sat there long when someone called out, sarcastically,

> "Oh, we must treat our former solicitor general properly. We must give him a good chair to sit on. Not *that* kind of chair."

And so, someone behind me replaced it with a proper chair. Then I saw a silhouette of a man seated behind the desk opposite me, obviously a senior ISD officer, who asked me whether I knew why I was there.

"I do not," I replied as calmly as I could.

And I asked him why I had been arrested; but he replied that I should know the reasons why, for the ISD did not arrest any one without any evidence. Someone testily bellowed out,

> "We are wasting time. It's no use being nice to him. He is still behaving as if he is still solicitor general, who is in charge of the interrogation. Take the bloody chair away from him."

And so, it was taken away. I was compelled to stand. I tried to reply, as quietly as I could, when somebody launched into a belligerent tirade:

> "Look, cut out all your court English. This is not a court of law. The rules of evidence do not apply here. We make the rules here. This is a kangaroo court. No one can help you, no one. All the human rights organizations can do is to make a little noise, but how long can they keep it up? After a while, you will be forgotten. Patrick Seong has already fixed you up. He has told us all about you and Hank Hendrickson and all the rest of them. And you had better answer truthfully all the questions that we put to you. Otherwise, we can throw the bloody key away, and keep you in here for as long as we like. What have the Americans promised you for going into politics? Now, who is providing you with funds?"

"What funds?"

"Funds for the general election! You are finished, do you understand?" he shrieked his lungs out. "You are finished!" I initially did not appreciate the thrust of those questions. With no frame of reference to assist me, I was puzzled at this persistent line of questioning. I could not believe the government was seriously tilting at American windmills. I could understand that my sudden interest in politics and critical public utterances on the national issues of the day could have given rise to the prime minister's and his party's fears of the growth of a credible opposition coalescing around me; but American connections! Many of those issues on which I spoke deserved ventilation; it had nothing to do with America and the Americans but, because of the controlled news media and the ambience of fear, few Singaporeans were bold enough to voice them, as they feared it might bring the prime minister's wrath down on them and their loved ones. Any critical, albeit constructive comment that questioned the official line or policy was looked upon with disfavour and suspicion. Dissent was suspect and considered disloyal and therefore subversive. I had always been known as a bit of a maverick. I saw no reason why I should not be able to criticize the government, if it deserved criticism. Someone had to do it. Given my background, I thought I was better placed than most to do so; but, unfortunately for me, the prime minister does not possess the political sagacity of Sir Winston Churchill, who once remarked:

> Criticism may not be agreeable but it is necessary; it fulfills the same function as pain in the human body, it calls attention to the development of an unhealthy state of things.[3]

Instead, he saw in me only a political thorn in his side, to be plucked out and crushed. Shades of Confucius—*Sha ji xia hou*! My letters to and interviews by the foreign press and attendances at international law and human rights conferences where I spoke vigorously on some of these issues only served to intensify the political pain and suspicion to chimerical proportions that there must be a motivational force behind me. It was no secret that I was friendly

---

3. Cited by William Manchester in *Winston Spencer Churchill, The Last Lion*, vol. 1, p. 348. Boston: Little, Brown, and Co., 1983.

with foreign diplomats. I had been seen in the company of Hank, a *political* secretary at the U.S. Embassy, with whom I lunched periodically at fine restaurants in town.

I had first come to know Hank Hendrickson over a case in which I represented an American client who had run afoul of the law, but who at the time had an intriguing claim to knowledge of missing American servicemen in the Vietnam. Hank had wanted to know about him. We spoke on other occasions as when he wanted elucidation on some aspects of our laws. In about July 1986, Hank telephoned me, as president of the Law Society, to say that a group of American judges from New York City would be visiting Singapore soon, and inquired whether the Law Society could host a function for them at short notice. He had approached Justice Punch Coomarasamy, our former ambassador to the U.S., but who because of changed circumstances, felt it was difficult for him to do so. I agreed; and instructed our executive secretary, Patrick Nathan, to arrange for a cocktail party to which we also played host to our High Court judges, including Justice Coomarasamy, the heads of legal and judicial departments, as well as some members of the bar. The function was held at the newly-completed Amara Hotel in downtown Singapore. Hank escorted the American judges to the party. The U.S. ambassador also attended. It was an immensely successful party. The local judiciary and the bar had an interesting and useful exchange of viewpoints, if not telephone numbers and addresses, with their foreign counterpart.

On October 24, 1986, Hank told me that his superior from the U.S. State Department, Joseph Snyder, was in Singapore and wished to meet some lawyers. I thought it a good idea for the Council members to meet him as well, and at a Council meeting that day brought up the idea of hosting an informal cocktail session for him. The Council agreed. During the reception at the Amara Hotel, I was introduced to Joseph Snyder and some other U.S. Embassy officials.

Coincidentally in the fall/winter of 1986, Mei was in New York with U.S. Socfin, doing a course in investment banking and finance management. We had planned beforehand that I would join her for a short holiday towards the end of her course. I told Joe about Mei and that I would be in the States later in the year and asked whether we could call on him so that he could show us round the city if circumstances permitted. He gave me his address and telephone number.

As luck would have it, Mei had a free weekend, and we decided to go to Washington, D.C. where I met him again. Because he was at the time about to be transferred to another departmental posting, he introduced his successor, Colin Helmer, to me.

"Why should he do so?" a voice in the darkness thundered at me.

I thought it was the most natural thing for him to do so; but they were trying to read more into the introduction than the situation warranted it. It was only devious minds that could possibly conceive anything sinister in a simple introduction. I shrugged it off, and kept silent. Unbeknown to me, a U.S. State Department official, one David Lambertson, after seeing the prime minister in Singapore, had inquired about me.

"Why did he ask for you? Why? Why?" they screamed to know.

Not having heard of the man or the name before, I was extremely perplexed at this repeated questioning.

Given his innate distrust of American political *dilettantism*, the prime minister perceived these events as political straws in the wind. *Eureka!*—an American connection! As I stood there listening to the ceaseless barrage of questions and innuendoes hurled at me in obnoxious and objectionable language, it struck me that the prime minister was using the ISD as the instrument to pluck the political thorn out from his side.

Among the very first salvo of questions fired at me with increasing stridency were:

"Why are you going into politics?" "Who are behind you?" "Who is David Lambertson?" "What is he to you? He had met Patrick. Why should Lambertson be asking about you?" "Why is he so interested in you?" "Who is more important, Patrick Seong or you?"

I was absolutely nonplussed. I had not heard of him. I denied knowing or any knowledge of him. Insisting that I knew him, and to "stop pretending" that I did not know him, they screamed back at me, calling me, "a bloody fucking liar," amongst other expletives. They grilled me at length about him. Believing they had caught me out in a blatant lie, an ISD officer, with an evil sneer on his ugly face, came up to where I stood and triumphantly waved a xeroxed copy of a legal notepaper with the name David Lambertson on it in front of me, saying it had been seized from among the papers on my desk. He thrust it under my nose. It was the instructions noted down by Roslina after her interview with Patrick. I had not seen it until then. I maintained my denial that I knew nothing about him. They did not believe me, accusing me of being a "damn good actor."

David Lambertson, the deputy assistant secretary for East Asian and Pacific Affairs, was, I learned much later, in Singapore to see the prime minister on some official matters. Hank had thereafter arranged for him to meet me and some lawyers, but I was then overseas. He had however met with Patrick, but missed meeting some other lawyers, who had mistaken the tryst in the maze of plush hotels in downtown Singapore. At the meeting, Lambertson had apparently asked Patrick pointed questions about me, which the ISD tried to spin out as confirmation of his [Lambertson's] satisfaction with Hank's supposed political talent scouting and recruitment of me.

They abruptly switched the line of interrogation:

"Now, where did you get the money to pay your debts?" they demanded to know. "Who is financing you?"

"From my law practice and from my friends." My reply was met with continuous guffaws of skepticism.
They returned to the "American connection" insisting that the Americans were backing my entry into national politics.

"I have not quite made up my mind whether or not to enter politics." This was greeted with howls of derision and vulgarity.

"We have irrefutable evidence that you are recruiting lawyers and others to contest the general election. Who and where is the source of your funds? We know you are going to contest all seventy-nine seats.[4] Where are you getting the money to finance

---

4. The number was later raised to 81 electoral divisions: See the Parliamentary

them? Who is providing you with the funds?" they shrieked and screamed one question after another, without any letup.

My denial of American funding only met with more abuses and obscenities. Each candidate, they yelled out in near unison, would need to spend about S$10,000.00, discounting the individual initial deposit of S$1,500.00.[5] In other words, I would require, according to their shocking computation, about one S$1,000,000.00!

In view of the difficulty in finding viable candidates in a tight, fearful island in the time remaining for the general election, I had revised my original thinking and number to about fifteen to twenty young men and women who were expected to fund themselves. I did not think that the election campaign expenses would require more than a couple of thousand dollars per candidate, but they laughed it to scorn. I was admittedly a political ingénu. As it turned out, my own personal expenses at the 1988 general election were about S$2,100.00. The amount did not differ much from what the other candidates themselves had incurred. Unperturbed, I replied that in order to minimize costs I had also considered mailing of letters and/or handbills to constituents and, where necessary, doing away with as many street rallies as possible. They screeched in ridicule. Before I could answer a question, another person would scream profanities at me, and followed by yet another. None of them was really interested in my answers.

Someone behind me bawled into my left ear,

"So, you think, you can take on and bully the second-generation leaders?" Before I could recover from its deafening effect, he continued,

"Well, our job is to make sure that you do not succeed. We are here to neutralize you. You know, to neutralize you! For your information, Lee Kuan Yew is running for another term. And you will be locked up here for at least two years, if not more. So, where will you be? You can give up all your ideas of going into politics."

Elections (Names and Boundaries of Electoral Divisions) Notification 1988, S.L. Supp. No. S 144/88.

5. The deposit (which is forfeited, if a candidate fail to secure one-eighth of the total votes cast) was raised to S$4,000.00 before the 1988 general election. See section 28, Parliamentary Elections Act, Cap. 218, as amended.

I wanted to retort that, save for the trappings of power, I did not think he was the kind of man, who would give up real power to another easily. But my tormentor, urged on by his strident accomplices, plunged on in a torrent of words,

> "You think, you can just dip your hands into our billions of reserves. Award lucrative contracts to your friends and cronies and dissipate our hard-earned reserves, huh?, huh? Who are the people behind you?"

As I turned round to confront him in the darkness, another person from behind bawled into my right ear that I was "a fucking, bloody liar," whilst a chorus of voices accused me of being supported and financed by the Americans. It was not only bewildering but terrifying. It was absolute bedlam. They were persons who had gone berserk. I kept whirling around to identify and meet the thrust of those shrill, shrieking voices. I suddenly began to comprehend that they were not really interested in hearing any answers. It was an awesome exercise to disorientate, malign, and humiliate me. It was the vaunted "psychological pressure and technique" of Brigadier General Lee Hsien Loong, the eldest son and political heir of Prime Minister Harry Lee Kuan Yew. He should have been there to watch his maniacs in action! The word *"neutralize"* was etched indelibly in my memory. It was intended to frighten and neutralize me from entering opposition politics. And to serve no doubt as a warning to all the professionals whom I had tried to cultivate for the general election. *Sha ji xia hou!*

I decided to erect a wall of silence around myself by shutting my ears to the ceaseless bombardment of accusatory abuses, vulgarities, and obscenities. My silence began to infuriate them. A well-built, bespectacled, mustachioed person who, by his features and accent, was unmistakably a Malay, emerged from out of the darkness. He came to where I stood and vociferously threatened to assault me on a couple of occasions if I did not answer them. I suddenly noticed he was dressed in warm woollen clothes over which he still wore a windcheater. He swung his hand at me. I braced myself for the blow. But his fist stopped short just inches from my face. He looked like a thug. He behaved like a thug. He was a thug. He repeated his threat. I remained silent. Amidst deafening obscenities, he swaggered up to me and repeatedly blew thick clouds of cigarette smoke into my face. He had shouted himself hoarse. I then noticed for the first time that the room was thick with cigarette smoke, tracing weird patterns as it curled and coiled lazily up the shafts of the spotlights. Venting his frustration at my continued silence, he demanded that I take off my shirt leaving my upper body bare under the air-conditioner duct. No one stopped him. I reluctantly complied. It was cold. Very cold. Very, very cold. And the wind chill or draught factor made it more unbearably so.

A tall Chinese, about 40 years old or so, clad in a long-sleeved woollen cardigan over which he too wore a windcheater, emerged from the shadows and took over from him. He had a weird hairdo, probably a wig to disguise his appearance. He was as threatening and as vulgar and as obscene as his Malay colleague, warning me that he was a hot-tempered man and could not control himself as well as his Malay colleague. Unless I spoke out, he threatened to hit me and, as I persevered in my silence, he swung his fist at me. I braced myself for the blow, again, but his fist, too, stopped just short inches from my face. They were without any doubt the goon squad. They were nasty, ugly—like men deranged.

Then, the brawny Malay lout, who had recovered his voice, came back fulminating and, pressing his hideously florid face close to mine, said:

"You have been fixing up a lot of police officers in your time." [He was alluding to the days when police disciplinary proceedings were referred to me as solicitor general for instructions.] "Now is the time for you to be fixed. You think you can pull strings; but I also can pull strings."

As he said that, he yanked loose the drawstring which held up my pyjama trousers. For some inexplicable reason, the law of gravity was suspended that night. My trousers did not drop to the floor. I kept very still. I was already bare from the waist up, and barefooted.

I never saw the Malay ruffian nor the Chinese hoodlum after that night. I learnt later that Patrick and some others were stripped stark naked and sprayed with water to intensify the cold treatment. As a result, they developed very bad cases of cold and flu requiring visits to the Toa Payoh General Hospital.

The senior ISD officer, who had been watching silently the circus performance of his buffoons and goon squad, rose from behind his desk, came round to the front of the desk and, leaning against it, slowly folded his arms across his chest. In the spotlight, he turned out to be a balding Indian of about 43 years old and, like the others, dressed in warm clothes, a long-sleeved maroon woollen pullover. Remarking in perfect good temper, "You must be very strong, not to feel the cold." He told me to re-tie my trouser's drawstring, and put back on my thin loose blouse. I am not sure to this day whether it was intended as a compliment or not. I was seething with inner rage, and kept close custody of my tongue.

Taking over the interrogation, he spoke in a low, measured tone. He was the foil. I asked him again for the reason of my arrest, but he told me I was there to answer questions. He advised me,

"Come clean, and do not waste everybody's time. The ISD does not arrest people for nothing unless it has the evidence, and it has a lot of evidence against you."

So, I told him to let me hear the evidence that it had against me. It was not for the ISD to disclose its evidence. It was for me to tell them and that was the reason why I was there. They would compare what I had told them with what they had in their file. And if they were satisfied that I was telling the truth, then, maybe, I could leave that place very soon. I reiterated I could not still understand my arrest and I had not done anything against the security of the state. He replied that that was what I claimed, but their evidence in hand suggested otherwise and, therefore, unless I told them, it was going to be a very difficult time for me. They did not want to keep me in there longer than was necessary. I told him that I would be "happy" to tell them whatever they wanted to know. It was, perhaps, a wrong choice of word, an untimely slip of the tongue in the circumstances. The reaction was understandable. Someone cried out at the top of his voice in derisive disbelief:

"He is *happy*. He still does not know where he is. He is *happy*," spitting out the word with vehement disgust.

I surmised they construed it as indicative of the fact that, notwithstanding my discomfiture, I was still much in command of the situation.

The Indian ISD officer said nothing, but changed tack. In seductive tones, he began to purr that I should really be in Kuala Lumpur together with Mei Siah who would be lonesome that evening. And who would miss me and be worried at my failure to turn up.

"Have you thought to yourself, what is she doing now?"

"Of course, she would be worried. It was only natural."

"Don't you want to join her?"

"Of course."

"Look, in that case, why don't you tell us everything, and you won't have to be here too long. You have missed being with her this weekend, but you could be with her the next weekend," he slyly insinuated.

"I do not know what you people really want. In any event, I have nothing to hide. What is it you all want to know?"

He disclosed that they wanted me to admit to an American black operations which, until then, I did not know had even existed, except in the febrile imagination of an overly suspicious prime minister. I denied that there was any such dark conspiracy. Black operations in ISD parlance refer to clandestine operations organized by foreign governments or their agencies to cause internal disruption and subvert the PAP government of Singapore. This line of questioning went on and on and on. As soon as one team of interrogators felt uncomfortably cold or exhausted, they would sneak out of the interrogation room and a fresh team of interrogators would relieve them. It was difficult in the darkness to detect the number of times the teams were changed. One only became aware of a change when a new voice was heard or when the shift and pace of the interrogation altered. This went on right throughout the night. Amidst the distractions of sound and fury, I did not notice that the Indian officer had slipped quietly away in the darkness. I never saw him again in that room. He had probably stood in for someone that night. Save for the driver of the car, he was the only Indian whom I saw throughout my entire detention.

At some point later in the inquisition, I became aware of a senior-ranking person seated behind the desk, whose face in the lurid darkness was concealed by a black porcine-like mask whose snout-like contraption scrambled his voice whenever he spoke. He was undoubtedly someone known to me, but whose fearful shame of discovery of his identity and participation in this monstrous inquisition had driven him to seek anonymity behind that grotesque mask. This surely was the stuff of Orwellian fiction! There were moments when they threatened me with dire consequences and, at other moments, reminded me of my grave responsibility towards my family who were the ones who were going to suffer if I were to be detained indefinitely, and in whose and my own best interests I should disclose all that they wanted to know. As that failed to elicit the desired response, the brute threatened:

"We have enough circumstantial evidence to hang you—in fact we have more evidence than you had to hang Sunny Ang."[6]

"Look, I don't know anything. I don't even know the reason for my arrest. And, as for going into politics, it is true that I was considering it, but I had not yet made a final decision."

Ignoring my reply, they began to zero in on my family, saying there was nobody except my son Ashleigh, who had still not yet qualified as a lawyer, to look after my law firm. And that he was running impotently around Singapore like "a blue-arse fly" trying to secure my release. Therefore, who was going to keep my firm going? It would "go to the dogs." My law firm was not doing well, and the longer I remained inside there, the greater would be the chances of my firm collapsing with no one to manage and run it. They reminded me of André, my 15-year old son, who had been heartbroken, they lied, upon hearing the late evening's television news announcement of my detention, with no one to care for him, without any financial or moral support, if I were to be kept long in detention, and so forth and so on. But the day came, when they spoke admiringly of Ashleigh, especially Deputy Director Sim Poh Heng, as a loving and filial son of whom I should be justly proud. They had kept him under constant surveillance!

Interrogation as to the imaginary source of money to fund all seventy-nine candidates at the general election continued unabated. I was not, I repeatedly replied, going to contest seventy-nine seats.

---

6. See chapter 3 above.

Several of them yelled out together that I was a liar, and that I was trying to field all seventy-nine candidates for which I had received or had been promised money from the Americans. I denied this. Where had I stashed the money away? Was it not in Switzerland? It was so ludicrous. I told them to prove it. They replied that it was for me to disprove it. If not in Switzerland, where was it? This senseless exchange went on interminably. Teams of interrogators focused on this issue, and grilled, and probed for hours on end, as well as for other sources of funds. I found myself repeating *ad nauseam*:

"I have none. No foreign backers."

At one stage, they excitedly accused me of having gone specially to Hongkong to solicit money from Hong Leong for the general election. I was totally mystified at this new twist to the interrogation. Hong Leong is a large Singapore public conglomerate,[7] which at the time spans "finance companies in Singapore, Malaysia and London, a bank in Hongkong, hotels, office blocks and stockbrokers, nail factories, concrete pile casters and tile makers," but which, through no fault of its own and not for want of trying, does not enjoy much rapport with the government. I denied any such solicitation. They had the evidence to show that I had been to Hongkong for that purpose. I denied it again; but they kept pressing me and shouting that I was a liar. I was curious for a long time at this accusation.

It was some time much later that I recalled that Mei and I had been in Hongkong in 1987. Mei had called on a Singapore acquaintance, Chiang Wee Tiong, then a managing director of Hong Leong Securities Company at Wheelock House. I had accompanied her there. Chiang had previously been a director of a Singapore firm of stockbrokers, which was liquidated as a consequence of the Pan-El debacle—a public company listed on the Stock Exchanges of Singapore and Malaysia—and had left Singapore to work in Hongkong. There was another male Singaporean Chinese, Ng Hong Leong, formerly of Standard Chartered Bank, Singapore, present at the time. Mei was mainly interested in ascertaining from Chiang the financial climate and investment opportunities in Hongkong after which, in

---

7. See *Far Eastern Economic Review*, December 5, 1985; November 2, 1989.

the course of an idle conversation, one or the other of them asked me whether I intended to stand as a candidate in the forthcoming general election. I recalled saying lightheartedly that I might give it a shot if there was sufficient support from them. Nothing further of import passed between us, if his casual inquiry could be so termed. What was so terrifying however was that a distant, half-forgotten, innocuous, private social conversation could reach the ears of the intelligence agency of government and become twisted out of shape and context into an idiom of oppression.

Shortly after my arrest, rumours abounded in Singapore and the Asean region, including Hongkong, that Hong Leong was under criminal investigation by the government. And when charges were subsequently preferred against its billionaire chairman for abetting an offence of criminal breach of trust by a nephew-director of a related company within the conglomerate of a relatively paltry sum of S$842,892 and receiving stolen property worth S$500,000, (said to have been committed about a decade ago), the public swiftly concluded it was because Hong Leong had financially supported my election campaign. If so, it had been most cruelly maligned. But, whatever you will, it illustrates one of the negative aspects of Singapore's closed society. Whilst I was still trying to recover from this latest vague onslaught, an ISD officer surprised me by asking:

"How well do you know Daim?" referring to the Malaysian minister of finance, Datuk Paduka Daim Zainuddin.

"I do not know him."

By now, I realized that they were groping for evidence of source of funds—any source—even though they might not be from the Americans. They persisted. I remembered Mei knew him through some business transactions some time ago long before he became finance minister. They wanted to know, however, of my *own* connection with him. I had none. They did not quite believe me. They claimed they had a copy of my telex to him on some monetary matters, which they had found in my office. I was momentarily dumbfounded. And then, I realized that it was a case of mistaken identity. I told them. An officer re-examined the telex and confirmed it. Sheepishly, they shifted on to other matters.

Given my life style I was not a political animal, they concluded, and my sudden interest in politics at the median of my life was sufficient cause for suspicion and suggestive of the fact that there was some one behind me. And it must be the Americans! They obviously had not heard of or, if they had, had forgotten, the aphorism: better late than never. I conceded that I was not initially interested in elective politics and the aetiology of my interest began with the Select Committee hearing on the amendments to the Legal Profession Act. I was until then quite contented to be the president of the Law Society and to work within the parameters of the Act and the law; but it was none other than the prime minister himself rather than the sinister forces of either extremity of the political spectrum that had sparked off my transition into elective politics.

They disliked the way I answered them and reminded me repeatedly that I was no longer the solicitor general and I was not in a court of law. They made the rules here and I had better speak the whole truth. But I kept telling them:

"Look, if you have the evidence against me, let me hear them so that I could at least reply to each and every allegation that had been made against me."

"We are not here to tell you what we have in our files. It is for you to clear yourself, and tell us everything that we want to know," they invariably answered.

They evidently had not heard of the burden of proof, that he who asserts has to prove the allegation. Not for them the rules of evidence and procedure! In this, they sadly echoed the prime minister, who had set the dubious example.

The absurdity of this exchange eventually reached an impasse. It became increasingly plain that they were trying to make bricks without straws. They were trying to make an ugly picture out of a black conspiracy from disparate, unconnected, mosaic pieces of social meetings with Hank and Joseph Snyder, (who was at the time director of the Indonesia, Malaysia, Brunei and Singapore affairs in the U.S. State Department) and the subsequent brief luncheon meeting with Joe in Washington, where he had introduced me to Colin Helmer, his successor in office as the Singapore desk officer. A former senior ISD officer's fatuous remark to a subordinate officer while berating him for an inconclusive police investigation, in the days when I was still in the service came forcefully back to me.

"In the ISD, we can make mountains out of mole hills. So, why can't you?"

I recalled joining in the laughter at that asinine remark as typical ISD mentality. Now that it was happening to me, it was not a laughing matter. They could, indeed, make mountains out of mole hills—and it was for me to disprove it! It was a horrifying thought! I was unaccustomed to a changing burden of proof.

The interrogation shifted from subject to subject and back again with sudden swiftness. I was asked about my interest in human rights activities and organizations and the identity of the person or persons who were instrumental in inviting me to speak at those international conferences. Param Cumaraswamy,[8] chairman of the Malaysian Bar Council and a notable human rights advocate, had invited me to speak at the 1987 Lawasia biennial conference in Kuala Lumpur, Malaysia. On hearing his name, they snorted in recognition and disgust:

"Oh yes, we know all about him."

And, from there, I was invited to speak by other organizations. True to his reputation, Param campaigned so vigorously for the release of the "Marxist" detainees at international law and human rights conferences that the Singapore government declared him *persona non grata*. It banned his entry into Singapore as an undesirable, even to the petty extent of denying him transit facilities at Changi International Airport, a primary international air junction.

On June 29, 1987, my robust address at the Lawasia biennial conference on the detention of those twenty-two ISA detainees and my appeal to concerned and caring international organizations gathered there to exert pressure on the Singapore government to put them on trial in a court of law or release them won thunderous ovation. As already noted, the prime minister had, at a hastily convened joint press conference with Archbishop Gregory Yong, dismissed any such appeal. However, it is worthy of note that some years before, he told a press conference of Malay journalists:

---

8. He later became president of Lawasia and, in July 1994, was appointed U.N. Special Rapporteur on the Independence and Impartiality of the Judiciary.

I give this warning to extremists who make use of religious or other sentiments. I shall not arrest them under the Emergency Regulations or the Preservation of Public Security Ordinance. *They will be brought to court. Evidence will be produced. Let the judge decide. Let the people know and understand in what way these people have sinned ... have sinned against the citizens of Singapore.*[9] [Italics added]

Many listeners at the conference openly expressed the fear that, upon my return to Singapore, I would probably be detained for having made that lively speech. The speaker, who followed immediately after me, prefaced his speech by offering me a safe refuge in the Philippines "if Singapore does not want him." I was deeply touched by the spontaneous offer of refuge and was intrigued at the identity of the speaker who was by his accent a Filipino. After he resumed his seat, he leaned across and passed his business name card over to me. His name was Sedfrey Ordoñez, the secretary of justice to the government of the Republic of the Philippines. I spoke at subsequent international legal workshops, seminars, and conferences on human rights. All these seemed to have irked my prime minister and his government.

My interest and involvement in the Law Society and my subsequent election by the Council members as president were well documented by the news media at the time. Apeing the prime minister at the televised Select Committee hearings, my horrid inquisitors tried to drive a wedge into my friendship with Soh Lung by insinuating that she had, together with Fong Har, made use of me in the Law Society for her own ends. It was so preposterous that I laughed it to scorn and, after a few more pathetic attempts, they abandoned it. But *The Straits Times* emblazoned it, nonetheless.

They already knew the identities of my supporters and sympathisers in the Law Society, but nevertheless directed countless questions about them in typical ISD style. They placed before me a list of names. It read:

"[Rajaratnam] Ramason, J.S. Khosa, Mirza Namazie, Mohan Das Naidu, Chandra Mohan, Jacob Chacko, Warren Khoo and [Thillagaratnam] Scott."

---

9. August 11, 1965.

"Well, what about it?" It did not appear anything unusual or unique to me.

"Can't you see?" they shouted out, incredulously.

"See what?"

"They are all Indians!" they scornfully cried out in unison.

"Your supporters are all Indians."

"So what?" I replied.

The fact that Warren Khoo is a Chinese, albeit a lone Chinese, among Indians, did not faze them. Until the matter of race was drawn so dramatically to my attention in that cold room, I had not spared it a moment's thought nor looked at it through their jaundiced eyes. The prime minister holds certain racist views of ethnic groups, which he articulates not without gusto from time to time. Indians, he observed, are "by nature, fractious and contentious." See his racist slur in a speech to undergraduates at the National University of Singapore:

... The Indians never vote, never agree to vote for any single party. They like contention. It is in their blood.[10]

What a sweeping condemnation of a race! In the early days of PAP rule, Singaporeans were slapped down for much less. But the times have changed. Divisive politics are now the vogue under the guise of preservation of one's language and culture. Needless to say, all my ISD interrogators were Chinese save for the Malay and Indian officers mentioned earlier and who, incidentally, were not apparent at this stage of the interrogation.

"Well, what's wrong with it?"

"Indians are trouble-makers.[11] You were being made use of by them and, at the first signs of trouble, see, they have abandoned you."

"Indians are fond of taking up law and medicine. There is a great disproportion of Indian lawyers to Chinese lawyers at the bar. Something should be done about it. This imbalance should be

---

10. December 12, 1986.

11. See, also, speech by C.V. Devan Nair to the National University of Singapore Society, June 23, 1987.

corrected,"[12] someone remarked, echoing the prime minister's chauvinistic sentiments.

Could all this in the course of the argument, be a matter of national security interest? It is frightening to speculate the other uses to which the ISD is being put by the government. Meanwhile, it was sad to witness the prime minister's reversal on the concept of a *Singaporean Singapore* striking root in the civil service and the increasingly lopsided emphasis on the importance and necessity of Chinese dominance, which cannot bode well for the long-term welfare of the country.

From the tenor of questioning, it was unmistakable that the ISD was well informed and had studiously catalogued the idle talk and gossip in the bar rooms of the subordinate courts and the supreme court. The ISD was well tuned into the profession. To my involuntary exclamation of surprise at their fund of trivia on the profession, an ISA officer crowed: "There are lawyers who are PAP members," from which it was to be implied that PAP lawyers were the source of their information. It was deliberately intended to throw me off the scent as to the identity of the claque of ISD informers and agents in the profession. It is an open secret at the bar that, in addition to PAP lawyer-sympathizers, there are also ISD informers.

They interrogated me at length about my unsuccessful bid for the presidency of the Automobile Association of Singapore (AA) at its last annual general meeting,[13] my motives, and the financial position of the Association. They charged me with trying to turn the Automobile Association of Singapore, an organization catering to the needs of the Singapore motoring public with reciprocal privileges with other national motoring clubs, into a power base to launch my political career; and obliquely hinted it as a source to delve into its financial reserves for my own purposes. They charged me further with trying to politicize the AA and embarrass the government over future increases in road taxes and other related issues. I was astounded at such a cynical interpretation of my bid for the

---

12. Recent intakes of Indians and minority races into the Faculty of Law, National University of Singapore, have reportedly been reduced.
13. April 29, 1988, AA premises, River Valley Road.

presidency. Indeed, such a charge could be brought home with greater precision against the government. The AA annual general meeting was packed with PAP members and supporters, almost all of whom were brought to the meeting in specially chartered buses to ensure that their nominee was elected president. It was they, and not I, who were politicizing it. The AA was the last place, I retorted, to turn into a political power base. Its members comprised disparate groups of persons who came from different backgrounds with different political persuasions, including a large number of PAP members and sympathizers. But they remained unconvinced.

Turning to my bid for membership of the committee of the Singapore Turf Club—the local equivalent of the Royal Jockey Club of England—of which I had been an ordinary member for the last fifteen years or so, they made similar charges against me of desiring to turn it into a vehicle for my political aspirations. There was again the oblique reference to the club's financial reserves. It was so laughably absurd. As its name implies, its members consisted mainly of lovers of equestrian sports and it was supported by members of the public who enjoy their weekly flutter. The club is probably the most exclusive club in Singapore with an ordinary membership ceiling of one thousand members. Stringent rules and regulations and a conservative admissions committee ensured that its ordinary membership was kept select and low. And, at the time of my arrest and detention, its ordinary members numbered no more than four hundred.

A year before my bid for a seat on the committee, in 1987, the minister for law, Eddie W. Barker, a sportsman and horse racing enthusiast, had made a similar bid. He sent out a personal appeal, under the Law Ministry's official letterhead, to all ordinary members of the club soliciting their votes for his candidacy; but he was ignominiously defeated. Knowing all too well the vengeful character of the prime minister, I grasped at once that he would construe the defeat of a close ministerial colleague's candidature as political *lèse-majesté*, and that it would not be long before he would wreak vengeance on the club and its members for this affront.

Shortly afterwards and unknown generally to the public, the chairman of the club was subjected to harrowing hostile surveillance and investigations into his personal and corporate finances by the Corrupt Practices Investigation Bureau and the Inland Revenue Department. At the same time the accounts of the Singapore Turf Club were heavily audited. Nothing irregular was found in either instance. But it was only a prelude to what was yet to come.

It came as no surprise to me when, a year later, the government introduced legislation in Parliament to acquire the club compulsorily. The club had been in existence for more than 150 years, and this action was taken on the outrageously spurious ground that the committee could dissolve the club and distribute its huge reserves amongst themselves to the detriment of the racing public. Today, Eddie W. Barker is the chairman of the Singapore Turf Club renamed the Bukit Turf Club.

I had lost all sense of time. I had been standing there under the pitiless glare of the spotlights. I felt the urge to go to the toilet. I told them. Two Gurkha guards appeared and escorted me to the toilet. Having stood almost motionless at one spot for so long I had great difficulty in walking. I found myself rooted to the ground—a term more descriptive of the reality of the situation than a mere figure of speech. My limbs were stiff all over. I was unsteady. The two Gurkha guards on either side of me supported me under my arms. I staggered out of the interrogation room, half carried by them, along the dark corridors up two flights of stairs to the ground level of Block C, along a corridor, to a toilet located in an empty cell in Block D. I blinked at the unexpected harsh light of day. I was quite shocked. The urge to go to the toilet was forgotten for a moment. I asked one of the two Gurkhas for the time of day, but, as he appeared somewhat nonplussed at my question, I grabbed hold of his wrist to peer short-sightedly at his wristwatch. It was 11:30 in the morning. I was astounded. I then realized that I had been standing in the interrogation room for about sixteen hours warding off questions thrown unremittingly at me. It seemed improbable to me that I could have stood at one spot, almost motionless, for that length of time. I recalled with shame that, when my detainee-clients had previously complained to me that they had been forced to stand for as long as 72 hours at a stretch, without sleep, I had great difficulty in believing them. I thought that they were exaggerating; but, incredibly, I, too, was undergoing a similar experience! But for the intervention of nature I could also have stood for as long as 72 hours or more in the circumstances. I thought long and hard about this phenomenon and I came to the conclusion that it must have been due to the adrenergic reaction of an animal at bay.

I noticed, too, dried sunburnt blisters peeling from the skin of both arms. I could not at first comprehend how I could have acquired them until I realized that I had been burnt by the powerful rays of those spotlights, which had also dried up the moisture in my eyes. Cold rashes had broken out all over my atrophied limbs under my clothes. Unlike many people who are sensitive to sunburn, I am susceptible to cold rashes. It was always troublesome for me whenever I had perforce to travel abroad during winter. In this instant case, as if signaled by a faithful built-in thermometer, the rashes broke out in chilling confirmation of the coldness of the room. My interrogators had swaddled themselves up in warm winter clothes and left it, time and again, whenever they could no longer withstand the wintry cold.

From that room I was escorted to the medical room. I was bone-weary and exhausted. The doctor was a turbaned Sikh, a kind and understanding man, whom I came to know as Kuldip Singh Vaswant. He examined me. With his stethoscope he probed my chest around the cardiac region for an abnormally long time. Through my sleep-weary eyes, I could sense he was concerned about something. I was not aware that the stress of the ordeal had caused my heart to misbehave or that he was feeling concerned that I should be warded in an hospital for a more thorough examination than he could possibly give me with the meagre medical facilities at his disposal in the Centre. I surmised later that he had tentatively questioned the wisdom of continuing with my interrogation under those inhospitable conditions. He prescribed the necessary medications for my skin and my eyes, after which I was sent back under the same escort to the interrogation room.

On re-entering the room, the blast of cold air sent me into a sudden paroxysm which lasted for about five to ten minutes. It occurred each and every time I was taken out of and returned to the interrogation room. The doctor later told me it was the body's defensive reaction to the intense cold in order to generate heat. An ISD officer immediately sent for a cup of hot tea which I gratefully accepted with eager trembling hands. I had great difficulty in holding the cup of tea which I hastily swallowed down. After a time, the paroxysm subsided.

A little while later, the phone in the room rang. I could not make out what was said. The ISD officer put down the telephone, and, with a mocking smirk on his face, said:

> "I think we better give him a chair to sit down on. He has a heart problem."

I was in fact grateful to be able to sit down. It did not matter then whether it was on a three-legged chair or otherwise. Another ISD officer, dripping with heavy sarcasm, said:

> "Yes, yes, let him have the better chair. We don't want our ex-solicitor general to die here, to be found dead in the Centre. So, we better treat him properly."

The interrogation continued, but on a less intensive or abusive note. It was suddenly interrupted by the telephone ringing again. I could not make out the conversation. But I was sent back to the medical room, and there, Dr. Kuldip informed me that he was sending me to the General Hospital for a medical checkup. I had to change into my street clothes and put on my shoes. I noticed for the first time that my feet were filthy, covered black with grimy soot from the floors of the interrogation room and the Centre. There was no ready means of cleaning myself. The medical room had the fortuitous luxury of an attached toilet. I splashed some cold water on my face from a faucet over the wash basin and, using a comb therein, groomed myself as best as I could.

On Saturday, May 7, 1988, the MHA released a statement to which was attached another statutory declaration purportedly made by Patrick, stating, *inter alia*, that—

> ... Hank then asked [me] why professionals were not coming forward to stand in the elections. I replied that Francis Seow had already made known his intention to stand for election. Soh Lung had expressed interest before her arrest but after her release, I did not know whether she had become dispirited. Hank was interested to know who were the lawyers who could be potential candidates. I told him that Francis Seow was trying to get a group of professionals to stand

and that A.S.K. Wee[14] was one of them. Hank then asked whether I was standing for election myself. I told him that Francis Seow had invited me to join him to stand for elections but that I was unlikely to stand. I said that I valued my private life and that I was not cut out for public speaking.[15]

The MHA statement alleged that—

> On another occasion, when one of Hendrickson's contacts told him that the opposition would need substantial finance in order to contest all seats in the coming general election, Hendrickson responded that surely money should not be a problem.

An exultant Brigadier General Lee Hsien Loong, minister for trade and industry and prime minister apparent, hailed it as an indicium of the nefarious hand played by Hank and his superiors in the U.S. State Department, but any amateur detective could have told him it was not evidence of a smoking gun. It does not even remotely suggest that the U.S. government financed or was going to finance the opposition in the forthcoming general election. Nay, the gun was not even loaded and, what was more, it had no firing pin!

---

14. A.S.K. Wee wrote to *The Straits Times* denying it.
15. Statutory declaration dated May 3, 1988.

9

At the General Hospital

> Nor stony tower, nor walls of beaten brass,
> Nor airless dungeon, nor strong links of iron,
> Can be retentive to the strength of spirit.
> —William Shakespeare, *Julius Caesar*,
> Act I, sc. 3, 93

I was brought blindfolded by ISD officers in plainclothes in an unmarked ISD car to the accidents and emergency department of the Singapore General Hospital at Outram Road. Gurkha guards are normally used for static duties within the Centre. The route to the General Hospital is as straightforward as it is well known to all Singaporeans. I could not possibly conceive through what other secret ways or devious byways they could have brought me there and back, which required the use of a blindfold. It was, in truth, a graphic example of mindless obedience to procedure. The time was about 2:55 p.m. There, I was examined by a young medical officer-in-charge of the accidents and emergency clinic, who, in spite of my dishevelled state and absence of glasses, recognised me immediately. I had momentarily forgotten that the news of my arrest had been widely reported and televised the previous evening. I could sense an instant empathy. He wanted to ask more questions about my plight but was inhibited by the presence of the Argus-eyed officers. As Dr. Kuldip Singh had, he also detected the arrhythmic condition but, as it was outside his area of medical expertise, decided to send me for examination by a cardiologist. I did not wish to be wheeled in a chair to the cardiac unit, but he advised it was indicated. I thought it was best to accede to his professional advice. In any event, I was too weary to argue. Although I did not have my prescription glasses on, I became conscious, as I was wheeled through the corridors with the ISD officers in tow, of being the cynosure of much interest and curiosity.

There, in the cardiac unit, I was made to lie down on a hospital bed where a young Chinese male cardiologist examined me and, after looking long and anxiously at the electrocardiogram, consulted a fellow cardiologist. I was vaguely aware of some excitement. But I was extremely weary and exhausted and tried in vain to catch up on lost sleep whilst in bed. But I was, however, constantly interrupted by eager-beaver nurses, who subjected me to several tests for evaluation by the cardiologists. Why all these procedures could not be done at one and the same time I really do not know! I suppose there must be some good medical explanation for staggered measures. Later on, I became aware of the presence of a consultant cardiologist who had been called in by his two colleagues. I became the subject of intense medical debate and I gathered that their professional assessment was that I should be warded for observation. But, unbeknown to me, pressure was being brought to bear on them to discharge me, as the ISD itself was under intense pressure to complete the interrogation. I overheard the name of Dr. Kwa Soon Bee, permanent secretary to the Ministry of Health and a brother-in-law of the prime minister, who had been consulted because the other specialists were not prepared to assume responsibility for my premature discharge. To resolve their dilemma, Professor Arthur Tan, the head of cardiology at Singapore General Hospital, was summoned for urgent consultation and made a surprise appearance at my bedside. He studied the results of the tests and examinations. A lengthy conference took place. After an interminable time, he returned to my bedside and, bubbling with a confidence which I did not share, good man that he is, smilingly allowed the state's demands to prevail over the welfare of his patient, assuring me that I should not be unduly worried, "as the muscle walls of your heart are strong." But, nonetheless, as a precautionary measure, he had prescribed or endorsed the prescription of a long-lasting medication known as *digoxin*, a cardiac glycoside group of drugs, which would raise the digoxin level in the body and slow down any erratic palpitation of the heart. He would leave, he further assured me, certain instructions with the medical officer at the Whitley Detention Centre to monitor the situation closely and, if there were any contraindications, the matter would instantly be referred to him for re-evaluation. With those comforting words, he cheerfully allowed me to be discharged into the tender care of the ISD to be returned to the Centre. It was about 9:00 p.m. Medical professionalism, alas, lost sorely out in this brief encounter with the state. It exemplifies vividly the gospel preached by my dear prime minister that the state takes precedence over the individual. Twisting the knife yet further into the wound, a cynical hospital secretary, on May 12, 1988, sent a bill to my law firm for payment of the hospitalization and treatment.[1]

Interrogation resumed for a few more hours. The fierce venom with which the interrogation had been carried out seemed to have lost its sting. At that point I was escorted back to my cell. I was so tired and exhausted that I did not feel the hardness of the wooden bunk as I laid my body down sinking almost at once into elysium.

> Weariness
> Can snore upon the flint when resty sloth
> Finds the down pillow hard.[2]

The news that I had been warded into the cardiac ward of the Singapore General Hospital spread like a prairie fire. Rumours proliferated that I had suffered a massive heart attack. Newspapers like *The Asian Wall Street Journal*,[3] among others, carried news of it. Unbeknown to me, an anxious Ashleigh, after urgent consultation with Mei, had written a firm letter to the minister for home affairs to put him on notice that, given my medical condition, he would hold him responsible if anything untoward should happen to me in detention.

---

1. Bill No. I 166906 was for S$70.00, after discounting a subsidy of S$56.50. Several reminders were sent. After it became publicly known, on July 23, 1988, the hospital secretary wrote to ignore the request for payment.
2. Shakespeare, *Cymbeline*, Act III, sc.6, 33.
3. *The Asian Wall Street Journal*, Review and Outlook, May 17, 1988.

10

Still in the Eye of Harry—Interrogation Continued

> I know not whether Laws be right,
> Or whether Laws be wrong;
> All that we know who lie in gaol
> Is that the wall is strong;
> And that each day is like a year,
> A year whose days are long.
>
> —Oscar Wilde, *The Ballad of Reading Gaol*

Interrogation continued. It was less ruthless and relentless, but it was nevertheless the same, old, tedious line of questions. I was eager to get out of jail. And I had told them at the very outset that I had absolutely nothing to hide and that everything that I did was above board. I was quite willing and, indeed, anxious to assist them in every way I could so that I could clear up this ghastly error as quickly as possible and satisfy them that I could not possibly be what they had claimed me to be. But this made no impression on them.

On Sunday afternoon, May 8, 1988, I was left alone in my cell. I was mulling over the events. I had been accused of being involved in a conspiracy with the American diplomats who had "incited," "instigated," "egged on," "encouraged," "urged," "nudged," me, or what you will, to enter into opposition politics in connexion with which they had surreptitiously financed me, which I had vigorously denied. I naïvely thought that if this were the crux of the problem, I could speedily resolve this perception by undertaking in writing to forsake national politics and to promise that I would not participate in the forthcoming general election provided that I was released immediately and Mei were allowed forthwith to return to Singapore. At the time, the more I turned the matter over in my mind, the more attractive it seemed to me. Convinced of my plan's reasonableness, if not the logic of the situation, I knocked hard at the cell door to draw the attention of the Gurkha guard on duty. Through fractured English, signs, and gestures, I told him that I wanted to see S.K. Tan, who was up to then the most senior ISD officer around dealing with me. This news reverberated throughout the Centre.

At about 6 p.m., I was taken under escort to the interrogation room to stand before Tan and an assemblage of high ISD officers. There was keen expectation in the air that I was about to make a contrite confession confirming my prime minister's worst suspicions of me and the exposure of a villainy specially endemic to America and Americans. I related my proposition. I had expected it to fall upon receptive ears, but the reaction was one of crushed disappointment. Their countenance changed. They looked at one another. Tan spoke, almost resignedly I thought, that that was only one part of the picture, but their instructions were to ascertain the identity of the persons behind me. We were back again to the Americans, their names, addresses, and telephone numbers! I told them emphatically that there was no one, not even a lurking American; but they did not believe me. We were back at the impasse. And so, the interrogation continued.

Sometime on the third day, in order to monitor my heart and blood pressure, Dr. Kuldip Singh, who was also the medical officer-in-charge of the police academy nearby, relocated its electrocardiograph to the Centre. That night, I was surprised to see two doctors in attendance—Dr. Kuldip and his nervous relief, Dr. Ngoh, the owlish, bespectacled Chinese doctor. They were all thumbs as they tried to fasten the electrocardiograph sensors on to my chest. It was plain that they had not touched an electrocardiograph since leaving medical school. After several unsteady, hesitant attempts at locating the vital areas, they finally accomplished the task. I later observed that scene of comic relief to the director, Tjong Yik Min, on one of his postprandial perambulations through the Centre in the company of his ISD officers. He was quite amused and, breaking into a good-natured guffaw, disclosed that, no thanks to me, the two doctors had had to undergo a refresher course on the use of an electrocardiograph at the General Hospital earlier that day.

On Monday, May 9, 1988, whilst in the interrogation room, I happened to look up at the ceaseless cataract of freezing cold air pouring down from the air-conditioning duct above, when I felt a sharp pain in my left eye. A grit of some description had fallen into it. My spectacles had not yet been returned. I tried to remove it off with a *Kleenex* tissue which the interrogating officer handed to me; but the dreadful pain persisted. I was taken to the doctor who, after some attempts at swabbing, prescribed some ordinary eye-drops. It did not alleviate the pain but restored some valuable moisture to the eyes. In the ensuing days, it became all too clear that an eye infection had set in. Pus had formed and I could hardly open my left eye. The doctor varied the prescription to antibiotic eye-drops, which reduced the redness and the swelling but did not erase the irritating pain. Finally, Dr. Ngoh, in probing the cause of the persistent pain, managed to dislodge a minute piece of metal filing from the eye. It was fortunate that it was removed in good time before irreparable damage was done to my sight. It is an ill draught that blows nobody any good. I remarked to the interrogating officer that this unpleasant experience would not have happened if I had my glasses on. He made a pathetic pretense that he did not know that I had not had my glasses returned to me yet. He ostentatiously ordered them returned instantly for which I thanked him most profusely. It was all of course a charade, a terribly serious charade. The other resultant good was that I moved my chair to the far edge of the desk away from the direct cascade of the cold arctic air. The room was still cold, very cold. Sometime later, the doors were kept open to allow the cold air to flow out onto the corridors and, yet later still, the air-conditioner was switched on and off to maintain an agreeable temperature.

For the first three consecutive days, I was not provided with any mattress, pillow, or footwear. I went about barefooted. I slept on the hard wooden bunk; I was not given a change of clothes until the fourth or fifth day. Unkempt and unwashed, I went without soap. I did not even have a toothbrush or toothpaste, soap, or comb. My mouth furred. I could feel plaque forming on my teeth. I requested a toothbrush and toothpaste as well as a comb, but was told that the issuance of these bare essentials lay within the discretion of the individual case officer. I had to earn them, which meant that I had to be cooperative in giving my statement. Accustomed to daily showers and change of clothes, I found it strange and distastefully unpleasant to wear the same dirty clothes and walk about with soot-blackened feet. When I first asked for a comb, they coldly told me: "Over here, there is no need for it." Although I disagreed with their observation, I decided not to pursue the matter. I, however, reminded myself that it was important for my own self-respect, dignity, and morale that a minimum standard of personal grooming and hygiene within the constraints of the Centre had to be assiduously maintained. I had noticed a comb in the toilet of the medical room and, whenever opportunity presented itself, I used it to manage my hair. I used my forefinger to clean my teeth, and the soap there to wash my face, arms, and legs. It was distressing enough to have the Gurkha guard escort in trawl wherever I went in the Centre; but I thought it especially objectionable to have him inside the medical room observing the medical examination. What do medical ethics have to say about it? But the respective doctors exuded an air of pitiful impotence, born no doubt out of long experience and resignation to their inability to preserve the privacy of a medical examination. Whenever I made use of the toilet, the Gurkha guard would, sentry-like, be outside the partially opened door. It was most disconcerting to have someone nosily pacing up and down outside the door, impatiently waiting for me to complete my natural functions. During the first three days, I was unable to comply with the natural urge, with constipation as an inevitable consequence. I was also unaccustomed to the squat-style trench toilet, to which some conditioning was required. That, too, in no small way contributed to my temporary disorientation. I sought medical assistance, and was prescribed some laxative. Gradually, I was able to adjust myself to the presence of a Gurkha guard outside the toilet door.

At the end of the fourth day, I was provided with two sets of old prison clothes, a cheap toothbrush, a tube of toothpaste of an unknown brand, a cake of inferior green, toilet soap with an obscure label, and an uneven cube of coarse washing soap. I had to do the laundry myself. There was no laundry service. Hence, the cube of washing soap. In addition, I was provided with a small, thin, cotton *Good Morning* face towel, a standard issue of the Japanese conquerors to Allied prisoners of war during their occupation of Singapore and Malaya. I remarked that it was insufficient to dry my body with. And, in a magnanimous gesture, they gave me an extra piece of the *Good Morning* towel. Bath was taken under a cold water tap. There was no hot water at all.

The cleanliness of the cell depended upon the energy and resourcefulness of its occupant. No paid staff maintained it save for the rare appearance of a cleaner, whose perfunctory efforts extended only to the corridors outside the cells.

Each morning at about 7:30, a Gurkha guard would noisily open the spy hole and announce in incomprehensible English the arrival of breakfast which he would slip through the spy-hole. Breakfast consisted invariably of a plain, English-style, egg omelette sandwich—not the gargantuan American variety—together with a small paper cup of hot sweetened tea with milk. Later, at my request and with the doctor's concurrence, it was changed to thrice a week. On alternate days, sardine sandwiches were served. The bread used was the non-enriched white Hainanese genre, devoid of vitamins or minerals. I commented on the nutritional quality of the bread. Someone took heed of this observation for I was pleased to note a dramatic improvement in quality. There was, as stated, no table or chair in the cell. So, breakfast had to be consumed either sitting on the bed or the filthy floor. After I had my breakfast, I would knock hard at the cell door to call the Gurkha guard who, after inquiring the purpose of the summons, would let me out for the morning's ablution and constitutional around the corridors of the block for about twenty minutes. As I was the only one occupying cell L-9 in the whole Block L, I was allowed to remain a little longer outside my cell.

I would then return to my cell, which the Gurkha guard would lock, while I waited inside for the inevitable summons for interrogation. No reading material of any kind was provided. The doctor examined me every morning at about 9:00 before I was taken for interrogation. In view of my cardiac condition, interrogation was interrupted by a medical examination every three hours, the final one of which was at the end of the interrogative session, regardless of the time it ended. Interrogation began at about 9:00 in the morning and lasted until 2:00 or 3:00 the next morning with short breaks for lunch and dinner.

Lunch was served at about 12:30 and dinner at 5:30 every day. The menu was unimaginative but the food was palatable. Rice was the staple diet. It appeared to be a fairly well-balanced diet. However, after my release, I discovered from a chance reading that a well-balanced diet is a medical myth. After a fortnight or so, one knew by rote the menu for each day of the week. The best meal of the week was the Saturday lunch, which was fried *beehoon*, a kind of Chinese rice vermicelli, with a fairly generous garnish of shrimps, cuttlefish rings, vegetables, and onions. That was the only meal in the entire Centre menu that I rather enjoyed.

Served by two Gurkha guards, the meals were prewrapped in clear polyethylene and brown paper secured on the outside with a thin elastic band, together with disposable plastic eating utensils. One of the guards carried a battered tin kettle from which he poured out into a paper cup a rather indifferent but hot Chinese tea. In between meal times, coffee or tea was served to the ISD officers doing the recording and who, as a social gesture, offered it to me. Coffee, comparable to the common Chinese coffee-shop variety, was laced with more chicory than coffee grounds and seemed to be the preferred drink among them. I commented on the quality of the coffee and the inelegant paper cups in which it was being served. To their credit, upon being told of my coffee preference, immediately thereafter provided me with *Nescafé* in a pot, served in real china cups on a proper silver tray. The standard of service improved from zero to two stars with another star for effort, but accommodation did not rate a single star. Unless one was in the interrogation room, all the meals were served and taken inside the cell itself. However, during those times, I was fortunately able to partake of my meals at the guard's table outside my cell in splendid isolation in the block.

Soh Lung complained in an affidavit in her *habeas corpus* applipcation—in which Anthony Lester, Q.C.,[1] now represented her in my

---

1. Now the Lord Lester of Herne Hill, Q.C.

stead—of the "very oily" food, which she found difficult to consume and which gave her a skin problem. I thought it was a just comment. I found it so, too, and brought it to the attention of the ISD officers who, in fairness to them, tried to redress it. There was no improvement in this regard. As any cook knows, an over-generous amount of cooking oil makes for easy frying—and so the food remained awash in oil!

Propaganda aside, there was some concern shown over my weight as a result of my medical condition. A careful watch was kept on it. A slight loss in weight provoked worried observations from doctor and ISD officers alike. On one occasion, my uneasy jailers inquired of me what I would like to have for dinner. I indicated a yen for a grilled country-killed spring chicken from the Goodwood Park Hotel, a first class hotel, steeped in historical associations, and serving excellent English afternoon tea and an even better grill room fare. Someone was sent out to buy it but he telephoned to say it was not available. I suggested the de luxe Royal Holiday Inn across the road. It was not available there either. I finally settled on the Penang-style, fried chicken, from the nearby family-size Sloane Court Hotel; but the results were dreadfully below expectations. The morsels of chicken were not only minute but over-fried almost to cinders. So much for grilled country-killed spring chicken from the Goodwood Park Hotel! We were more successful, gastronomically speaking, with meals purchased from the ubiquitous hawkers' centres dotted over the island. Each morning soon after I was escorted into the interrogation room, I would be asked my preference for lunch and dinner before the commencement of the recording session. I would indicate my choice for the day, after which an ISD orderly would be detailed to acquire it from the fastfood centre specializing in that particular cuisine. The way to a man's heart, as the saying goes, is through his stomach. I am pleased to record for posterity that it is an article of faith in the Whitley Detention Centre, too. Besides, the ISD officers themselves welcomed a change in the bill of fare for oftentimes they also placed their orders for a particular take-away meal.

The changing of the Gurkha guards in the block took place every two hours. Upon the new Gurkha guard taking over, he would, as a matter of routine curiosity, open the spy hole to peep inside, presumably to check whether the prisoner was still around and alive, and not up to any mischief. But in drawing the bolt each time, he created a sharp and horrible noise of infernal doom.

It was crucial during the first week of my confinement that I should make a confession as quickly as possible to enable the prime minister and his government to justify my arrest to the world in general and Singapore in particular. It was equally crucial that, before its publication, my confession had to be approved by the cabinet, especially the prime minister who was away on a short visit to Bangkok, Thailand. The dateline was his return from overseas. Hence, interrogation continued until those unearthly hours of the mornings in chilly and forbidding surroundings.

S.K. Tan turned out to be my case officer. He wanted me to write out the statement myself. But I refused. His immediate interest was Hank and the two U.S. State Department officials. As stated, I did not at the time appreciate this interest in the American connection which was, as far as I was concerned, completely innocuous. They had seized my office desk diary from which they noted my luncheon meetings with Hank, around which they were trying to build a case. I told him that, because he knew best the scenario he wanted, he should write it out himself. We had a lively exchange of words over it.

The "softening-up period" was over. The tigerish snarls had turned to the phantasmal purrs and grins of a Cheshire cat. But there was nothing to prevent a reversion to type if one failed to "cooperate" with them. One is painfully aware of being helpless in a hellhole, where the conditions and length of time in it depended greatly upon cooperation with the ISD and, ultimately, the political caprice of the prime minister. Cooperation meant saying the things the prime minister wanted to hear.

The serious business of interpreting, bending, and manipulating the facts to accord with the prime minister's beliefs and agenda began in earnest. S.K. Tan finally agreed to write it down. He had not written two or more paragraphs before he abruptly stopped, put his pen down, and exclaimed with poignant veracity that the prime minister, mark you, the prime minister would never believe the statement was mine, because it would not be in my distinctive language and style. I told him that was his problem. He was in a quandary.

As if on cue, a personable but astute ISD officer, Benny Lim, who had majored in English, walked in. The entrance and egress of these officers seemed choreographed to a hidden agenda. Benny and I shared a common love for English literature and poetry, and he was thus able to strike some mutual ground. He was familiar with my style of presentation and so, between the two of them, they completed the statement, intermittently pausing to check certain facts or figures and the use of proper words and phrases with their registry. They were overly anxious to incriminate Hank and the U.S. State Department officials and wanted me to agree that they had "instigated or egged me on" to enter opposition politics. I was not prepared to say it. The truth, the plain and simple truth was that neither Hank, Joe, nor Colin, nor any other U.S. official for that matter, had "encouraged or discouraged" me from contesting the forthcoming general election during our several meetings. But, as this was contrary to their hidden agenda, it was therefore unacceptable. Benny suggested instead the word "nudged," as being less forceful. I rejected it, too. They were not prepared to accept that our conversations had been innocuous, and wanted me to paint them in vibrant colours acceptable to them. I refused to agree to anything that I considered derogatory or defamatory or untrue of our acquaintanceship. They spent several days going over a thesaurus of relationships, seeking a label for ours, and, finally, in order to overcome my resistance, disclosed for the first time that Hank had already been "expelled as undesirable from Singapore." I was shocked. I did not believe it. And I told them so. They disclosed that Hank had been expelled on the basis of Patrick's statements the day after I was arrested. Four days later, the U.S. government, in a tit-for-tat, expelled from the U.S. a Singapore diplomat, Robert Chua, in Washington, D.C.

They revealed that Hank had once been stationed as a consular official at Udon Thani, Thailand, a town close to the Laotian border, which could only mean, they insinuated, that he was involved with or had CIA connections. After that, he had been posted to the

Philippines as an advisor to Mrs. Corazón Aquino, the future president of the Republic of the Philippines, during which he had carried out covert CIA operations. In any event, because he had already been expelled, I should have no qualms in stating what they wanted me to say about him; I could not possibly hurt him.

Furthermore, they argued that Patrick had already in his statutory declaration "exposed Hank's undiplomatic activities," wherefore he was expelled from Singapore. Therefore, whatever I agreed to say about him would not make the slightest difference to him as the expulsion was a *fait accompli*. I should not thereby have any compunctious visitings of conscience to shake me from making the statement, which could significantly hasten my own release from the Centre. Overwhelmed by this sudden revelation of Hank's expulsion, I resigned myself to let them record the statement in accordance with their agenda. We ended the recording in the wee hours of the morning. In the meantime, I was still worried, and pondered over the truth or otherwise of Hank's expulsion. Were they putting one over me? I had no means of verification.

After a short break, the recording resumed. I was weary and about done in. My doubts returned. It would be wrong to make a statement about a person that was untrue, and that was what they were persuading me to do. I told them that I would not sign anything about what they had written about Hank or the U.S. State Department officials. I repeated that neither Hank nor Joe nor Colin had "encouraged or discouraged" me from entering opposition politics. They were utterly dismayed. They refused point-blank to write down what I said. It was vitally important for the prime minister's case that the U.S. government was shown to be involved and, if not the U.S. government directly, then its officials as having acted out of hand, outside of their authority.

Furthermore, I did not believe Hank had been expelled from Singapore. They stressed that Hank's expulsion had been announced on television and in the other news media. I asked to see a copy of *The Straits Times*, which they promised to show me—a promise as lightly given as it was quickly forgotten. For, with each passing day, no such news report was shown to me. Upon my reminders, it was against orders, they claimed, to show me any newspapers at that stage of the interrogation. They beseeched me to trust them. Just then, a senior ISD officer walked into the interrogation room. He noticed the impasse and inquired the nature of the problem.

Having appraised himself of the problem, he disclosed his identity with a candour uncharacteristic for an ISD officer, as "Sim Poh Heng, deputy director of ISD," and solemnly assured me that his officers' account regarding Hank's expulsion was true. A matter of such gravity as a diplomatic expulsion, he asserted with a flourish, could "not be cooked up." It was a serious matter. No harm could come to Hank now, he pronounced. He was no more in Singapore. And nothing that I would agree to say could possibly affect his career. More importantly, I should think more of myself, for if I were to make the required statement, it would affect my early release. His earnest and logical appraisal of the situation seemed compelling. I relented and agreed to the continuation of the recording of the statement. But, as I continued to object to the use and meaning of the words "egged on," "encouraged," and "nudged into" opposition politics, Benny Lim substituted the words "supportive of" instead as a compromise. What I had failed to appreciate was that such a statement was still useful to buttress Patrick's alleged statements, even though it would not have had any influence on Hank's professional career. In hindsight, I had been, to borrow Brigadier General Lee's fulsome expression, "suckered" into agreeing to allow them to weave a pattern of untruth in the statement.

I had originally maintained that our meetings were largely sociable in character and did not include discussions on politics. Granted their sociability, Benny reasoned that as Hank's designation in the U.S. embassy was First Secretary (Political), his area of interest would be in political matters. I agreed. And that it would be only natural for him to seek my and other persons' views on the burning political topics of the day, such as the Legal Profession (Amendment) bill, the Newspaper and Printing Presses (Amendment) bill, the political succession issue, the respective capabilities of the PAP second generation leaders, the Group Representation Constituencies (GRCs), the disbarment of lawyer-politician J.B. Jeyaretnam as a member of Parliament, amongst others. We could have discussed one or more or, indeed, all of those topics of the day. Nothing malignant flowed from any such discussion.

Whilst I was incarcerated inside the Centre, the government announced on May 10 that a *spontaneous* rally of about 4,000 "enraged" trade unionists would take place the next day, outside the U.S. embassy to protest against the U.S. government's interference in Singapore's internal affairs. The Singapore government is egregious in organizing spontaneous demonstrations. But only 2,000 unionists or so turned up. The wrath of the rest had presumably consumed itself by the next morning, despite the monetary incentive provided to sustain their "spontaneity" of outrage at perfidious America and the Americans. There was later some lively, if not altogether droll, dissension in public as to what amount of money each and which trade unionist had or should have received for his participation in that spontaneous demonstration. *Spontaneous*—a favourite metaphor of Singapore's officialdom which has yet to learn its true and full meaning!

Contrary to the ISD's braggadocio, there was a crescendo of international protests and expressions of concern over my arrest and detention by governments and leaders of governments, international human rights groups, law societies and bar associations and caring organizations, some of which even called for a tourism boycott of Singapore. As usual, Amnesty International, Asia Watch, and the International Commission of Jurists were foremost among them.

11

Devan Nair and the Asylum

> My colleagues and I have been personal friends and political colleagues for 15, 20, years now, and we have been through fire together .... And you build a camaraderie that these little things [split or disagreement] cannot break; and they are all thinkers.
>
> —Lee Kuan Yew[1]

> I assure him [Devan Nair] from this Chamber that there is no reason why he should always be on parade. ... There is no reason why, however, at ease or in mufti, he should not continue to be his old self. Indeed, his best contribution is to be himself. ... Those who meet Devan Nair will recognize that he is a man out of the ordinary. He will not diminish the high standing of the office of President.
>
> —Lee Kuan Yew[2]

They verbally assailed me for having gone to Washington D.C. for the purpose of arranging an asylum for myself. I was completely astounded at their construction of that wonderful stray weekend, which Mei and I had spent in that capital city, as a trip specifically made in perpetuation of a growing black conspiracy with Joseph Snyder and Colin Helmer. Pursuant to his secret agenda, the prime minister perpetuated the same deliberate distortion in Parliament.[3] I was indignant at the preposterous charge that I had met Joe for a controversial or subversive purpose or had sought assurance of an

---

1. To Fred Emery, *London Times*, August 13, 1965.
2. Parliamentary Debates, October 23, 1981, col. 230.
3. Parliamentary Debates, June 1, 1988, col. 325.

asylum in the United States should anything go drastically wrong in my debut in national politics. The question of an asylum or a permanent stay for myself in the United States was never within my contemplation at the time. My belief, however, that Joe and Colin could be useful to me or my friends at some remote future date was anything but sinister. I tried to convince them that our visit to Washington was not for the specific purpose of arranging an asylum. What, then, was the purpose of the trip? I explained again it was my first trip to the American eastern seaboard. I had never been there before, and, as it was a stray weekend, Mei and I had decided to go there sightseeing. I had called Joe from New York to inform him of our visit in the hope that he could also show us the sights and sounds of the city, requesting him at the same time to arrange for us inexpensive accommodation. They asked me whether I knew Tommy Koh, our ambassador in Washington. I knew him. Why, then, did I not contact Tommy for that purpose? Why did I contact Joe whom I had met only once before? Surely, the object of the meeting was to develop the American connection and the black conspiracy begun in Singapore. Tommy was indeed on my list of persons to see but, time and circumstances not permitting, we never got round to him. There were shouts, abuses and obscenities of ridicule and disbelief. Where did I meet Joe? What did we discuss? I did not recall them. Joe unfortunately had a prior appointment. We had a very brief luncheon meeting at a fastfood restaurant whose name I could not recall. They burst into an unrestrained bout of asinine laughter, saying:

"So, you expected to be treated to a fancy restaurant, huh?"

Given his *metier*, they argued in familiar fashion, the conversation would in the nature of things have been largely on politics in Singapore. I agreed we could have discussed them during the brief lunch; but contended that, in any event, I could not see any harm in it. And so, as I yielded to an admixture of inveiglement, weariness, and sleep, ISD officers of no mean talent slowly wove a plausible story and script of our Washington encounter:

… Mei and I went to Washington for a weekend as well as to see [Joe]. I was then contemplating entering politics and it would be useful for me to build up my relationship with State Department officials if anything should happen to me in that eventuality. By then I had already raised the subject of seeking asylum in the U.K. with Sir Ham, the British High Commissioner then, but got a negative answer. I thus wanted to look up [Joe] to renew our acquaintance and to size up his disposition towards and usefulness to me. ...

My thinking was to get as many professionals as possible to come in with me. [Joe] was pleased and generally supportive of it. He liked my style of approach and saw me as a potential leading opposition personality. I sensed that Joe was well-disposed towards me and my political intentions, and that he would help me to emigrate to the U.S. should I ever want to do so. ...

I felt comforted that I had friendly faces in the State Department who were supportive of my plans and willing to help secure refuge for me when needed. ...

I maintained cordial relationship with [Hank] as he had been most supportive of my political intentions—which I found most encouraging. Having a direct line to a diplomat in the U.S. embassy here would also be helpful in case things should turn sour after I enter politics, and I need assistance to settle in the U.S. expeditiously. In retrospect, I would say that Hank's interest in me was extraordinary compared to that of other diplomats I had come into contact with in Singapore. But this did not occur to me earlier because I was keen to cultivate his friendship just as he was keen to seek me out. ...

After the Select Committee hearings, I was encouraged by some friends to consider going into politics. My interest was aroused and the idea of going into politics intrigued me. I sought the views and opinions of political veterans like Devan Nair. I began to build upon my contacts with diplomats, including some officials of the U.S. State Department. I wanted a line to such diplomats so as to be prepared for any eventuality including asylum should that ever become necessary. I told them of my political intentions. The State Department officials I met and Hank of the U.S. embassy here were most encouraging and supportive of my political plans. I felt reassured that assistance to secure refuge in the U.S. would be forthcoming if and when needed. Although the likelihood of emigration was then remote, I was comforted that this nagging problem at the back of my mind had been settled.

This was the version of the events which they wanted and which they were bent on having, and which they eventually crafted. No other interpretation was possible or acceptable. It is not only an example of ISD creativity in making stories to order, but also a testimony to its skill and expertise in storytelling that, from molehills of disparate facts and information and half-truths, it could make veritable mountains.

They asked for my opinion of Colin and the part he had played in the meeting. Colin did not, as I recalled it, take any notable part in the conversation. Some months thereafter, he came to Singapore, but I did not meet him as I was out of the country on business.

The ISD inquisitors asked about my association with Sir Hamilton Whyte, the then British high commissioner, to which they listened with strange and almost annoying disinterest. They were most understanding, incredibly temperate in attitude and in language. They were almost benign. No attempt was made to spin any dark conspiracy into our several meetings and conversations. They were not particularly interested in pursuing the British High Commission officials whom I had met and known. Of course, I did not know that the U.K. government or its officials abroad were not on the secret agenda.

I first met Sir Ham when I was the president of the Law Society. My elder brother, Gerald, who was working in the British High Commission, asked me one day whether I could arrange for an invitation to be sent to Sir Ham to attend a Law Society's function, as he had evinced an interest in meeting me. Consequently, I revived the practice of the Law Society inviting high commissioners of Commonwealth countries and the U.S. ambassador to the Society's annual dinner functions.

In about the first quarter of 1986, I telephoned Sir Ham to invite him to lunch, but he instead invited me to lunch at Eden Hall, his sprawling official residence, at Nassim Road. Mei knew him, and Sir Ham told me to bring her along as well. He was good company and was very interested in the Law Society. Our discussion centred mainly on the Law Society, Singapore politics and personalities.

I returned the lunch at the brasserie at the Marco Polo Hotel subsequently. By then the Law Society's press release on the Newspaper and Printing Presses bill had exploded onto the pages of the domestic and international press. Sir Ham asked me about it. He thought that I was taking a courageous stand in the face of the government accusation that the Law Society was becoming a pressure group.

I called him again at the High Commission inviting him to lunch indicating that I wished to discuss a matter of confidence. But he suggested that we lunch at Eden Hall instead. Mei came along, too. As soon as we walked in, Sir Ham remarked that I was drawing a "lot of flak" from the prime minister. This prompted me to ask him whether, given the prime minister's vengeful streak, if I were to go into politics and things turn sour, I would be able to emigrate to the United Kingdom. Sir Ham was not familiar with the U.K. immigration rules and policy regarding entitlement or eligibility of persons, who, like myself, were former subjects and citizens of the United Kingdom and colonies, to permanent U.K. residence. Sir Ham said that as it was a Conservative and not a Labour government, there was stricter interpretation of the immigration policy. But he promised however to inquire about it. Although I did not seriously expect to emigrate, I thought there was no harm in exploring the possibility and, in any event, it was useful trivia knowledge. Besides, Mei was toying at the time with the idea of emigration, and, among the countries we discussed, England was topmost in my books.

Sir Ham had a very good knowledge of Singapore politics. He told me that it would be an uphill task, that the odds were weighed against me. I told him the prime minister was pushing me into it and I would nevertheless give it a try. About three or four weeks later, Sir Ham invited me and Mei to lunch at Eden Hall again. Sir Ham said that he was afraid that emigration to U.K. was a "no-go" situation. I then asked him whether it could be treated as a request for asylum. I mentioned in passing, the case of Tan Wah Piow, the Singapore University student leader who became a victim of a political frame-up and was given asylum in the United Kingdom. Sir Ham was not familiar with it and said he would check on it. The upshot was similarly in the negative. So, I let the matter drop. I told them too that Sir Ham had neither encouraged nor discouraged me from entering politics, using the very same expression I had used when they interrogated me on Hank. In startling contrast to Hank and the U.S. State Department officials, they recorded it without the slightest hassle.

The ISD officers insisted that Sir Ham's conduct in his dealings with me was right and proper as compared to Hank. I disagreed; but they insisted that there was a difference. Wisdom whispered that one should not antagonize one's captors. So I let it pass. As far as I could see, it was a distinction without a difference. But then the Van Goghs in the ISD had painted a different word picture of the truth and the reality.

They suddenly switched to Devan and pointedly asked me whether I had seen him in the States in 1986. This was a test question. Mei and I had met him briefly at the *Quo Vadis* Restaurant on East 63rd Street in New York in the winter of that year. He had come up from Bloomington, Indiana; over an excellent dinner and drinks, we had renewed our acquaintance and regaled each other with tales of Singapore, its grim politics, and grimmer personalities. He was doing some lecturing, research, and writing at Cornell University in Ithaca, New York and showed me for my comments a few pages of a manuscript which he had begun on his chequered political life. He told me that he would be attending a forthcoming conference in Manila and of his intention to return via Singapore to the U.S. I did not think it was wise for him to do so, because as president of Singapore he was a repository of state secrets, a fact which could easily be manipulated by a spiteful prime minister as a pretext for placing him under house arrest, even though he had been most careful in that regard.

There were two male Caucasians sipping coffee, seated at a table nearby, whose undisguised interest in our conversation made Devan and Mei suspect them as agents of the Singapore government employed to tail one or both of us. I dismissed it then as unlikely and a sheer waste of public funds. But, sad to confess, how terribly mistaken I was. I had underestimated the depth of my prime minister's paranoia, which was subsequently borne out by an exposé in *The Wall Street Journal* of a covert surveillance on me across the length and breadth of America in 1988 and 1989 by private American investigators hired by the Singapore government.[4] When asked in Parliament, the minister of law arrogantly disdained to disclose the cost to the Singapore taxpayer, except to say with tongue-in-cheek that it was "money well-spent," and "well within the budget."

I had known Devan for some time, as long ago as 1948, when he was a young school-teacher at Saint Andrew's School, Woodsville,

---

4. February 15, 1989. See, also, "Dissident under watch in New York—Eyes on the job," *Far Eastern Economic Review*, January 26, 1989.

although I do not think he remembers it. I met him through the introduction of my English language teacher, P.V. Sharma, at the Singapore Teachers' Union, then located in the Liberty Cabaret building, North Bridge Road, (on which the present Bras Basah Complex stands), a sprawling, bustling den of social and political associations and organizations. Sharma was a good and cerebral teacher at Saint Joseph's Institution, Singapore's premier Christian Brothers' school. He was later arrested, together with Devan, by the colonial government as a communist and deported to India from where he made his way to Peking, China, where he made overseas propaganda broadcasts for the Peking government until recently.

Looking back through the arches of the years, it explained why I used to receive through the mail the proscribed Anti-British League literature which abruptly stopped with his arrest. The ABL samizdat was so badly printed that it was unreadable in parts, testifying to the difficulties of clandestine operations. In any event, it made no impression on me, a young student then preparing to leave for England for further studies.

I had met Devan again on several other occasions, both before and after he had assumed the illustrious and exalted office of president of Singapore. I saw him also after he was forced by the prime minister to step down as president of Singapore, not "for reasons of health" as in civilized countries but, more specifically and brutally spelled out, for "alcoholism," which had caused "impairment to [his] judgment and perception" and which, according to the prime minister and his team of medical advisers, was irreparable.[5] Devan has denied the diagnosis of alcoholism.

I digress to record that, notwithstanding that vicious announcement, Ashleigh subsequently had a drink or two with Devan at his grandchild's birthday celebrations in Singapore. He betrayed no signs of alcoholism. And I am pleased to record, too, that, whilst staying with him in snow-swept Bloomington, Indiana, during the Christmas of 1988 and numberless times thereafter, the two of us did Johnny Walker proud over his premium export. Devan's mind was as sharp as his intellect was keen as I have always remembered

---

5. Lee Kuan Yew's letter, March 5, 1985, "A Reply to Devan," *Far Eastern Economic Review*, April 22, 1985.

him. Had I met Devan after my return from the United States? It was another loaded question to test whether I had told Devan of my Washington rendezvous with Joe and Colin.

"Yes, I had."

"Have you told him about seeking asylum in the United States?" they asked me in unison.

I did not recall at that time having ever used the word "asylum" to him. I denied having said it, whereupon a number of them pounced on me, shouting and screaming, amidst a volley of vulgarities and obscenities, that I was a liar, a bloody, fucking liar. They had evidence, they charged, that I had mentioned to him about seeking asylum in the United States. And, to reinforce their charge, they revealed that Devan's second son, Janamitra Devan, was also present at the discussion.

I had, indeed, tried to persuade Janamitra to contest the general election, but he had declined because he was not certain that in the time available a cohesive group of professionals could be formed that shared the same ideals. Besides, his wife Sabrina was in the family way. I cast my mind back. I then remembered the substance of that conversation, and recalled having used the word "asylum." I had told Devan that, as he would be returning to the States to take up a fellowship at Cornell University where he would remain for a long time. Joe and Colin would be valuable persons to know in any contingency, for they would be able to help him. I conceded that I could have uttered, perhaps half-in-jest, the word, "asylum." I recollected leaving on the coffee table a piece of paper on which I had written their names and telephone numbers. Observing my amazement at the accuracy of their information, they could not suppress their professional conceit, boasting that it had been obtained through "bugging" Devan's house. I then realized that I had been taken in, as the conversation had not in fact taken place at Devan's house but at someone else's residence. Nevertheless, the substance was fairly accurate. I was not concerned about it *per se* as much as I was interested in the source of the leak. I raked my mind as to who it could be. There were several possibilities. One was that the ISD did bug the residence where the conversation took place. The other possibility was that someone had leaked the conversation, as one of

Devan's close friends was partly privy to it and could have wittingly or unwittingly disclosed it to the ISD. Given Singapore's tight island milieu, this scenario could not be discounted altogether.

I did not discuss seeking an asylum in the United States with any one at all. They were not convinced. They wanted me to admit that I had requested for asylum and had been assured of it by Joe, which was wholly untrue. I did not know at the time that this was the core of the prime minister's complaint against the U.S. government and his case against me. We spent hours disputing over this. Weariness and sleep deprivation finally overcame truth: I left Washington *"comforted* that I had friendly faces in the State Department who were supportive of my plans and willing to help secure refuge for me when needed." Following public disclosure of my statement, *The Asian Wall Street Journal* editorialized:

> Mr. Seow also confessed that he looked for a country of possible asylum, should his venture into opposition politics prove overly hazardous. On the evidence, that was prudent.[6]

They sedulously interrogated me on the nature and content of the advice Devan had given me on politics. It was basically that it was not wise to underrate the second-generation leaders, and, in particular, First Deputy Prime Minister Goh Chok Tong, Minister for Foreign Affairs S. Dhanabalan, Minister for Education Dr. Tony Tan and Brigadier General Lee Hsien Loong, the eldest son of the prime minister and the fastest rising star on Singapore's political firmament. They were, in his view, forces to be reckoned with, and I should not go unprepared into the political arena. That made a lot of sense to me.

"I have no intention whatsoever of charging into any issue like a bull in a political china shop," I replied.

It was important that I should bone up on economics, an important topic in Singapore politics having regard to its strategic geopolitical position.

Devan, however, disagreed with Dr. Toh Chin Chye, whom I had also consulted, as to the wisdom of joining a Workers' Party

---

6. Review and Outlook, May 24, 1988.

Alliance. Devan thought that I should contest as an independent. As the general election was around the corner, several opposition parties had discussed contesting the election under a grand alliance with the Workers' Party spearheading the alliance and thus avoiding three-cornered or more fights. In the past, opposition votes had been badly split among warring political parties. Devan took the view that the Workers' Party had been largely discredited in the public mind and, if I joined it, there was a possibility that I might be tarred with the same brush. His view was, however, not shared by Dr. Toh, who felt that, if there were a sufficient number of fresh faces lined up in the Workers' Party, he could not see what possible harm it could do. Alternatively, the Singapore Democratic Party, (SDP) was equally available. The SDP was a relatively new political party, and Chiam See Tong was its secretary general. The advantage in joining an existing party was the organizational infrastructure and the ready availability of experienced, knowledgeable staff and personnel. As there appeared to be a divergence of views, I had not, as yet, decided which advice I should follow or whether I should pursue an independent course and persuade like-minded young professionals, such as lawyers, doctors, and engineers to join in with me. They wanted to know how I proposed to go about it. I told them we could stand independently on a common platform but as part of the same team united by the same political beliefs or manifesto.

Dr. Toh was not especially attracted to the idea of forming another new political party because there are already about twenty or more parties, most of which are inactive or defunct, registered with the Registrar of Societies. Many registered political parties were guilty of infringements of the Societies Act for noncompliance with its provisions. But the government, for its own political ends, had seen fit not to have them de-registered, so that it could always point to the number of political parties on the register to quash awkward international inquiry or suggestion that opposition parties have been suppressed out of existence.

During the initial interrogation, a white-haired, insipid-looking, hollow-faced Chinese ISD officer of about 45-years old, with droopy eyes and a rough complexion, would interlope into the room and, in an abrasive voice, interrupt the sessions with gratuitous remarks. The recording officer would patiently pause for the interruption to pass before resuming his writing as if nothing had happened. I was already seething with a mixture of anger and annoyance at the preposterous allegation that I was involved in and had been the recipient of a black money conspiracy. I told the recorder that the easiest and quickest way to resolve this bizarre allegation was to check with my past and present clients and friends. I had already given him names and addresses and, in some instances, their telephone numbers and the amount of money they had paid or given me. Whereupon this doltish officer, who had been sitting there listening, interjected:

> "Yes, yes, we will do that. In any event, even if we can establish from them that what you say is true, it will not mean a thing."

I was startled at the premise. I resented his gratuitously insolent interjection and, leaning back in my chair, angrily retorted:

> "If this represents the attitude that is being adopted by the ISD, then, I see no useful purpose in my giving a statement or answering any further questions."

If I had been my normal self and more perspicacious, this portentous slip of the tongue that the ISD was only interested in establishing its own agenda and not in the truth of the matter would have put me on my guard. Those words pregnant with evil portent carried more than a grain of truth, which I, in my annoyance, had failed to see. On looking back now, could it be that he was trying to tell me something? I have often wondered?

At about the time of my angry outburst, Deputy Director Sim Poh Heng walked in and, sensing something was amiss, inquired as to the reason. In the meantime, this dunderhead had slunk quietly out of the room. I told him of my grave misgivings and unhappiness at the revelation that the ISD was really not interested in ascertaining the truth of the matter. He quickly assured me that Paul Pry had no business whatsoever to be present in the interrogation room and even less business to make any comments; and that he would give specific instructions that, from henceforth, no persons other than those properly authorised should be present. He reassured me the ISD would investigate fairly my statement which, if it were proven true, would be a factor in my favour. Upon his solemn reassurance, the interrogation resumed.

Thereafter, the stern, officious visage which Deputy Director Sim Poh Heng had been affecting up to then melted into a smiling mask of affability and sweet reasonableness. His steps, too, had a discernible quality of buoyancy—all told, a man satisfied with the progress he was making.

12

The Closing Society

> I'm told [repression] is like making love—it's always easier the second time. The first time there may be pangs of conscience, a sense of guilt. But once embarked on this course, with constant repetition, you get more and more brazen in the attack and in the scope of the attack. All you have to do is to dissolve organizations and societies and banish or detain the key political workers in these societies. Then, miraculously, everything is tranquil on the surface. Then an intimidated press and the government-controlled radio together can regularly sing your praises, and slowly and steadily the people are made to forget the evil things that have already been done. Or if these things are referred to again they're conveniently distorted and distorted with impunity, because there will be no opposition to contradict.
>
> —Lee Kuan Yew[1]

On the night of Thursday, May 12, 1988, Smiley Sim came prancing into the interrogation room where a number of ISD officers were gathered and handed over to me a xeroxed copy of a feature article, captioned: *Singapore's Closing Society*, which had appeared under my name in *The Asian Wall Street Journal*:

> Prime Minister Lee Kuan Yew argued brilliantly from a jesuitical brief, for a poor case, before a polite and civilized gathering of the American Society of Newspaper Editors in Washington on April 14. His audience was reportedly impressed by the eloquence and *sang-froid* that went into his justification of his government's restrictions on the foreign media. Mr. Lee expatiated on the horrendous consequences for a multicultural society of an American-style free marketplace of ideas.

---

1. Legislative Assembly Debates, October 4, 1956, col. 322.

But in a speech to the Singapore Graduates Society in June last year, C.V. Devan Nair, the former president of Singapore, and an intimate comrade-in-arms of Mr. Lee for over 30 years, reminded Singaporeans that 24 years ago, in December 1964, their prime minister also had delivered an even more brilliant and altogether more convincing brief for an open society in the Malaysian Federal Parliament. He then sat on the opposition benches as a member from the constituent state of Singapore. We might recall that Malaysia at the time was, and still is, a nation plagued by potentially lethal inter-communal antagonisms. This was what Lee, in a truly spellbinding oration, said on that occasion:

"Let us get down to fundamentals. Is this an open or a closed society? Is it a society where men can preach ideas—the novel, unorthodox, heresies, established churches and established governments—where there is a constant contest for men's hearts and minds on the basis of what is right, of what is just, of what is in the national interest? Or is it a closed society where the mass media—the newspapers, the journals, publications, TV, radio, either by sound or by sight, or both sound and sight, feed men's minds with a constant drone of sycophantic support for a particular orthodox political philosophy? That is the first question we ask ourselves. And let me preface my remarks with this: that it is not only in communist countries where the mass media is used to produce the closed mind, because the closed society must produce the closed mind. I believe that Malaysia was founded, if you read its constitution, as an open society, constituting peoples of various languages, of varying political beliefs, in which the will of the majority will prevail, and in which a large dissenting minority will not be crushed and intimidated and silenced. ... I say let's pause and ask ourselves ... I am talking of the principle of the open society, the open debate, ideas, not intimidation, persuasion not coercion."

Today, under Mr. Lee's government, Singaporeans are no strangers to the "closed society—where the mass media—the newspapers, journals, publications, TV, radio ... feed men's minds with a constant drone of sycophantic support"—which Mr. Lee had so eloquently argued against in the Malaysian Parliament. Thoughtful Singaporeans are unimpressed by the positions Mr. Lee espouses now. Americans are not likely to be hoodwinked for long either by a well-argued but fundamentally flawed case. The flaws are excruciatingly clear.

Lee told his American audience: "Singapore's domestic debate is a matter for Singaporeans." Irrefutable. Only, what domestic debate was Mr. Lee talking about? The "constant drone of sycophantic support" for the official line from the local media cannot by any stretch of the imagination be mistaken for public debate.

The rules of the democratic game have been systematically and drastically changed since independence to ensure, among other things, a tightly controlled media. Mr. Lee's mention of Rupert Murdoch being able to purchase the independent TV stations of the Metromedia group in 1985 only after acquiring U.S. citizenship is surely specious in reference to Singapore, for the good reason that we have no independent media group. No branch of the media in the republic can claim ownership and editorial direction independent of the powers-that-be. Government nominees oversee every newspaper to ensure that there is no departure from the official line. Hardly a journalist exists in Singapore who would not offer a silent prayer should he decide (which never happens, of course) to write an original article. A William Safire or a George Will is simply inconceivable in Singapore. And a Derek Davies would find himself in the jug as a "Marxist conspirator."

Things are no better in the political arena, heavily mined as it is with legal booby traps to maim the unwary. Most U.S. Congressmen and British or Indian MPs one can think of would be hauled up for contempt of Parliament if they were transposed to the Singapore republic. Parliamentary proceedings, unless Mr. Lee is himself lecturing everybody else, serve admirably the purpose of political sedation.

Mr. Lee's constant theme these days is that Singapore is not another Western society. Of course, it isn't. He goes on that even among non-Western Asian societies it is unique. It is most certainly, and in very positive ways, all thanks to the highly successful social, educational, cultural and economic development policies implemented over 25 years by the founding fathers of the People's Action Party, of which Mr. Lee himself was (and still is) the secretary general. We are the best educated population in Asia after Japan. We are not far behind in our standard of living either. And above all, Singapore can claim the unique distinction of being about the only heterogenous society in Asia that effectively defused inflammable emotive issues of race, language, religion and culture. Indeed, in the early years of independent Singapore, Mr. Lee and his colleagues were lionized in the Western media for precisely this singular achievement. Yet today Mr. Lee chooses to sing an altogether different tune about how the foreign media, unless controlled (or gazetted), might spark an inflammable multicultural mix.

Singaporeans still gratefully remember the vigorous contention of Mr. Lee and his party comrades, when Singapore was still part of Malaysia, that in an equal multiracial society there should be no talk of majorities and minorities, of Malays, Chinese and Indians, but only of Malaysians. After Singapore was booted out of Malaysia in 1965, Singaporeans rallied round Mr. Lee when he passionately declared that in Singapore there would be no majorities and minorities, but only Singaporeans. An entire new generation was brought up to believe that it was part of an equal multiracial society.

The 1960s and '70s saw in full swing the most intelligent and dynamic nation building program in all Asia. But the '80s were to find

Mr. Lee announcing new fundamentals that effectively betrayed the credo he had started out with. Singaporeans heard with alarm his *Eureka!* when he discovered eugenics. From now on Singaporeans would be classified according to assessments of their genetic makeup. And we heard lectures *ad nauseam* about intense achievement-oriented East Asians, and about other less intense and more easygoing Asian cultures. Then *Eureka!* again when Mr. Lee made his next earth-shaking discovery. This time it was poor old Confucius, disinterred from the cultural cemetery of feudal China, and installed as the patron saint of Singapore-style progress in the technological age. Confucian social conformism and docile deference to the powers-that-be would free Mr. Lee's genetically superior breed of new Mandarins to pursue the creation of a Brave New World of science and technology, without distraction by un-Confucian rumbles of discontent.

Singaporeans are not amused. Nothing is better calculated to disturb the equilibrium of a hitherto stable multiracial society right in the middle of Malay-speaking Southeast Asia than Mr. Lee's volatile mix of eugenics, Confucius, speak-Mandarin campaigns and the like. Recent constitutional changes to provide for minority representation in Parliament have served only to revive and reinstate in the polity of the republic the minority syndrome which an earlier generation of leaders (Mr. Lee was still captain) had succeeded in almost erasing from the political blood-stream of the nation.

But the aging captain has developed obsessions that increasingly threaten the hard-won social and political stability of Singapore. Indeed, with enviable economic success, everything else should be going for the political leadership. It clearly is not. Obsessive fixations, a political self-righteousness intolerant of dissent, the arrest and rearrest without trial of well-educated social activists whom the generality of Singaporeans regard as anything but "Marxist conspirators" have all served to sour public opinion.

Singaporeans might take legitimate pride in Mr. Lee's international reputation as a cerebral Asian statesman if they did not also know his other face as a crude, visceral politician at home.[2]

Grinning widely, Smiley Sim said,

"The 'old man' wants to know who really wrote this article.
He does not believe that you had written it. The style is not yours."

The op-ed article was a collaborative work. After my return from Kuala Lumpur, I discussed the implications of the ISA detainees' rearrest with Devan in course of which we discussed the prime

---

2. May 10, 1988. A shorter version appeared in *The Wall Street Journal*, May 11, 1988.

minister's defence of press restrictions in Singapore before the American Society of Newspaper Editors in Washington on April 14, as reported in *The Straits Times*. It was a brilliant presentation but it contained certain basic flaws with which the American audience would not be familiar. I wanted to reply to it but, in view of the pressure of the aforesaid *habeas corpus* applications, Devan undertook to prepare a draft incorporating the points discussed for further discussion. I made several suggestions and changes to the article. Sim told me to underline our respective words, phrases, and paragraphs, and those which were jointly ours. It was not easy to dissect an article in the mode and manner requested as it embodied our thoughts and ideas. It was mainly the language used which differed. Any one familiar with our respective styles could detect the difference just as I could detect the hand and style of the prime minister in official statements.

On Saturday, May 14, 1988, after innumerable amendments, corrections, and additions on reams upon reams of paper, a statement was at long last whisked out of the word processors into final form. It had been, to borrow the current ISD's favourite expression, "fine-tuned." I had, by then, read and re-read them in bits and pieces, paragraph-by-paragraph, page-by-page, topic-by-topic, and statement-after-amended statement, at the end of which time it was no longer easy to see the wood for the trees.

Deputy Director Sim, a-beaming with smiles after reading it, remarked rhetorically:

"The 'old man' will like it. I am sure the 'old man' will like it."

The other senior ISD officers present nodded in agreement. Otherwise, one or two of them resignedly declared, it would mean more nights redoing it to his satisfaction. It was sent for "the old man's" perusal and approval, and everyone waited apprehensively for his reaction and comments.

On Sunday, May 15, 1988, sometime in the afternoon, Smiley Sim returned, announcing with great aplomb that "the old man" was satisfied. He wanted to know—as if I had any real choice in the matter—whether I was prepared to have it put in statutory declaration form. My passport to freedom, having now received his crucial imprimatur, I was able to leave, or so I thought, and, in my over-anxiety to leave the Centre, I wearily answered: "Yes."

CHAPTER 12

On Monday, May 16, 1988, a commissioner for oaths, who was also a Chinese interpreter based in the subordinate courts, turned up for the purpose. I recognised him from my days in court prosecuting peccant citizens. He was quite uncomfortable to see me in a new role in unfamiliar surroundings. Discounting the usual niceties, he briefly asked me whether I wanted to read the statement which an officer had handed over to him. I did not. I was completely disinterested. I was bored. The statement had turned stale beyond belief. Truth no longer seemed to matter as much as the visa in the passport to freedom. Truth had in the event been twisted out of recognition and given an unacceptable face. No free man or woman would readily swear to such statements extracted under such tortured circumstances. Thus, one phase of the interrogation ended only to have the next stage begun.

On Tuesday, May 17, 1988, a boyish-looking ISD officer, Eric Tan, a public accountant by training, took over from S.K. Tan. Overflowing with patriotic fervour and purposeful enthusiasm, he exuded the smug confidence of the new Singaporean in his eagerness to please authority and, at the same time, to display fairness and impartiality. He, however, withheld from me the vital fact of the income tax officials' involvement in his interrogation. For whilst his namesake and side-kicks were busily grilling me, he was quietly going through and exchanging information with them on my personal records and office books of accounts seized by the ISD. Confidentiality is at best a myth and even less so when the name of security is invoked. It was at once apparent to him that the hoary spectre of a black money operation did not exist, a fact which made him acutely uncomfortable, which he repeatedly betrayed in his conversations with me.

A nasty feature of the prime minister's political style is his use of tax audit as an instrument to keep political opponents, critics, or those who have fallen out of official favour in check, off-balance, or preoccupied with endless tax queries. Other government departments also are sometimes used as tools of harassment and repression. It struck me that the seizure of my law firm's account books was a devilishly cunning stroke to kill three birds with one stone, viz. to seek evidence of possible receipt of American or foreign funds, tax, or other financial irregularities, which could expose me to a tax or criminal prosecution. Whichever it was, he would have scored a decisive political victory by deflecting the mounting international protests and pleas of concern relative to my arrest.

Here in the cold, dark, soundproof interrogation room with its fierce spotlights trained on me was the ISD officer, Eric Tan, uttering rather anomalously to me that my financial affairs would be of more interest to the income tax department than the ISD, which had not known of my overseas sources of income. Nonetheless, in defence of the arrest, he intoned that the ISD had to satisfy itself that the funds had not come from the U.S. government, the CIA, or its agencies. I told him the ISD should have investigated first before arresting me, to which he replied *ad nauseam* in the all-too-familiar cliché that "Patrick was really responsible for your arrest." He was not the only ISD officer to parrot this tedious rite of self-exoneration, as if by invoking the name of Patrick it would in some vague way explain away my arrest. Patrick was responsible for involving me in this dark complicity in his statutory declaration, which he had written out, they stressed, in his own hand. In the same rhetoric of his other comrades, Eric asked me if Patrick's allegations were untrue, why then did Patrick say what he did about me? I could not, of course, speak for him but, as far as I was concerned, there was absolutely no truth in them at all. When they persisted, I dared them to bring Patrick (who was still under detention) bodily before me so that I could confront him one-on-one on the trumped-up allegations, but they visibly balked at the challenge and changed the subject.

On May 17, 1988, Patrick was released with no conditions, after having been jailed without trial for exactly one month. It was felt that he had learnt his lesson well. It was the prime minister's concept of crime and punishment, for having acted as a conduit of information for international human rights groups and the foreign media during the 1987 detention of alleged Marxists, later ignominiously dismissed by him as "do-gooders."

After combing through my personal and my firm's accounts, only one item remained for verification—my offshore accounts with the Standard Chartered Bank in Hongkong. The ISD had no access to my bank accounts in Hongkong, although it tried to invoke the assistance of the Hongkong Special Branch. The bank had, quite properly, refused to accede to its demand for copies of statements of account without my consent or an order of the Hongkong High Court. It was refreshing to note the stand adopted by the bank on the privacy of banking transactions. On the other hand, the Bangkok Bank in Bangkok, Thailand capitulated by giving the ISD information on my accounts fearing possible reprisal to its branch in Singapore if it did not comply with the request for information. The Malaysian-based United Malayan Banking Corporation also capitulated in the same way. The climate of fear even overhangs the fields of commerce and banking, mocking Singapore's status as a regional financial centre. Anyway, I felt that this was no time for standing on the niceties of banking confidentiality. The ISD encouraged me in the belief that, if my accounts were satisfactorily explained, the matter of my detention could be quickly resolved. Having nothing to hide, and, in order to expedite the receipt of the statements of accounts, I offered to and did write out a letter of authorization, which was urgently telefaxed through my law firm to the bank. This was in the first few days of June 1988. With rising hopes, I looked forward thereafter to an early release from prison but, sad to say, I had not counted on the personal *animus* of one man with a stiletto memory: "People with long histories have long memories. And I happen to have a long memory."[3]

On Friday, May 20, 1988, the MHA released my statutory declaration, but not before it had deleted the names of David Lambertson, Joseph Snyder, and Colin Helmer and replaced them with Mr. X, Y, and Z, as it did not wish, it unctuously claimed, to aggravate their embarrassment. But the U.S. government squashed this puerile cloak-and-dagger nonsense by disclosing their names. My statement was slavishly serialized in the controlled news media.

As with so many of my friends, Devan was naturally distressed at my arrest and awaited my inevitable statement with great interest or, as ISD Director Tjong put it, he was "acting like a cat on hot bricks." As soon as it was published, Tjong said Devan had "slipped

---

3. Liquor Retailers' Association, October 3, 1965.

out" of the country, and, shortly afterwards on May 21, 1988, from the relative safety of the capital city of Kuala Lumpur in Malaysia, issued a press statement supportive of me and my action, criticizing the government's interpretation of my declaration,

> ... which would do justice to a spy thriller on the best seller list. ... Mr. Lee and his government have never lacked the kind of vivid imagination which suspects the presence of communists or CIA agents under every bed. ... in lobbying for foreign support with the Americans, Mr. Seow had done nothing more than Prime Minister Lee and others did more than two decades ago when they sat on opposition benches in the Malaysian Parliament prior to the time Singapore was ejected from what was then the Federation of Malaysia.[4]

The government denounced Devan as "dishonest" for his public defence of me, to which Devan rejoined, on May 22, 1988, with a hard-hitting press statement:

> Torturing facts to yield his own bizarre interpretations of reality is the forte of Mr. Lee Kuan Yew. His Press Secretary's response to my statement on Francis Seow's statutory declaration once again proves the point.
>
> Other versions of the history of Singapore's brief experience as a part of Malaysia tell a rather different story. One of them is that of Tungku Abdul Rahman, Malaysia's first Prime Minister, who told me not long ago that he had all the facts at his disposal to warrant the arrest of Mr. Lee Kuan Yew when he was the most vociferous member of the Malaysian opposition.[5] But being cast in a more humane mould, and possessed of the kind of soulcraft so totally lacking in Mr. Lee, he resisted all pressures to arrest Mr. Lee.
>
> True, Mr. Lee and his party colleagues, including myself, did not ask for asylum like Mr. Seow. We never thought of it, for the good reason that the Tungku was a far cry from the incarnation of self-righteous intolerance Mr. Lee himself was to become. But in courting and sedulously cultivating a whole variety of foreign establishment and opposition circles, we did what precisely Mr. Seow is supposed to have done in his meetings with the U.S. State Department officials, who turned out to be rather small fry. Mr. Lee had courted far more powerful figures in the countries concerned.
>
> Incidentally, as the sole DAP opposition MP after Singapore was evicted from Malaysia, I did keep in frequent touch with foreign embassies in Kuala Lumpur. And I did so openly. This was widely

---

4. The Straits Times, May 22, 1988.
5. This sentence and the two sentences in the following paragraph formed the basis of Lee's defamation suit against Devan Nair.

known to the Tungku and his ministers. But they did not treat me in the way Mr. Lee is treating Mr. Seow now.

Mr. Seow's soundings about the possibilities of asylum in the U.S. and Britain are a damning indictment of the climate of fear and insecurity Mr. Lee has managed to instil in Singaporeans who seek political change. Or is Mr. Lee angry with Mr. Seow for not preferring the asylum he provides for dissenters in the Whitley Road Detention Centre? How honest is Mr. Lee's pretence that Mr. Seow and others like him do not have anything to fear in Mr. Lee's Brave New World, where statutory declarations of incarcerated opponents, and not the testimony of free men, are waved as infallible witnesses to truth.

On May 23, 1988, the MHA issued a press statement assailing Devan, who vigorously responded the same day with another press statement:

> First, we were treated to the sinister American Connection. We were told that Mr. Francis Seow was arrested for interrogation about his complicity in foreign interference in Singapore's internal affairs.
>
> But now comes the Singapore Connection. We have dubious revelations about Mr. Seow's connections with Singapore's citizens. Devan Nair and his son Dr. Janamitra Devan. Where, pray, is the threat to national security in all this? The brazen abuse of the powers of the ISA and of statutory declarations obtained from detainees under duress of detention must now be evident to the most blind.
>
> My own recollections of what transpired between me and Mr. Seow are, to put it mildly, rather different. Nonetheless, I must decline comment as a matter of principle. For that would be to confer respectability on statements from captives so shamelessly flaunted by their exulting jailors. I shall raise my own questions with Mr. Seow, but only when he is a free man.
>
> I need only observe, at this stage, that if giving political advice and assistance to a fellow Singaporean makes him my mouthpiece, then Mr. Lee Kuan Yew has also shared that distinction. I had occasions over a lengthy period of years to assist Mr. Lee with drafts and opinions on a variety of subjects.
>
> In addition to everything, Mr. Lee's favourite prize fighter, S. Rajaratnam, has now been unleashed on me in the columns of *The Straits Times*. The PAP government juggernaut is clearly on the move against every critic, whether foreign or domestic. I do not have anything like the formidable means at Mr. Lee's disposal to counter his government's campaign of systematic misinformation.
>
> But Mr. Lee should know me well enough. I revel in battle, however solitary I may be. I wish Mr. Lee good luck. He badly needs it.

I recalled those overseas trips which the prime minister and other PAP ministers made during the heady but uncertain days, when

Singapore was a constituent state of the Federation of Malaysia, to countries of the Commonwealth and the Third World, to drum up support for Singapore and his concept of a Malaysian Malaysia. His international image-building at the expense of the Malaysian government and its leaders upset, more particularly, the Malay *ultras*. One would have thought that what was sauce for the goose was sauce for the gander unless of course it was the PAP gander. For his act of political courage and decency, Devan was rewarded with a writ of summons for defamation, commenced at the suit of the prime minister in the High Court in Singapore.[6] But, significantly and largely unknown to the public, Devan's press statements had put the cat among the PAP pigeons, creating consternation and confusion in the cabinet and complicating their predicament over my arrest and detention.

Dr. Toh indicated that he wanted to speak on the orchestrated government motion in Parliament on the ISD detentions, but was dissuaded from it by the pleas of Deputy First Prime Minister Goh Chok Tong, who felt it would further compound the government's difficulties over the arrest. Thus, Dr. Toh did not participate in the debate and remained an interested observer. Not all among the PAP faithful believed the monstrous lies about me and the American connection.

On Thursday, May 26, 1988, the U.S. embassy in Singapore issued a Washington press release, dated Wednesday, May 25, denying the Singapore government's allegations that U.S. diplomats had engaged in undiplomatic activities:

> In spite of our denials, the Government of Singapore continues to allege that U.S. diplomats engaged in activities not in keeping with accepted international practice and interfered in Singapore's domestic affairs. The United States is not and had not been engaged in interference in Singapore's domestic affairs. All activities of U.S. government officials in dealing with Singapore have been legitimate and in full accordance with customary diplomatic practice. The public campaign being waged by the Government of Singapore and its allegations of wrongdoing are groundless.
>
> As we have said repeatedly both publicly and privately, Mr. Lambertson, Mr. Snyder, Mr. Helmer and Mr. Hendrickson (the individuals

---

6. Singapore High Court Suit No 1042 of 1988. It was, however, settled in court on April 19, 1993, through the mediation of a mutual friend.

cited in the Singapore government's statements) were engaged in normal diplomatic activity in meeting with Singaporeans in and outside of the government. What our embassy officers do in Singapore is no different from the normal diplomatic contacts of our diplomats in every country of the world. It is also no different than the conduct of Singaporean diplomats in the United States. Attacks on their intentions and their character are gratuitous and unfounded. The constant repetition of the baseless charges against them and the U.S. government can only serve to damage the traditionally close and cooperative relations between our countries.

We regret that the Singapore government did not attempt to resolve this matter privately, in a manner befitting relations between friendly countries. The U.S. government has stressed in all of its public statements, and in our diplomatic exchanges with the Government of Singapore, that it values the mutually beneficial relationship it has had with Singapore and wishes to see bilateral relations stabilized.

On Saturday, May 28, 1988, the MHA released a second statutory declaration on my finances, which the controlled news media once more gave full prominence. The ISD issued a separate statement that its investigations into my finances were "inconclusive, and have not revealed any evidence of payments of U.S. government funds to Francis Seow." What is a dispassionate observer supposed to make out of all this? In stating its investigations were inconclusive, ISD officers told me that they had tried to be fair to me. It was strange logic, indeed.

A responsible investigative branch of government should have ordinarily carried out preliminary investigations to establish a *prima facie* case so as to justify an arrest of a suspect. It applies with even greater force to arbitrary arrest and detention without trial, where the suspect has no recourse through normal channels for vindication. In this case, save for the prime minister's paranoiac suspicions, the ISD had no evidence against me when it first began and absolutely no evidence at all at the end. To top it all, the MHA statement said:

Seow's links with the American officials and diplomats have now been exposed ... it's unlikely Mr. Seow can obtain fresh backing or funding from any foreign source before the next general election. Therefore, the government will not detain him longer than necessary to deter him from reverting to his former activities.

A classic example of chop logic! My meetings with Hank and Joe were nonconspiratorial, in the open and in some of the best restaurants in

Singapore; but, notwithstanding, PAP MPs in the parliamentary debate on the arrest parroted on cue that they had been "covert." They are not so blind as those who would not see! As I had never received any funds or financial backing from the Americans or any foreign sources, what *further* fresh funds or backing were being denied me?

In a press interview, stressing there was nothing in my sworn statements so far to show evidence of subversive activity, Ashleigh called my continued detention an act of "political timidity." Not one minister had dared to order my release without the cachet from the prime minister himself. Ashleigh nailed the MHA's declaration on its head: "They know if they keep him there he will not be able to ring people to get them to run in any forthcoming election."[7] The neutered *Straits Times* editorialized the prime minister had no choice:

> To release the man would be an admission that it had been wrong to arrest him, and such an admission would confuse all those who have believed in the Government.

Therein lies the nub! Within the strict parameters laid down by the prime minister himself that "the U.S. cannot be pictured or portrayed as an enemy,"[8] PAP backbenchers and government ministers acted out a parliamentary burlesque *debating* a government motion supporting the use of the Internal Security Act to prevent subversion by imaginary foreign interest groups. With its massive parliamentary majority, the end result was never in doubt. Lee displayed his parliamentary skills and oratory. In a two-hour long speech, marking the "*dénouement* of a sometimes nasty debate on the alleged role of U.S. officials in encouraging opposition candidates to stand in the forthcoming parliamentary elections, Prime Minister Lee proposed the U.S. government submit to an inquiry by a neutral committee of three international experts to determine whether Hank and the State Department officials acted properly in Singapore 'as a simple way to put the matter quietly to rest,' and if the committee found that their actions were 'legitimate and did not

---

7. *The Asian Wall Street Journal*, June 6, 1988.
8. Parliamentary debates, June 1, 1988, col. 339.

constitute interference in Singapore's domestic affairs, the Singapore government will withdraw its protest and apologise to the State Department.'"

Referring to a letter from Secretary of State, George Schultz, who had "asserted strongly that the U.S. officials had conducted themselves in an entirely appropriate manner, and that it was totally untrue that the U.S. government funds had been provided to opposition elements," the prime minister had recalled Tommy Koh, Singapore's ambassador to the United States and Kishore Mubhani, permanent representative at the United Nations, in his search for a rationale for the alleged U.S. interference in Singapore politics, to explain why the U.S. officials had acted the way they did. They told him that "the behaviour of U.S. diplomats is not surprising, as they cultivate opposition and dissident figures all over the world. And that U.S. diplomats often feign sympathy for the causes of opposition figures in an effort to elicit information."

The "Reagan Administration is deeply committed to supporting democratic forces around the world," and that the U.S. "since its founding, has felt it has a divine mission to be a beacon of democracy to the world;" and that some Americans "feel they have an obligation to actively promote the cause of democracy in the world and, if necessary, to do so by intervening in the internal affairs of other states." Hank was "probably just such a missionary." But the prime minister said that, despite U.S. attempts to coax and cajole Singapore toward a less authoritarian political system, "my colleagues and I are well-versed in the theory and also the practice [of democracy], and we know what will and what will not work."

Challenging opponents of the government, particularly those who backed the joint statement by the detainees, "to get together, present an alternative government, and contest against the PAP," the government would, he said, defend its use of the Internal Security Act. "There is nothing to stop you, to stop all noncommunists who want to work the system, to do that;" but he warned that those "who intend to take on the government should know that there are few karate blows we do not know how to deliver."[9] The motion was

---

9. *The Asian Wall Street Journal*, June 2, 1988.

overwhelmingly approved by a PAP-dominated Parliament with the lone opposition member, Chiam See Tong, opposing it.

On Thursday, June 2, 1988, my solicitors, Murphy & Dunbar, handed over to the ISD facsimile copies of statements of accounts from the Standard Chartered Bank, Hongkong. After the ISD's accountants and staff had examined them, they were more disconcerted than ever that "someone had jumped to a very hasty conclusion." I could see they were plainly troubled by my continued detention in the Centre and sought half-heartedly to justify it:

> "Well, there are still a few more persons from whom we have not yet received any confirmation of their having paid money to you."

I had readily revealed the names of all those persons who had paid for services rendered or lent or given me money over the years. They told me they were only interested in my accounts from the year 1986 when I became president of the Law Society but, in truth, their action again did not match up to their word. Their interest in so-called national security went way back to 1970—the year I commenced private law practice! Perhaps they thought I had already been suborned a U.S. mole by the U.S. government or its agencies. My clients and friends were interviewed at length by ISD officers causing them no small amount of disquietude. They corroborated my statement, except for an unfortunate friend, Tang Tuck Wah.

Irrationally terrified at possible retribution from a vengeful prime minister, he foolishly lied to the ISD officers during interrogation that a loan he had made to me was actually money placed with my law firm for the purpose of engaging a Queen's Counsel for a legal case in which he was the appellant. The tame news media, of course, made capital out of it. The matter was referred to the Commercial Crimes Branch, CID, for investigations into a penal offence of criminal breach of trust. There are so many ways of skinning a cat—if they could not involve me in a black money conspiracy, they might succeed in a charge of a criminal or a tax offence. Tang's report was shown to be false. It is a dreadful indictment of the climate of fear that pervaded and still pervades Singapore and of the wanton abuse of the Internal Security Act.

The notoriety generated by my detention sedulously fanned by the government-controlled news media resulted in the abrupt withdrawal of Mei's secured overdraft facilities by her bankers, Banque Nationale de Paris, and the cancellation of a mortgage loan application already approved in principle by it, "because of the discord you have with the Singaporean authorities which we have just learnt about today."[10] It repercussed on my circle of friends and acquaintances, among whom was an old and valued friend, Julius Teo Joo Lai, chairman and managing director of Teo Teck Huat Co. Ltd. and several other companies, a successful land and building developer, who had his companies' books of accounts seized by the comptroller of income tax within a week of my arrest. With remarkable *sangfroid*, he accepted the tax investigations into his wealth, explained the reasons for the loans to me, the manner and method of their record in the books of his companies. Another person would have been vexatiously terrified by the combined attention of the Internal Security Department and the Internal Revenue Department! But, seriously enough, what Julius Teo and all the others had to do with the American connection, it was very difficult to see!

News of these harassments reached me through Ashleigh and my solicitors during their visits to the Centre. It angered me. I was powerless. They were deliberately creating unnecessary difficulties for Mei and my good and helpful friends and clients, some of whom foolishly but understandably made themselves prisoners of their fears. I berated the ISD officers for the harassments, but they disclaimed responsibility. All this they shrugged off as nothing but self-induced fear. Whilst the disclaimer might have some grains of truth, the ISD could have done something to ameliorate that cold grip of fear. But then why should it go out of its way to do so? It serves the ISD's purpose to let the canker of fear feed upon itself, making it easier for its covert actions, surveillance, and subsequent investigations. On the other hand, it is difficult to blame the public for succumbing to and accepting the unwholesome tenet of state supremacy in their daily lives.

---

10. *The Asian Wall Street Journal*, June 1, 1988.

On Saturday morning, June 4, 1988, they told me that they had discovered that my law firm had a safe-deposit box with the Hongkong Bank. I had forgotten all about it. My personal assistant, Ruby Koh, was the only one who operated it. I did not know what was kept in it. Anxious that it should not be used as a pretext to delay my release, I immediately gave S.K. Tan a personal handwritten note instructing Ruby to accompany him to open it up so that the ISD could satisfy itself I had not stashed away any hidden American bounty. But, strange to relate, Tan was not overly keen to do so. Inwardly, we all knew that there were no American or foreign funds involved and that it was largely a figment of the prime minister's fevered imagination. I had to prevail upon him and his colleagues to go and verify it that very same day. They returned from the bank that afternoon, the results of the search plainly written over their crestfallen faces. The safe-deposit box had not been opened for the last two years and it contained nothing but wills of clients. One nagging suspicion of hidden loot was put to rest.

Sunday, June 5, 1988, would be exactly thirty days since I was first detained. The ISD had virtually completed its investigations and submitted the necessary documentation and recommendation to the prime minister. The order for release should be imminent at any moment. Everything now depended upon *him* and on *him* alone. At midday, a dreadful premonition suddenly swept over me that made me voice my fears aloud to the ISD officers that *he*—without mentioning any name—would try to exact vengeance against me for having crossed him at the Select Committee hearing on the Legal Profession (Amendment) bill. They tried to reassure me that they were "professionals" and had not been influenced by any extraneous considerations in their report and recommendation. They appeared almost as anxious as I was at the decision. We spoke in as normal a voice as we could muster, but we all were tense for the air was charged with great expectation. They looked at their watches every now and again to see whether the news of the decision was on its way.

Director Tjong Yik Min accompanied by some senior officers walked into the room. We exchanged looks; I looked at Tjong but he was deadpan. He sat down amongst us without a word and, to my anxious query, claimed that he knew nothing of the prime minister's decision, which I did not believe. He was, after all, the head of the Internal Security Department and would be the first to be informed before the news, good or bad, was broken to me. Shortly afterwards, at 3:15 that same afternoon, a subordinate ISD officer came in and confirmed my worst fears.

Under the intent gaze of Director Tjong and his coterie of officers, he served me with an order of detention for one year. It read:

To: The Director of Prisons,
Singapore

The Commissioner of Police, Singapore,
all other police officers and to all others whom it may concern.

WHEREAS the President is satisfied with respect to one FRANCIS T. SEOW NRIC 112608-A of 31 Balmoral Park, #06–31, Singapore 1025, that, with a view to preventing him from acting in any manner prejudicial to the security of Singapore or to the maintenance of public order or essential services therein, it is necessary to detain him:

NOW, THEREFORE, the Minister for Home Affairs, in exercise of the powers conferred on him by section 8 of the Internal Security Act, has directed—

(a) under subsection (1)(a) of section 8 of the Act that the said FRANCIS T. SEOW be detained for a period of 1 year with effect from the 5th day of June 1988; and

(b) under subsection (4) of section 8 of the Act that the said FRANCIS T. SEOW be detained at Whitley Road Detention Centre or at such other place as he may from time to time direct.

Made this 5th day of June, 1988.

Sgd.   BG (Res) TAN CHIN TIONG
PERMANENT   SECRETARY
MINISTRY OF HOME AFFAIRS
SINGAPORE

No one uttered a word for what seemed to me to be an interminably long time. I felt greatly let down. I articulated my deep disappointment. It could not have been more than a few minutes during which time an uncomfortable Tjong left the room with his entourage leaving me to the company of the other officers. It mocked all my earnest efforts to clear my name and my action. It went against the very grain of truth. I thought of myself as a gambit in a bigger political chess game. When the bombshell burst on me, I was sorely disappointed, and yet, in some ways, I was not altogether surprised. Personal spite rather than professional consideration had momentarily triumphed.

Later that same night, Director Tjong Yik Min returned and handed me a copy of a MHA statement and this time sheepishly asked me what I made out of it and, in particular, paragraph three. I read it through carefully, as follows:

EMBARGOED TILL 1700 HRS, 5 JUNE 88.
SINGAPORE GOVERNMENT PRESS STATEMENT
(Issued by the Ministry of Home Affairs)

1. The Government has today issued a Detention Order for a period of one year against Francis Seow to prevent him from acting in any manner prejudicial to the security of Singapore.

2. The Government does not believe that Seow has revealed the whole truth in his Statutory Declarations. However, what he has admitted to clearly establishes that Seow had been courting if not colluding with an American diplomat and senior State Department officials to lead a group of lawyers and professionals into opposition politics. He had cultivated the Americans to seek their backing for his political plans and to provide a safety net. The Americans encouraged Seow, supported his political plan, and instigated other dissident lawyers to join his ranks. They also gave him the impression that asylum would be forthcoming when needed. Seow was thus beholden to the Americans for their support and prospect of asylum. He had made himself a willing party to interference in Singapore's domestic affairs by foreign representatives.

3. That Seow intended to contest the General Elections is public knowledge. Seow's links with the American diplomats and officials have now been exposed. It is unlikely that he can obtain fresh backing or funding from any foreign source before the next General Elections. The Government will not detain him longer than necessary to deter him from reverting to his former activities. So that there can be no doubt over the reason for this Detention Order, the Government intends to release Seow shortly, before the expiry of his Detention Order and in time for the General Elections.

4. Seow's release will be subject to conditions to prevent him from associating with foreign diplomats or travelling outside Singapore without the consent of Director ISD. But there will be no restriction on Seow's political rights. Like any other citizen who wishes to, he can stand for elections.

I looked at paragraph three, again. What had they really exposed? Absolutely nothing! It begged the question. My association and meetings with Hank and the others were not in the slightest bit conspiratorial. They were all in the open, in full view and within earshot of the public. What former activities have I indulged in that were inimical to the security of Singapore? Where was the evidence that I had obtained foreign funding? There was absolutely no equivocal evidence whatsoever unearthed about any funding. The ISD statement had said as much and, yet, in the face of the evidence, the government had still persisted in Goebbelsian disinformation—if one repeats an untruth long enough it may be believed! But for the time being, the punctuation mark in the last sentence of paragraph three provoked a lot of speculation among my gaolers as to the author's meaning and the intention.

The ISD officers assured me that none of them was responsible for the MHA statement or consulted on it. Some of them appeared genuinely disappointed at the issuance of the order of detention but, as good civil servants, they held their counsel and tried to mollify me that it would not be long before I would be released, given the comma in the statement. How very brittle is liberty to have to hang upon one little comma!

We discussed as dispassionately as we could, or at least I tried to, the significance of the punctuation mark—the all-important comma—in the syntax. Each gave his understanding of the key word "shortly," and the consensus was that my period of detention would be no more than three months, probably less. It was however no consolation to me. As far as I was concerned, I had already been detained thirty days too long. We all knew who the *éminence grise* of my detention was. It is especially noteworthy that the ISD officers to a man claimed they had done all they could and had made the necessary recommendation, but the matter of my liberty was no longer in their hands. It now rested, they repeatedly stressed, "on an emotional plane between you and *him*." We all knew who was the *him*. It did not require those words to confirm my own worst suspicions. They rationalised their action and, Pilate-like, tried to wash it off by shifting the blame for my arrest and detention on to their political masters.

On Friday, June 17, 1988, I was served with the grounds on which my detention order was made under section 11(2) of the ISA, and informed that I could make representations in connection with the Order.[11] On Saturday, June 25, 1988, my solicitors, Murphy & Dunbar, sent my representations pursuant to section 11(2) of the ISA to the Chairman, Advisory Board.[12]

Meanwhile, enraged by Devan's open support for me and his critique on the misuse of the ISA and topped by his call to him to step down as prime minister, as all the other old-guard PAP ministers had done so, the prime minister gave an unparalleled exhibition of the depths to which he was capable of sinking by mounting a vicious, vindictive, and vitriolic *blitzkrieg* on "one of [his] closest comrades." He opened the floodgates of squalid and sordid minutiae on Devan's alleged alcoholism, womanizing, and wife-beating in a White Paper,[13] which he caused to be tabled in Parliament on June 29, 1988, "so that Singaporeans can understand [Nair's] motives and see through his statements."

On July 9, 1988, Devan rejoined in a long, scathing open letter to him,[14] which was published in *The Straits Times* and other newspapers and periodicals, questioning, amongst other things:

> Where in the civilized world is sordid political capital so shamelessly squeezed out of a medical condition? ... You know the answer: only in a society governed by a man like you.

Although Brigadier General Lee Hsien Loong was publicly quoted as saying that "a proper statement on Mr. Nair's open letter to the prime minister would probably be issued in due course,"[15] no reply was ever made to Devan's devastating rebuttal of political revenge and dementia. The next day, Goh Chok Tong, in response to questions from journalists, said: "The bitter row that has erupted over the publication of the White Paper on Devan Nair should not drag on." He felt more exchanges could only prolong the agony for

---

11. For Ground and Allegations of facts, see Appendix 3.
12. For Representations, see Appendix 4.
13. Command No. 8 of 1988.
14. An abridged version appeared in the *Far Eastern Economic Review*, July 21, 1988, captioned "Politics of the gutter." But for the full letter, see Appendix 5.
15. *The Straits Times*, July 11, 1988.

the former president and his family and embarrass Singapore. "We should not drag on the exchanges between Mr. Devan Nair and the government. They make for sorry reading."[16] In the circumstances, it is exquisite irony to recall what the prime minister had once said of his longtime political comrade and friend: "He is anything other than one of [my] closest comrades. There are bonds which cannot be broken."[17] That was probably true, so long as one did not dissent from him! And, incredulously, since then, horripilant obsequiousness aside, First Deputy Prime Minister Goh Chok Tong has hailed him as the advent of a "modern Confucius"—no doubt to the perturbations of the spirit of that ancient sage!

On Wednesday, July 13, 1988, I was served with a notice of hearing of representations before the Advisory Board scheduled for Saturday, July 23, 1988, at 10:30 a.m. at Court No. 6, High Court. The chairman was none other than Justice Sinnathuray.

---

16. *The Straits Times*, July 12, 1988.
17. Press conference, City Hall, August 26, 1965.

13

Dr. Toh Chin Chye et al.

> Within this democratic system everyone has the right to compete, to preach his political views, but the competition must be for the purpose of working the system, not destroying it. These [emergency] powers will not be allowed to be used against political opponents within the system who compete for the right to work the system. That is fundamental and basic, or the powers will have destroyed the purpose for which they were forged. If, in using these powers you, in fact, negate the purpose for which you made them, then you end up with a situation where force, and more force, will become increasingly necessary.
>
> —Lee Kuan Yew[1]

> [T]he ultimate answer to the communist challenge is not provided by this type of legislation giving the executive emergency or extraordinary powers. Ultimately, it is the economic, social and political conditions and the battles on these planes that will decide whether Singapore ... will grow from strength to strength as a democratic state in which the more tolerant features of human civilization are preserved whilst the economic needs and necessities of the people are rapidly met, or whether a more totalitarian system will succeed the democratic system to cater for these economic needs. These powers can only provide a temporary damper against those who set out to wreck the democratic state.
>
> —Lee Kuan Yew[2]

I was closely questioned on my relationship with PAP members and leaders, amongst whom were the former PAP founder-chairman, Dr. Toh Chin Chye, Jek Yuen Tong, and Ong Pang Boon—all of

---

1. Legislative Assembly Debates, October 8, 1958.
2. Legislative Assembly Debates, October 14, 1959.

whom had at one time or another held ministerial portfolios in the government—and other personalities. They were reportedly more individualistic in temperament and character and did not quite enjoy the unquestioned confidence of the prime minister. But as with other PAP ministers, they had been prematurely put out to grass by the prime minister for his own personal and political purpose. The public perception was that they were insurgents and precariously beyond the pale. Wherefore I was accused of trying to glean dark secrets from them for my own selfish ends at the impending general election.

They laboriously recorded statements concerning them but, oddly enough, all references were subsequently surreptitiously excerpted from the statutory declarations released and put in cold storage. A day or two later, when I had regained some composure and orientation, it suddenly occurred to me that I had not seen any reference to Dr. Toh and the others. I queried the omissions, but they tried to fob me off with one excuse after another. I demanded to see the original statements, and only then did they reluctantly admit their names had not been included in the statutory declarations. But why then were the references to Devan included? The answer was because "the old man" already knew about our connexion whereas, in Dr. Toh's case, there was no need to create any "unnecessary trouble" between him and "the old man." The ISD was as full of guile as ever. Devan's courageous public defence of me had created a credibility problem for the government; this might replicate itself with even uglier repercussions, if any reference to Dr. Toh was similarly published, as he would unlikely have allowed it to pass without comment, which would queer the political pitch for the government. Dr. Toh was much too shrewd a politician to fail to read the handwriting on the wall!

Why had I consulted Devan and Dr. Toh instead of Eddie W. Barker, the minister for law, my former minister, or Dr. Goh Keng Swee, the minister for defence, with whom they knew I was on nodding terms and whose basket of ideas and breadth of vision, intellect, and energy in overseeing the economic miracle of Singapore I respected? I knew Eddie well enough not to broach the subject with him. He was at the time essentially apolitical and had gone into politics more for reasons of friendship at the behest of the prime minister. And where Dr. Goh was concerned, he was not easily accessible, as oftentimes he was reportedly away or in China on special assignments for the PRC government.

They were not altogether satisfied with those answers and denounced me for seeking Devan and Dr. Toh out, because they were perceived as PAP dissidents, so that I could pry out from them the shadowy secrets of the PAP's inner council. What dark secrets had they revealed to me, they repeatedly pressed me; but I dismissed their question out of hand as an insult to the intelligence and integrity of Devan and Dr. Toh. They asked me about the lesser lights in the PAP firmament. Although I knew some of them in varying degrees of friendship, I had not sought them out. Implicit in this line of questioning was a certain political naïveté. And in any event readers, pray tell, what had all these to do with national security necessitating my arrest and detention under the ISA?

Tan Boon Teik

Tan Boon Teik was the attorney general and public prosecutor of Singapore. His care-worn, wizened face and prematurely whitened hair make him appear older than his 60 odd years. The state of the AG's chambers often depended on which side of the bed he awoke or on the state of his digestive secretions that morning. As related, we were both appointed to our respective positions on the same day. Almost to a man, the director and his officers made no secret of the fact that they did not like him. "We do not need his counsel or advice." "We do not seek his advice." "He rants and raves like a mad man." "There is no reason for us to call him 'Sir.'" "We hear he is a nasty, little bully." "We try to have as little to do with him as possible." These are some of the many comments made in tones which have to be heard to appreciate the impact or depth of the articulators' sentiments. The ISD had obviously noted a lot about him. His tantrums were proverbial in the chambers and to those who had any truck with him. His quick tongue and violent temper were well-known in and beyond the civil service.

I pause to recall that the attorney general's chambers originally were in the stately Colonial Secretariat building, at Empress Place.

But, in June 1959, when Lee and his PAP government took over power, we were purposedly moved out to the unkempt Ministry of Labour building at Havelock Road that often reeked with half-forgotten men seeking social welfare assistance on the fringe of Singapore's Chinatown. It was not a suitable location; but our new political masters in their infinite wisdom had decreed otherwise. It was never built to house the legal department of government and it was itself overcrowded. In the result, the chambers were split and scattered untidily throughout the length and breadth and height of the Labour building, requiring of its occupants a determination and purpose before they ventured forth to the respective locations. Indeed, most of them found the telephone or the intercom more convenient and a less exacting form of communication. It was, to put it mildly, a most unsatisfactory arrangement.

My own chamber, including the crime section, was on the ground floor at one end while Boon Teik occupied a large, commodious office at the opposite end on the top floor of the building. The civil section was perched on a hastily-constructed wooden mezzanine floor overhanging the labour secretariat, whilst the legislation section shared insufficient space cheek by jowl with the attorney general and his staff on the top floor. The library was everywhere. It was an office planner's worst nightmare. We remained there until many years later when we were able to relocate close to our source and origins to a building once occupied by the public works department, which had shifted to the modern multi-storied Ministry of National Development building at Maxwell Road.

In the maze of offices which was the AG's chambers, Boon Teik sought companionship in my office almost daily and, on occasions, several times a day. The frequency and duration of his visits depended upon his humour on that particular day. When he first burst into my room in a foul mood, it was in mute fascination that I beheld an angry man silently pacing the room, now and then venting his frustration and anger in kicking at my chairs and the legs of my table as if they had stood deliberately in his way or had in some way been responsible for some recent mishap to him. When after a while I quietly told him to desist from kicking the furniture about, more out of concern that he might injure his feet or his shoes than the chairs or the table, he burst out in a volatile mixture of vexation and laughter: "How can you be so damned calm about it?" It was to become a familiar scene. In the course of time, I discovered that the source of his tantrums was directly traceable to an acute sense of insecurity over a variety of causes. They ranged from his having been reproved by the prime minister or the minister over some legal advice or matter, to second-guessing the reasons why the prime minister had summarily summoned for his presence, to the condescending demeanor and conduct of the chief justice or the chairman of the Public Services Commission towards him, to his listing at public functions in accordance with protocol, and to his losses from share speculations. When I became more accustomed to his temper, I would let him work off his frustration or rage. Basically, he needed someone to lend a ready ear and to reassure him on his fears and disappointments.

These one-way visits did not go unnoticed among the staff and other civil servants, including the ISD, and became the subject of unpleasant rumours and idle conversations. I thought I should reciprocate his visits occasionally so as to counter these snide gossips. Almost the first time when I did so, I found him talking agitatedly on the phone to someone who, he later said, was his stockbroker. What impressed me, however, was the sight of the Singapore and foreign financial newspapers spread out on his desk and the financial periodicals and reports stacked at the side. It required a certain knowledge and expertise to read and interpret the facts and figures. I did not see anything amiss in the display of financial knowledge and intelligence before me, and I rather admired his far-flung interests in stocks and shares, the money and the bullion markets, and told him so.

One evening, Boon Teik asked me whether I would like to accompany him on a visit to his stockbroker, Robert Wee, at Market Street, who was, among several other stockbrokers, his main stockbroker with whom he studiously played the stock market. The wisdom in having a plurality of stockbrokers at call, I was told, was that in essence no one stockbroker could claim access to all market information, and one interpretation of the stock market was not necessarily the same as the next stockbroker. It made sense to me.

Having nothing particular to do that evening and wishing not to appear aloof, I agreed. About 6 p.m. or thereabouts, we went in his ivory-coloured Mercedes Benz car, SJ 2, driven by his Indian chauffeur. The prefix "SJ" on the vehicle registration plate indicated to the world that the car belonged to some august official in the Supreme Court, but the low single digit "2" narrowed down its owner, however, to none other than the attorney general. The registration plate prefix and number of the chief justice's car is SJ 1, followed by the attorney general with SJ 2, and thereafter by the judges of the Supreme Court in ascending number in accordance with their seniority. As the attorney general, he was entitled to a chauffeur whose wages were met partially by the state, but his unfortunate temper was such that he could not retain the service of these persons for long. There was a dearth of good chauffeurs at the time because of the establishments of new foreign embassies and many multinational companies in Singapore, whose top executives were not restrained in hiring them at market rates of pay. Be that as it may, he instructed the driver to stop at the road junction where Chulia Street meets with Market Street in front of a nondescript Chinese coffee shop, since demolished as part of the urban renewal programme, after which the chauffeur drove off to the Marine Police Station on the opposite side of the Singapore river to await us there. I was puzzled as to why we had alighted there, when we were still some distance away from the premises of Robert Wee & Co., Stocks & Sharebrokers, at 86–88 Market Street. He sheepishly explained that it was more convenient. Not long after, when his chauffeur had left his employment and he had to drive the car himself, he would park it in front of the Chinese coffee shop at Chulia Street. But in time, he felt sufficiently emboldened to leave it along Market Street but still some several doors' distance away from the premises. We then crossed Chulia Street and entered Market Street and walked along the crowded covered five-foot way, where scores of gunny sacks filled with different varieties of oriental spices were exhibited for sale. They jostled for space before the Indian shops that lined our route, interspersed with the Chinese shops of rubber importers and exporters. Each time we negotiated this route, our senses were assailed by a mixture of strong spicy scents which collectively vied to overpower the acrid smell of smoked rubber wafting from within the storehouses of the Chinese rubber merchants. One stray section of Little India was sharing an easy, albeit odoriferous, existence with the Chinese mercantile community, a small but significant symbol of a multiracial and multicultural Singapore.

It was about dusk. Vehicular traffic had thinned out. Most of the office workers had already abandoned the city to the gathering night. When we reached the stockbroker's premises, I noticed several latest model limousines parked on the same side of the street. Their respective chauffeurs were lounging and idly chatting among themselves nearby. I rather ingenuously remarked that their presence was a confirmation of my original belief that there would be lots of car-parking space available there. But Boon Teik appeared not to have heard. As soon as we entered, he made a beeline for the stairs leading up to Robert Wee's office, with me in tow and accompanied by Robert Wee's junior partner, Ong Thiam Hock, an amiable Chinese with a piercingly loud laugh, who had earlier intercepted his entry. I noticed the business premises were half deserted. The speculators and the remisiers had long gone, leaving only what I discovered were the firm's accounts staff to record and take stock of the day's proceedings and the cleaning staff to tidy up the mess left behind in the day's operation. A couple of business titans were waiting for Robert in his spacious office. Ong, with his round cherubic-face wreathed in smiles, proudly effected the introductions. I remember one of them was Tay Beng Swee, a sleeping partner, who held a glass of whisky in his hand. Beng Swee offered us a drink. He was surprised to see both of us together, as was Robert himself, when he joined us shortly. Robert Wee, a scion of a well known Straits Chinese family, was the shrewdest and most successful stockbroker in Singapore and Malaysia; his arrogant manipulations of the stock markets were in due course to gain for him a deserved notoriety.

Boon Teik was there to settle accounts with the brokerage firm and to find out about the day's market and the future prospects of selected counters. It was then an esoteric world to me, and, in some ways, it still is. But Boon Teik was in his natural element. I listened intrigued to Robert's prognostications of the market, the counters to watch, the dividend payable, the yield, the price/earnings ratio, and the high and low prices that could be expected of their performance. The man was obviously not hailed as "the emperor" of the Singapore and Malaysian stock markets for nothing. He was a generous host and lavish in his hospitality. He kept a good cellar of fine whisky and Cognac, including Armagnac. We were later joined by his other "big" clients of the firm. They were the giants of business and commerce, who talked and bought or sold in terms of tens of thousands of shares whose paper value ran into millions of dollars. They were the owners or the majority shareholders of public companies that were listed or about to be listed on the stock exchanges of Singapore and Malaysia, and they had come to pay court to the emperor. Those were the days before the boom was lowered on insider trading on the stock market, its practitioners, and players. Those were the days before the authorities took a closer look at Robert Wee and his "big" clients, precipitously sending him and several of them to Hongkong to continue where they had left off in Singapore.

I was often in court, and soon found out that the life of an active trial lawyer did not lend itself to stock or share speculations, more especially when he was a dilettante. It was virtually impossible to monitor the movements of the shares. For all the supposedly inside track, we lost a lot of money, and I decided to call it quits. But, my dear friend, Boon Teik was resilient and persevering. Once he asked me whether I wanted to go in with him in the Australian gold market, and, when I balked at the suggestion, gave me a score of reasons why it would be a safe investment. I told him candidly that I was unable to monitor the local market, as it was, and to venture into the overseas market was an invitation to disaster. I saluted his courage when he decided to go ahead, nevertheless. There he was, poring over the various financial reports to make informed investments, which I did not have the time nor the specific knowledge, let alone the courage, to do so.

We were at Robert Wee's office almost every day after work, with Boon Teik usually settling his accounts while I kept him company and enjoyed the fine whisky. Boon Teik rarely drank save for a soft drink. On other days, I would wait for him there while he first went to other brokerage firms to settle accounts. *Haud ignota loquor*—I speak of things by no means unknown. He lived in constant fear of discovery, of being misinterpreted in his actions, and of being the point of discussions of vicious tongues. Perhaps, it was a prescience of a survivalist, a talent which I readily confess I did not possess. But notwithstanding all those circuitous maneuvers, malicious reports abounded about his stock and share speculations some long time after I had resigned the service. It was this which interested the ISD.

The prime minister's surprising public exoneration of Boon Teik in Parliament of alleged abuse of office, dubious share dealings and financial improprieties intrigued the ISD officers. I could not elucidate for them any more than what they had already known about him and his penchant for speculation in shares.[3] I suggested that, if they wanted any further information on him and those activities, they should really contact his present and erstwhile friends, Wee Cho Yaw, the chairman of the United Overseas Bank; H.L. Wee, a lawyer and former president of the Law Society; and lawyer A.S.K. Wee and several stockbroker firms. Nevertheless, they still wanted a statement concerning him which they recorded at some length and, for the reasons mentioned, put in cold storage, probably for use at some appropriate time and opportunity as all the statements on other subjects and personalities.

It was, incidentally, not the first time the ISD had evinced a professional interest in Boon Teik. When I was being briefed on communism and the Communist Party of Malaya (CPM) in preparation for the commission of inquiry into the secondary IV examinations boycott, I was startled to see his name mentioned in a number of intelligence reports on the activities of certain left-wing lawyers. But my amazement was nothing compared to the rude shock I received when, among the voluminous files, I accidentally came across xeroxed copies of two air-letters of my apolitical wife, written in Finnish, to her parents in Helsinki, Finland, together with translations

---

3. *Allan Ng and his allegations against the Attorney General.* See Parliamentary Debates, January 27, 1988, cols. 470–74. He finally retired as attorney general on April 30, 1992, and was subsequently appointed Singapore's roving ambassador to Hungary.

in English by someone from the British Foreign Office. Whoever the translator was, he could not decipher her handwriting, as his translations contained many gaps of missing words and phrases and even sentences. The letters were absolutely innocuous. What they were doing in the files relating to Chinese schools and radical student activists, I am still uncertain to this day. Or, for that matter, in and among the files of the ISD! The mounds of useless, incorrect or irrelevant, if not misinterpreted, information that I came across was phenomenal. I later told Boon Teik of these discoveries and warned him to be careful of his association with those persons lest his actions or movements be misinterpreted by over-zealous security officials. I also encountered personal files of or references to lawyers and other well-known personalities, who could not by any stretch of the imagination be said to be political extremists of the right or the left variety; and thus when Chua Sian Chin asked to look at his own personal file, his suspicion of ISD interest in him was not entirely misplaced.

Tan Boon Teik was one of several personalities in whom the ISD showed, to me, renewed unhealthy curiosity, and who could not possibly be subjects of security concern. Therefore, the irresistible conclusion lies in the ISD's insatiable interest in building up or updating secret dossiers on well known personalities, including their private lives, proclivities, and prurient interests and anything usefully incriminating so that they could, should the circumstances warrant it, be held as hostages to fortune.

14

Cell L-9, Block L

> I have been studying how I may compare
> This prison where I live unto the world.
> —William Shakespeare, *King Richard II*,
> Act V, sc. 5, 1

And now to return to cell L-9. My toiletry set was kept in an unlocked locker outside the cell behind a desk at which sat an eagle-eyed Gurkha guard, who without fail went through its contents after each morning's ablution. Whenever he noted a comb, toothbrush, or shaving razor missing from amongst the items in the bag, he would question its absence. Inadvertently, I would have left something in the bathroom, which I had to retrieve and hand to him.

During the day, the cell became unbearably warm, oven-hot, turning on one occasion within minutes several chocolate bars, which I had received as part of a food parcel, into a glorious sticky mess. The cell was eerily quiet during the day and night except for the ceaseless whirring of the electrical extractor fan that valiantly tried to expel the hot, humid air from within. Its perpetual whirring sounded like the rolling of distant Chinese temple drums during festival days. In time, one became accustomed to its constant ululation. Because the lights burnt brightly, night and day, one had to learn to sleep with them on. In order to overcome the unaccustomed brilliance, I had asked for and received from home a Singapore Airlines' cloth nightshade, but, alas, I had perforce to abandon it when the unrelenting heat caused my head and whole body to break out in dire perspiration. Tiny pellets of perspiration trickled down my body into little rivulets which soon turned my clothes and the nightshade into a damp, soggy mess. It was maddeningly unpleasant and impossible to sleep.

During the first week or so in the sweltering cell, I had no, nor was I given any, reading matter. Later, after the interrogation was over, Ashleigh brought me several books, including *The Complete Works of Shakespeare*, Palgrave's *Golden Treasury of English Poems*, and *Waltzing with a Dictator*—a book on the rise and fall of President Ferdinand Marcos of the Philippines. A detainee was allowed about seven books at any one time. I quickly devoured Manchester's *American Caesar, The Life of General Douglas MacArthur* and *The Last Lion, the Life of Sir Winston Churchill*. I supplemented my book reading with old copies of the Reader's Digest lent me through the courtesy of an ISD officer.

After the release of my second statutory declaration and shortly after the orchestrated parliamentary debate on the government's action under the ISA, I was at long last given *The Straits Times* newspaper to read, with the express *caveat* that I should not upset myself over the "stupid," "idiotic," and "ignorant" statements made about me by the PAP members of parliament, whom they colourfully described as "political jokers and clowns." The statements of those "ignoramuses" did not, they claimed, reflect the true views or opinions of the ISD over whom they had no control. I was appalled at the way those fawning PAP minions fell over each other on cue in repeating blindly the official line, attempting to justify without question my wholly unwarranted detention, and accepting it as gospel. Apropos of those PAP MPs' statements, they said, "But we and you know better." I was angry, very angry; but there was very little I could do to correct the record, not while I was languishing impotently as a dissident in Lee Kuan Yew's prison.

I perused with fascination the growing saga of confrontation between the prime minister and Devan over my detention, and of his malevolence towards Devan, hitherto unequalled and unseen in the political annals of Singapore. The prime minister, slow to praise, had once described his erstwhile friend with feeling,

> What a singular privilege it has been to have been closely associated with the Secretary-General of the NTUC for all these years. I

know men; I know them when they have the guts and I know them when they haven't. And, I say, he has got guts.[1]

Forgotten in his heedless descent into the sewer of negative politics was this priceless encomium,

> Once in a long while, in any movement, you get a person of more than ordinary girth and more than ordinary weight. And Devan Nair was such a man.

Forgotten, too, was the fastidious distinction he drew between the communists and himself that, "unlike ruthless communist cadres, personal friendship and sentimental regard for old friends matter." In attempting to underscore his own humanity and quality of friendship from the likes of the communists, he excoriated the opposition *Barisan Sosialis* leader, Lim Chin Siong, in a radio broadcast thus,

> *Lim began to fight Devan Nair relentlessly and ruthlessly, by smears and intimidation, to destroy every influence that Devan Nair had with the workers and in the unions. His personal friendship for Devan Nair meant nothing.*[2] [Italics added].

How frightfully hollow these words must now sound in his mouth? He is guilty of the very sin for which he had so robustly condemned another erstwhile comrade, Lim Chin Siong. It is so easy to see the mote in another's eye!

I tried to draw the ISD officers out in a discussion on the prime minister's statement in Parliament and the allegations against Devan as contained in the White Paper, but they professed at first to have no views on them. On occasions, one or more ISD officers would warily deplore the prime minister's personal and vicious attacks on Devan. They were clearly distressed and conceded that the monstrous allegation that Devan had consumed "a bottle of whisky every night for a few months" was somewhat far-fetched and improbable. An hyperbole of Goebbelsian proportions! Given the wines and spirits stored in the *Istana* wine cellar, what do the cellar's records say? Why were they not produced in support of the allegation of the President's gargantuan thirst for whisky? Did the charge emanate from a liveried staff of the *Istana*? Or, was it solely

---

1. Opening of Trade Union House, October 15, 1965.
2. September 18, 1961.

a product of the prime minister's egregiously feverish mind? And where could Devan have possibly hidden the multitudinous empty whiskey bottles?

No one amongst the ISD officers thought much of the outbursts of Senior Minister S. Rajaratnam either, especially his strictures on Devan *via* silly, anonymous letters to *The Straits Times*, which, albeit in pseudonyms, bore unmistakably his unique paw marks. Were senior PAP ministers paid S$26,000 per month plus other generous perks and privileges of office to indulge in writing anonymous letters to *The Straits Times* annoying of the citizens? They shook their heads slowly in positive disbelief at the antics of their political elders. This penchant for anonymity, more understandable in members of the public than in ministers of government, preceded the subsequent and present official injunction against the use of pseudonyms by correspondents in letters to the editor, "as they should be brave enough to state their views, and stand by them."

The Straits Times newspaper was my main source of news of the outside world. It was a "privilege" to be provided for a limited time with newspapers to read, albeit dated, because the same newspaper was circulated among other inmates of the Centre. I was fortunate in a way to be able to peruse it first, even though somewhat belatedly, the same day before the other detainees. We had no access to foreign newspapers or periodicals, television, or radio broadcasts. Very privileged detainees are sometimes given an opportunity to watch television—a treat, a reward for especial cooperation. Pen and paper were rare commodities.

During those solitary moments, without a thing to read or do, I diverted my time by watching my other cell mates at work and play—the tiny, little ants of several genuses scurrying to and fro about the floor of the cell and the spiders in their webs. In the hustle and bustle of freedom, these lowly creatures rarely ever merit any attention from most persons, except that when they do, they usually invite their swift and sudden destruction. Here, in the drab, steamy-hot cell, it seemed wrong to kill or exterminate them. One could not possibly squash them out of existence for, in their busy search for scraps of food or whatever, the lowly ants, and even the ugly, repulsive arachnids provided momentary diversion, if not entertainment.

These cell ants did not strike me as robust or as energetic as the ants in my apartment, but were rather sluggish in their movements. Could it be that the prison environs had in some ways, also, affected them?

When he was not otherwise being interrogated, the Centre regime called for the detainee to be locked in his cell throughout the day and the night, the key to which was kept by the Gurkha guard commander. The Gurkha guard on duty outside the cell was himself locked inside the block. His only contact with the rest of the Centre was through an internal telephone to the Gurkha guard commander at the guard house some distance away. As there was no toilet within my cell, whenever I felt the call of nature at nights, I had to knock hard on the cell door to attract the Gurkha guard who, after having ascertained the purpose of the disturbance, would telephone the Gurkha guard commander, who would detail a Gurkha guard to go over with the key to open it. Sometimes, the Gurkha guard would come with the wrong key. In view of the distance he had to traverse and the hour of night, it could take as long as thirty minutes or so for the Gurkha guard commander to respond. And, if the call was rather urgent, a minor tragedy could occur. I eventually devised a way out of this nocturnal problem. The breakfast sandwiches were served each morning, in a small, white, transparent plastic bag, secured with a piece of rubber band. Sometimes, the rubber band was not removed by the guard. I began to save up those rubber bands and the plastic bags for this purpose, which I would discard during ablution the next morning.

Valley Wing

About a fortnight before I was suddenly released, I was "upgraded" to a cell in Block N, euphemistically called the Valley Wing by ISD officers but sardonically by the inmates, after the luxurious Valley Wing of the world-famous Shangri-La Hotel in Singapore. I was at first reluctant to accept the transfer as I had, curiously enough, grown accustomed to my tiny cell. But, upon informed advice, I allowed myself to be persuaded to change cells and, in retrospect, I was glad that I did. At the time I was upgraded to the "suite" in the

Valley Wing, K.C. Chew, who had had an involuntary experience in the Centre, was applying for a transfer. They delayed his application for a transfer as further punishment for his part in publishing the offending joint press statement.

The cell was indeed bigger and cleaner, tiled in parts and well-ventilated, measuring about forty-eight feet long by fifteen feet wide by fifteen feet high.[3] The wooden, flush, handleless door with its peephole was similar to cell L-9.

A low wall about three and a half feet high separated a courtyard or airwell from the sleeping space, where there was a metal spring bed of the type formerly used by the British Armed Forces and a foam-rubber mattress. Bed sheets and pillow cases were provided and changed weekly almost every Monday. A small, rickety desk and a tumbledown chair made up the additional creature comforts.

Another concrete wall, about five feet high, separated the sleeping space from a squat-style trench toilet. There was a rudimentary shower with a missing showerhead and a small concrete-tiled water receptacle, the use of which was discouraged because the water entrapped therein made it an ideal breeding place for mosquitoes.

The courtyard which was covered over head with wire mesh completed the amenities of this infamous suite. It was actually no different from the cages that one sees at zoological gardens, where dangerous animals are kept. The only things missing, to my mind, were a catwalk to enable visitors to view the dangerous political animals housed below in the Valley Wing and the signs *"Dangerous— Do NOT feed the animals."* As the courtyard opened up to the heavens one could tell whether it was day or night. The sultry breezes that blew outside also blew into and through the cell dispersing in its wake the stale, stagnant air. The Valley Wing was indisputably vastly superior in many ways to Block L. It was luxury, indeed.

After breakfast each morning in the Valley Wing, I exercised in the courtyard for about twenty to thirty minutes, except when it rained. Rain was a welcome relief as it cooled the cell. In the closed, cloistral conditions of cell L-9, I succumbed to the arms of Morpheus

---

3. See sketch at Appendix 2.

bathed in perspiration. In the Valley Wing, it was warm but airy. As I watched the sun trace its way daily across the heavens with its shadow lengthening across the inside wall of the cell, it occurred to me that the cell wall could be turned into a rudimentary sun dial. Soon, I could tell with reasonable proficiency the approximate time of day. Since I was now ensconced in the luxurious suite of the Valley Wing, with bathroom attached, there was no necessity for waking up the Gurkha guard in the dead of night to answer the calls of nature. This, too, was comfort.

The daily routine in the Valley Wing did not differ very much from that in Block L. We were awakened up at 7:30 a.m. each day without fail; and provided with breakfast. We did the morning's ablution and exercise and, if so minded, the laundry. Thereafter one settled down uneasily to await the dreaded summons for the assumption of sessions of rehabilitation, more crudely known as brainwashing.

15

Security

> Security is mortals' chiefest enemy.
> —William Shakespeare, *Macbeth*,
> Act III, sc.5, 32

Security was the watchword. It was tight at all times. In the name of security, detainees were discouraged from writing or composing poems and verses and drawings so that no covert or hidden messages were smuggled out through such means. Pen and paper were jealously guarded and rationed. Their application or use were under the jealous eyes of an ISD officer, who would send the completed labour of pen and ink for the censorship of his superior before it could be despatched to the addressee.

Simple English was the order of the day. Some noted literary works have incidentally been produced by persons whilst in captivity; but in Singapore, whether inside or outside of prison, the sterile environs, the inhibitive conditions are not conducive for great literary efforts. Creativity is suspect and discourages the production of even minor works. Soh Lung whiled away the heavy hours in sketching, drawing inspiration from the many genuses of insects in her cell, and composing laments to freedom and liberty. Some of her efforts found their way into magazines and publications of human rights groups when the flow of her aesthetic and literary efforts was suddenly stopped. The artistic efforts of K.C. Chew met a similar fate.

Detainees were locked up about twenty-three hours a day in solitary confinement in separate cells in separate male and female wings. Unlike ordinary prison life, where prisoners have opportunities to congregate for communal dining, recreation, or daily physical exercise, detainees however ate or exercised on their own in the strict privacy of their cells. In the 1987 mass arrests, some detainees were allowed to share cells and mix and mingle with one another, but in 1988, a stricter regimen was implemented "as punishment." Great care was taken to prevent contact and communication between the detainees. But, in spite of all these preventive measures, tidbits of news of arrest, detention, or release eventually filtered their way down to the detainees.

The administration tried hard to keep the inmates in the dark as to the identity and number of persons detained, especially during the early stages of interrogation. Notwithstanding stringent security arrangements, I ran into K.C. Chew, on two separate occasions, once, at Block C and, the other occasion, at the outhouse. We managed to exchange some brief pleasantries before the embarrassed guards hustled us along. These accidental encounters caused some consternation among the ISD officers in the Centre who feared these encounters "could create security problems for them." On February 20, 1989, K.C. Chew and another detainee were conditionally released as they had, according to the official statement, "responded positively to rehabilitation. The government is satisfied that they are unlikely to resume subversive activities and no longer pose a security threat."

The cells in the Valley Wing do not have a common party wall. There are six cells in a block. There is therefore no possibility of tapping on the wall coded messages to the detainee in the next cell. A narrow passageway divides the cells. Stories of communication by prisoners with one another through emptying out the water in the toilet bowls and using them as an internal underground telecommunication network belong to history, at least where the Centre is concerned. Some detainees were warned for trying to communicate with one another by throwing written messages through and over the wire mesh into adjoining cells, which is not an easy feat.

However, on the evening of the day I was transferred to the Valley Wing, I heard a detainee singing his heart out. I discovered later that the voice belonged to Kevin D'Souza, the young law graduate, who was among the eight ex-ISA detainees rearrested. On a couple of evenings, I did not hear him singing and, through discreet inquiries, discovered that he had been sent to the General Hospital for dental attention. I was told that one evening he sang out loud and long and did not stop when ordered to do so by the cell guard, who did not appreciate his musical talents or suspected that he was engaged in a lyrical passage of messages. His melodious persistence resulted in the Gurkha guard commander being summoned wherefore Kevin was subsequently deprived of privileges by a tin-eared administration. On March 11, 1989, he was released together with two other women detainees, after they had abandoned their renewed application for a writ of *habeas corpus*. But Soh Lung, who refused to cave in, had to undergo the full measure of her detention.

Counsel's Visits

On Wednesday, May 18, 1988—eleven days after my arrest—at 3:00 p.m., Howard Cashin, a senior lawyer and a dear friend, was allowed to see me. He brought news that Louis Blom-Cooper, a good friend, and an eminent English Queen's Counsel, whose forte is administrative law, happened to be in town and had agreed to represent me. Louis has since gone on to be the chairman of the U.K. Press Council, a prestigious appointment. Louis advised that I should not press immediately for a writ of *habeas corpus* but await the expiration of the one month when the minister for home affairs had to decide whether to release me or to order my detention for one or two years or whatever. I agreed to this course of action, although Ashleigh was, at the time, all gung-ho.

On Tuesday, May 24, 1988, at about 2:00 p.m., Howard came to see me again. I gathered that the public was skeptical of the government's allegations against me. The legal profession was sympathetic, but confused and afraid.

On Tuesday, June 14, 1988, at 3:00 p.m., Howard came to the Centre but could not see me, because of the unexpected visit by officers from the Commercial Crimes Branch, CID, who were interviewing me on Tang Tuck Wah's allegation of the offence of criminal breach of trust. The CCB interview took the best part of the afternoon. The

ISD officers were not particularly pleased at what they considered to be an intrusion into their sacrosanct precincts by CCB officers who, they felt, not without some justification, were trying to upstage them. I was quietly amused at this interdepartmental rivalry. Howard returned the next day to see me.

The MHA later released a press statement that Tang had retracted his monstrous allegation and admitted it was untrue. That night, Smiley Sim came into the interrogation room and spoke aloud to all who cared to listen to him that he did not think all along that Tang's allegation had any substance. "Francis Seow is not that kind of man. It was out of character." So, he claimed, he had told his superiors and all and sundry.

On Wednesday, June 22, 1988, at 2:30 p.m, Howard came to discuss the order of detention, the statement, and the allegation of facts on which the government relied as evidence of my being a security threat to the nation.[1] He promised to put up a draft representation to the advisory board for discussion.

On Friday, June 24, 1988, at 3:30 p.m., Howard returned with the draft representation, which, after some minor amendments, he submitted in due course to the chairman of the advisory board.

Family Visits

Visits are limited to once a week for half an hour by only two members at a time of a detainee's immediate family. A timetable was usually drawn up for visits by family members. The timetable was strictly kept. Any family visitor arriving late was allowed only the remaining time allotted for the visit. Distant relatives or friends were not allowed visits, except with special permission.

Family visiting days usually turned the Centre into a veritable beehive of activity. The personnel and logistics involved and the precision of times and movements required of the relative parties are not dissimilar to a minor military operation. Elaborate steps were executed to prevent the detainees from meeting one another through chance encounters.

---

1. See Appendix 3.

Because there was only one changing room, it was necessary to time the order the detainees were taken to the room to change into their own clothes, freshen, and groom themselves before being led out to the interview room. After the visit, they had to change back into their prison clothes.

On visiting days, or when the detainees were escorted out for interrogation, Gurkha guards were invariably on point duty at intersections within the Centre to direct pedestrian traffic so that no detainee would run into another one along the corridor either to or from his cell, changing room, or the interrogation room.[2] On those days, organized bedlam reigned as the Gurkhas shouted out in their incomprehensible language to one another warning of their approach down blind corridors with their charge. The absurd length to which the ISD went in the name of security to prevent these chance meetings within the Centre was reduced to nought, when the relatives and loved ones, all scheduled to visit on the same day within thirty minutes of each other, usually congregated beforehand at the foot of the hill where they traded the latest information with one another. As they say, even the best-laid plans can go awry.

Gift food parcels brought by visitors were carefully scrutinized to ensure that no unauthorised article was sneaked in with them. Home-cooked or prepared food was not permitted to be brought into the Centre. It was allowed during the days of the British *Raj* but, after Devan Nair and others revealed the methods used by their home folks to smuggle in messages to them through home-cooked curry meals, the practice was made forbidden.

Visits from members of the family provided a wonderful tonic to the spirit. The importance of pristine news to a detainee of the outside world cannot be over-emphasized. A letter or postcard or food parcel from loved ones or a friend could make a detainee's day and generate much feelings of joy and happiness.

Detainees are restricted to one incoming letter and one outgoing letter per week; but this restriction might be waived by the case officer. It is a great feeling to know one has not been forgotten, that one is missed and cherished, and that loved ones are waiting anxiously

---

2. See Appendix 2.

for the day of release. This spiritual and moral uplift is all-important to a detainee to sustain him or her through the long, dark, dreary days of detention.

Marjatta was gravely ill in an hospital in London, England, with only our daughter, Ingrid Annalisa, there to keep her company and minister to her needs. She was of the worrying kind, so Ashleigh and I swiftly agreed that the news of my arrest and detention should be kept away from her as it might aggravate her critical condition. It was, therefore, necessary that I should write to her as if nothing untoward had happened and, for this, Ashleigh provided me with a stack of blank picture postcards so that I could write to her, weekly. The charade ended even before it started.

Unbeknown to us, my sister Clare's son, Colin Looi, who was then finishing his master's degree in computer science at Cornell University, had read of my arrest in *The New York Times*. He had immediately telephoned his mother in Merritt, British Columbia with the dreadful news, and she in turn telephoned her eldest son, Mark, then in Ottawa. Mark contacted Amnesty International (AI), Canadian section and was referred to Margaret John, the irrepressible coordinator for Singapore and Malaysia, to whom he conveyed the news of my detention. Margaret advised Clare to approach her member of Parliament to raise the matter of my detention in the Canadian House of Commons to press for my release, which he did, and thereafter urged the Canadian government to take action. As in the 1987 arrests, Margaret, in the meantime, thrust AI's formidable machinery into top gear. The news of my detention was dispensed to journalists, the support of the Canadian government and sympathetic parliamentarians was sought, and AI members throughout the country wrote letters to the Singapore government. As AI Legal Network was about to generate further action, news of my release was announced. Mark, for his part, wrote to *The Wall Street Journal* highlighting my plight, whilst his wife, Susan, wrote to her U.S. congressman and, among the three of them, they had, in Ashleigh's words, burned the wires all the way from Merritt to Ottawa, to Washington, to London, and to Singapore agitating for my release.

Clare, who knew Marjatta was in London, contacted her about it. She was very upset and, although seriously handicapped by her illness, prodded Amnesty International, London and our English lawyer-friends and others to weigh in the good fight to secure my release. She bore the depressing news of my detention with characteristic Finnish *sisu*, a stoical calm and fortitude. Despite her own pain and suffering, she faithfully wrote to me weekly letters or postcards of love and prayerful concern. In this regard, the ISD, and my case officer in particular, were most compassionate in allowing me to receive and send her weekly loving letters and postcards. A great wife, a gracious and noble lady, and a wonderful mother to our children! Her untimely demise—*heu, pudet dictu!*—brought home to me a sense of prodigious loss, evoking within me the plaintive words of Othello, "whose hand like the base Indian, threw a pearl away richer than all his tribe."

The former chief justice of the Republic of the Philippines, Claudio Teehankee, and later permanent representative to the United Nations made a special visit to Singapore to see me in vain. He requested the Chief Justice Wee Chong Jin for assistance in arranging a visit to see me at the Whitley Detention Centre; but, as the chief justice was unable to do anything, Teehankee requested his own embassy to make the visiting arrangements. No approval was received from the Ministry for Home Affairs during his stay in Singapore, and he had perforce to leave the country. In any event, he left behind with the chief justice a book on his selected judgments, touchingly autographed, which came into my hands only after I was released.

I first met him in Manila, Philippines, at the International Conference on Constitutional Principles and Issues held in observance of the first anniversary of the Philippines' 1987 Constitution and the bicentennial of the United States Constitution, in February 17–20, 1988, and we became firm friends. But, before that, I had heard of him, by repute, as the intrepid Supreme Court judge, who had sworn in Mrs. Corazón Aquino as president, when it was considered not the politically correct thing to do. I had the pleasure of renewing our friendship in New York in the winter of 1988.

Giam Chin Toon, who succeeded me as the president of the Law Society, also tried to see me in vain. I also received a letter of encouragement and hope from a young Indian freedom fighter, a woman lawyer, Bahma Sivasubramaniam, whom I met at the Lawasia biennial conference in Kuala Lumpur, where I spoke vigorously on the arbitrary arrest and detention of the twenty-two young professionals under the ISA.

I was always very happy to see Ashleigh and André, who almost invariably brought gifts of fruits and food and, on one occasion, my niece, Caroline, who brought news of my mother who, in view of her age and health, was advised by my brothers from venturing a visit. I was equally happy to see my brothers, Gerald and George. They were like a tonic to my sometimes flagging spirits.

Ashleigh brought me news of Mei but, on Wednesday, July 6, 1988, I was especially thrilled to receive from her a solicitous letter dated June 19, 1988, care of the ISD, which really lifted up my sagging spirits and buoyed me up for many days. She ended the letter with a prayerful hope that I would be released in time to celebrate her birthday with her. All letters to or from the detainees were censored by the ISD. Her letter was similarly censored which probably accounted for the delay in reaching my hand. They knew the date of her birthday and, whenever opportunity arose, I reminded them of it and of her prayerful hope for my release before then. Solicitously, they inquired whether I had sent her a birthday card and suggested a bouquet of flowers through Interflora. I had sent it the Wednesday before her birthday through Ashleigh, who had been given special permission to visit me for discussion on an urgent legal problem with our London solicitors. This birthday card reportedly never reached her. To my constant inquiry as to a possible date of release, they were unable to say anything, as the decision lay in the lap of the prime minister. They had long ago stopped pretending that it depended on the decision of the younger ministers.

16

Method of Recording

> With as little a web as this will
> I ensnare as great a fly as Cassio.
>
> —William Shakespeare, *Othello*,
> Act II, sc. 1, 169

The softening-up period usually takes between forty-eight and seventy-two hours, involving deliberate physical and psychological abuse and harsh treatment, the intensity and length of which depends upon the psychological and physical make-up of individual detainees. The word "torture" normally evokes visions of medieval cruelty and violence, of racks, thumbscrews, and other exquisite instruments of pain and suffering. But the prime minister's version of the Spanish Inquisition is more subtle and no less effective. A detainee can be made to admit anything by the simple expedience of prolonged deprivation of his sleep—a most effective weapon in the ISD armoury of persuasion, which is its standard procedure.

Degraded and humiliated by being compelled to stand motionless, barefooted, and half-dressed or, worse, stark naked, in the cold, chilling air, before a fully-clothed ruffian band of aggressive inquisitors, confounded for hours on end by their relentless, strident barrage of questions interspersed with abuses and obscenities, and debilitated by long deprivation of sleep, a detainee in this extreme state of physical discomfort and psychological disorientation is easily reduced to a malleable and suggestible condition to agree to or make any statement desired by his tormentors. To hasten the disintegration process, physical force is freely administered and/or water is doused or sprayed over the detainee's naked torso. Many detainees have been known to plead in desperation for its cessation and clutch at vague promises of early release by making "cooperative" self-incriminating statements. A statement extracted by such methods is just as reprehensible as a statement extracted under ancient methods of torture. Brigadier General Lee Hsien Loong, in a BBC TV interview, in February, 1988, bragged:

> We have [not] in any way maltreated or ill-treated or tortured any of the detainees. ... We don't ill-treat people. We don't beat people.

And yet, in almost the very same breath, in a BBC World Service interview, admitted:

> The ISD does however apply psychological pressure on detainees to get to the truth of the matter ... the truth would not be known unless psychological pressure was used during interrogation.[1]

No one had stopped to ask him to clarify in detail the vaunted "psychological pressure." Remarks by Professor Jerome A. Cohen, former director of the East Asian Legal Studies, Harvard Law School, who visited Singapore on behalf of Asia Watch, the highly respected American human rights organization were quoted in *The New York Times*:

> "Given the ISD techniques, any statements from anyone detained used to substantiate the government's charges would be suspect. You can make your witnesses to order if you give them four or five days. They figure with soft people, the intellectuals, it's quicker." He found deeply disturbing both the use of psychological torture and what he called a "pervasive Singaporean, if not Asian view that if you haven't hit somebody, it isn't torture." Psychological disorientation is evil, whether it happens in South Africa, the Soviet Union, China, Singapore or the United States. Yet here they seem almost proud of their psychological tactics—of breaking down the defenses of people in captivity. They need to be more sensitive to the definition of what constitutes cruel and unusual punishment.[2]

Civilized people everywhere will find it difficult to disagree with the sentiments expressed in that statement.

---

1. *The Straits Times*, April 22, 1988.
2. *The New York Times*, May 12, 1988.

After the softening-up period, the detainee is usually told to write out his self-incriminating statement in accordance with the rehearsed scenario under the eye of ISD invigilators. As the statement is in the detainee's own handwriting, he would be hard put later to deny the voluntary nature of his statement.

In the instant case, the case officer, with the aid of another officer, Benny Lim, wrote it out after I had refused to do so; but, before he wrote it down, they went through with me the scenario and script on the American connection. How I had come to know Hank, our several meetings, the subjects of discussion at those meetings, the introduction of Joseph Snyder, and the subsequent meeting with him in Washington. Tan wrote it down, topic-by-topic on separate sheets of paper, aided by Benny, after which he sent the completed handwritten sheets through an ISD orderly to the administrative section upstairs where they were word-processed by the clerical staff.

A statement in draft was later returned to him, after which he corrected the mistakes, the English, the grammar, the words and phrases used, *et cetera*. He asked me to read it to see whether it reflected our earlier discussion, after which he sent it back for retyping. Benny was very useful in suggesting a word or words or a phrase or whole sentences whenever I disagreed with the text or substance as written by his ISD colleague.

The method of recording was such that the end result would inexorably wear an already physically exhausted detainee down to almost complete indifference. I remembered trying to read the first draft statement with as much care as I could muster and made several penned corrections which he sent back for retyping. While the first draft was being typed, Benny continued to record other matters or topics. There was no respite. The amended statement was later returned typed together with the original statement. I was asked to go through it. Brandishing the original statement with its corrections in his hand, he made a great play of tearing it up into two or four large pieces and, setting the torn segments ceremoniously aside, saying aloud more to himself than to me that he would discard them later. But they were in fact carefully preserved, as Minister for Home Affairs Jayakumar (who was the second minister for law) afterwards referred to them as supportive evidence of the voluntary nature of my statements. In the meantime, the ISD scribe found other mistakes in the typed statement and amended it. The amended statement was corrected and sent back for retyping. The retyped statement was brought back and, in exaggerated gestures of good faith, my scribe pointed out the parts he had corrected whilst remarking at the same time that he had "not inserted anything new." And then he would discover further typographical, grammatical, paragraphing, or numbering errors. It was sent back each time for retyping. Corrected new statements were produced. The statement was returned and one or another ISD officer who was assisting him would discover more typographical or punctuation errors and, after I had been asked to initial those particular corrections, the statement was repeatedly sent back for retyping.

As we came towards the end of the long recording ordeal, I was told the prime minister was very persnickety about the format of statements sent to him, which meant that it had to be typed again. The sequence of some paragraphs was found to be not in chronological order. The statement was changed and then I was told that the ISD research, formerly the collation unit, had cross-checked some events which, as stated therein, could not have occurred because they had not as yet taken place on the dates mentioned. A wrong sequential order of events would detract from the credibility of the statement, and had to be avoided at all costs!

After a profusion of editions and as we were about to complete the final version of the statement, several ISD officers warily sounded me about whether I really wanted the inclusion of certain comments on the prime minister *vis-à-vis* his relationship with Devan. The atmosphere in the interrogation room was no longer combative or hostile or even adversarial. It was guarded *bonhomie*. We had a lively discussion. They ventured their professional opinion that the inclusion of such comments in the statement would not help and, given the prime minister's known temperament, would certainly exacerbate the situation. "Well, you know the man. You have worked for him before. We leave it to you." I pondered it over. There was, of course, merit in the astute observation. This was, admittedly, not the time nor the place to do battle. The advantage was all with him. Better be a live adversary than a dead hero. I agreed to the deletion of luculent barbs from the statement, which necessitated another retyping. The paragraphs and the pages were renumbered and a fresh statement was produced for my perusal. I had to rely on their word that "nothing new" had been inserted.

Emboldened, another ISD officer suggested that I might also like to reconsider my pungent observations on S. Jayakumar, the minister for home affairs. After some animated discussion, I agreed to a similar deletion, after which the statement underwent the same procedure and result.

As we approached the end of the recording session, the statement had to be—to borrow Benny's pet *mot*—"fine-tuned" again; and was sent back to the research unit for one last final checking. They then disclosed somewhat diffidently that the allegations against Hank had been laid on "a bit thick," and should be "toned down." I had a silent chuckle over it. They were the authors, scenarists, and script-writers; I had vigorously objected to the story, but they had insisted on their inclusions. Weakly, they retorted that I had however agreed to them. So, once again, it was returned for deletion and amendment. I had lost count of the frequency of the amendments, alterations, additions, corrections, adjustments, and readjustments, deletions, and retyping of the statement. It was only a matter of time before one could no longer see the wood for the trees, become weary of the whole statement and begin to accept suggestions for change and accept the final statement as gospel. To say that there must have been at least a score or more of different editions of my statements would not be sheer hyperbole. There is much method in this seeming haphazardness and ineptitude. The end result was, to quote the imperious words of Professor Jayakumar at a press conference, "a craftily drafted document," an observation which many, and even I, would find it invidious to gainsay. The Oscars for production and direction, as well as screenplay and script, must unreservedly go to the ISD and its cast of talented officers. They had worked very hard at it. My contribution to craftsmanship was as minimal as it was unwilling. I was, therefore, not surprised to read that the principal and the supporting actors had been nominated and awarded the honours for their industry and creativity by the state in the National Day Honours List later that year. Speaking as dispassionately as I can, the awards were in my view well deserved. As related earlier, they had a deadline to meet and worked day and night on the statements to rush them through for the approbation of a fastidious prime minister the day after his return from his visit to Prime Minister Prem Tinsulanonda in Bangkok, Thailand.

Other ISD officers were also recording statements from me on the same topics. I repeated myself so often to so many of them, which they laboriously wrote down. What became of those same old statements, I do not know, but I suspect the object of this exercise was to check whether there were any deviations from the original version. This is an old but tried technique of interrogation. Whatever it was, there came a time when I objected having to cover the same ground over and over again with them. These secondary and tertiary statements were not shown to me although they were faithfully recorded.

Given the above circumstances, what, then, is the probative value of such a testament, albeit purportedly sanctified by an oath? None. It offends the fundamental canons of the law of every civilized country against the receipt in evidence of statements by any one, let alone detainees, made or given under any inducement, threat, or promise having reference to the charge against him.

17

Period of Rehabilitation

> We understand the mechanics of power.
>
> —Lee Kuan Yew[1]
>
> [I]f you can label a man ... as a Communist, then you can use administrative powers of arrest and detention without trial ... which means you just get stifled. ... you're scrubbed out.
>
> —Lee Kuan Yew[2]

On Monday, June 6, 1988, after the statements had been crafted by skilled and talented ISD draftsmen and approved by a pleased prime minister as hereinbefore stated, the period of rehabilitation began. During this period, which could be as long as several months, several officers took turns daily to "baby sit" the detainee, during which they silently assessed his response to rehabilitation which would form the basis of their recommendation for an early or delayed release. This period is also used to "mop up" bits and pieces of information, which had been neglected or overlooked during the interrogation.

An officer or officers beguiled the time in conversation with the detainee on topics with which he was comfortable, be they politics or otherwise. This was also the time when they would try to erase the detainee's ugly memories of induction into the Centre and to

---

1. Legislative Assembly Debates, July 30, 1963.
2. ABC Four Corner, Melbourne, Australia, March 29, 1965.

change his psyche by playing up their supposed personal or official difficulties, often ascribing them to the detainee's intransigence or lack of cooperation. Shades of the Stockholm syndrome! If a detainee was taciturn, they would not intrude upon his privacy but wait patiently for an opportune moment to win him over and ingratiate themselves into his good books. A far cry from the raging brutality of those early days! S.K. Tan used to say, with tongue-in-cheek, that every single detainee had complained about the frigid condition of the interrogation room, but he, too, was in the same room with him and had undergone the same privation. The fallacy of his remark was too apparent to need comment. And I let it pass.

I learned that the bar became restive upon my arrest and divided as to the course of action to take regarding it. But, as the shadow of fear lengthened across the profession, it was cowed into silence. One evening, they told me with grim satisfaction that the angry, surly bar was at long last settling down. I made no reply. I thought of the ancient Chinese proverb, "a closed mouth does not catch flies," and reminded myself to be wary of hidden traps or pitfalls even though our daily conversations seemed innocuous and cheerful enough. It was not easy to adhere to this sage advice unless, of course, one is a trappist. Man is naturally gregarious and craves the companionship of his fellow men. And, even if he is capable of weaving himself within a cocoon of silence, it might, nevertheless, be misinterpreted and end up as a minus factor in the rehabilitative process. This was the critical period, as already noted, when a detainee was being rated by his case and other officers whose recommendations were crucial to an early release.

I tried to steer these discussions into safer waters, but just as often found myself drifting into the murkier and more turbulent topical waters of national politics, the government, and its leaders. I spent several evenings reciting or discussing noncontroversial matters, like the works of Shakespeare and other English poets with them, especially with Benny Lim, whose partiality for Australian poets was understandable because he had studied in Australia. Director Tjong Yik Min, a 35-year-old Chinese-educated, engineering graduate of an Australian university, streamed in science, was all at sea. He was significantly a contemporary at school of the ambitious Brigadier General Lee Hsien Loong and appeared well-placed in his books, as, indeed, were other contemporaries and sympathizers across the civil service and the armed forces. Smiley Sim, on the other hand, seemed cut from a different cloth, a product of rugged Singapore and its university; he enjoyed those rehabilitative "evenings with Shakespeare" to such an extent that one evening he good-naturedly vociferated that ISD work would be much more pleasant if they had more detainees like me. I threw up my hands in horror, crying out in earnest, "*Heaven forbid!*"

We discussed the Pavlovian reaction of the younger cabinet ministers in agreeing to set up a commission to scrutinize the ex-detainees' accusations of torture and ill-treatment and then its abrupt cancellation. I had welcomed the announcement, and so had many other persons. I thought in this case the government had called for one commission of inquiry too many. The most conservative of judges would have had a near impossible task to close back the lid on the political can of worms once it had been opened, with an increasingly skeptical Singapore and the world's media focus on it. All it would have taken, to my mind, was to give the presiding judge "the long wait" in the interrogation room (as they do in the British Royal Navy, but in the boiler or engine room with unsuspecting visitors to naval ships) with the air-conditioner turned on full blast, as herein-described, for him to feel and accept the chilling truth of the cold treatment. Nothing like a personal experience to convince the most wayward of judges!

As I had long suspected, the announcement had been made without mature and proper consideration and, most incredibly, without reference to the department most affected by that decision—the ISD itself! The director and his senior officers disclosed their concern at the commission of inquiry, for no security agency in the world had ever withstood or survived intact the merciless and searching scrutiny for the truth, especially in an open inquiry before an impartial and independent tribunal. I could not agree more with him.

When the enormity of the possible horrendous consequences sank in the official consciousness, the government backtracked on its own stratagem. To box off its predicament, it came up with the bizarre idea of rearresting and detaining the signatories; and, dangling before them the prospects of immediate release, forced them to recant, on oath, the retractions of their "confessions and allegations of assault, abuse and torture," as if a solemn appeal to God as witness would sanction the truth of those retractions. Witness, alas, the infamous Spanish Inquisition! Aeschylus, the great Greek tragedian, once observed: "It is not the oath that makes us believe the man, but the man the oath." Writing in 1664, the English poet and satirist, Samuel Butler, seemed to have anticipated the People's Action Party:

> He that imposes an oath makes it,
> Not he that for convenience takes it;
> Then how can any man be said
> To break an oath he never made?[3]

But coming to more modern and recent times, the capital case of Samat Dupree, an odd-job Malay labourer, aged 30 years, who was charged in court with the murder of his friend, Salleh Misnin, an environment inspector, aged 38 years, graphically illustrates the perils of relying on "confessions" of prisoners in custody. Without any proper legal safeguards or the benefit of counsel, he "confessed" to the terrible accusation of murder, for which the supreme punishment is death by hanging! According to the Criminal Investigation Department, he had given a detailed statement admitting his guilt. But when he was finally allowed access to counsel, he protested his innocence. Fortunately for him, he was able to establish a cast-iron alibi—that he could not possibly have been at the *locus delicti* because he was away in Malaysia and had returned to Singapore three days after the death of the victim. His passport with its official date-stamps of entry into and departure from Malaysia put his contention beyond controversy. The public prosecutor, after verifying it, unreservedly withdrew the charge against him. The minister for law, S. Jayakumar, blandly stated later in Parliament that there was "no impropriety in the way the confession was obtained." He endeavoured to seek doubtful refuge in the fact that neither Samat Dupree nor his counsel had raised questions as to "voluntariness"

---

3. *Hudibras*, ib. pt. II [1664], canto I, l. 377.

of the confession or made "allegations of assault or threat until two years after it was made." The last word, however, properly belongs to Samat Dupree who, when he was questioned as to why he had made that hideous "confession" when he was totally innocent of the charge, remarked in pregnant prose: "I was scared. It's easy for people to ask why; but I am the one who suffered in the C.I.D." He refused to elaborate how he had suffered in the Criminal Investigations Department, except: "You never know what you are going to face in the C.I.D." He had spent two and a half years in jail awaiting his trial for a murder, which he had not committed."[4] In place of the name of Samat Dupree, substitute Teo Soh Lung and all the other detainees!

When I expressed profound skepticism at the alleged existence of a conspiracy to subvert the government and replace it with a Marxist state, they tried to convince me that there was indeed such a Marxist conspiracy involving my erstwhile clients. Tan Wah Piow, highlighted in the MHA statement as the mastermind, and Paul Lim Huat Chye were, they said, communists. But, as already noted elsewhere at length, the prime minister at a "secret" Istana meeting with Archbishop Gregory Yong, his priests, and the laity had contemptuously dismissed Wah Piow as "a simpleton" and "stupid" among other epithets, and the so-called conspirators, including my clients, as "novices" and "do-gooders." I was not aware of this secret assessment then, which was in direct contradiction to the MHA's own statement. There were reservations within the establishment itself that Lee and his government had overreacted in arresting the young professionals. Today, there is broad consensus that it was a bloody, knee-jerk action. What a high price those idealistic young social activists paid in terms of personal liberty!

On another day, I was told that Tang Fong Har was "definitely a communist." But when I requested for proof of it, they claimed they could not provide it for security reasons; but to believe them. I sometimes mused about whether her spunky statement to the BBC World Service from the relative safety of London, England, upholding the integrity of their joint press statement and pledging she

---

4. *The Straits Times Weekly Overseas Edition*, Saturday, March 20, 1993.

would work for the release of all the ex-detainee signatories, and of Chia Thye Poh, "for whom she had immense admiration," had anything to do with it. Needless to say, she, too, would have recanted the joint press statement had she been in Singapore and in the clutches of the ISD. Soh Lung was, they said, influenced by those persons, and I was being used by them. K.C. Chew was not a Marxist, and "should have concentrated on his business and not allowed himself to be used by [Tan Wah Piow and Paul Lim]" while Patrick Seong was arrested because he had become an irritant to their internal security operations and had to be taught a longlasting lesson. It was horrifying to observe with what insouciance the ISD speaks of the fundamental freedoms of an individual.

They freely conceded that the detainees' appearance on prime time television showing their "confession and contrition" in the Marxist conspiracy was, to quote them, "a total washout." It did not have the desired propaganda effect on the Singapore public for several reasons, in spite of the fact that the recordings were retaped several times. Firstly, given the time constraint, there were far too many detainees. Although TV Singapura was government-owned and -controlled television, it still could not allow prime time to be altogether swamped with "confessions." Thus, they had to compromise with a limited time slot, spread over several days. Because of the number of detainees involved, they were severely handicapped in creating and projecting a convincing tale to hold and maintain public interest. The difficulty was further compounded by the selected TV interviewers, who, instead of keeping to their prepared text and instructions, had departed from them, interrupted the detainees, and, in their eagerness to out-Harry Harry, put words into their mouths thus debasing the currency of several interviews. This revelation of their failure in the propaganda campaign confirmed what the public had already known or long suspected.

One day, Smiley Sim observed that my office newspaper clippings, *et cetera*, on the so-called Marxist conspiracy were more "thorough and complete" than the ISD own files on the subject. My press clippings were kept in two thick files and were among the numerous documents and files seized from my office by his department, which had made good its omissions, he said, by xerox-copying the "missing" pieces. For what it was worth, the ISD was apparently dependent to some extent on the Ministries for Foreign Affairs and for Culture for such information.

Inevitably, they repeatedly returned to the thorny theme of politics. Several officers counselled me against going into national politics, during which they used every possible blandishment and argument. I should concentrate on and worry about my law practice, rebuild it; or that, at my age, it would be much better for me to enjoy life rather than to descend into the rough-and-tumble of the political arena. I accused them of being responsible for the damage to my law practice; but the accusation washed over them with little or no apparent effect. With my patrician background and approach, they could not possibly imagine me in walkabouts in market places shaking hands with peddlars, hawkers, and shopkeepers, or kissing dirty-faced babies. To assuage their humour and end the colloquy, I agreed that they might well be right.

But the most disingenuous attempt to inveigle me away from opposition politics was the constant argument that, given Mei's status as a prohibited immigrant, if I were prohibited from leaving Singapore, I could no longer meet with her in Kuala Lumpur or elsewhere, save possibly at the international boundary in the middle of the Straits of Johore. Mei was a favourite persuasion ruse. They were aware that my outlook in and approach to life at the time revolved around her. And thus, on one particular day, Deputy Director Sim, unexpectedly brought up the vexed issue of her prohibition from entry into Singapore which, he hastened to add, had "absolutely nothing to do with the ISD or with national security." For what it was worth, he swore with almost convincing gusto that the ISD had maintained "no files" on her.

The general consensus was that the minister for home affairs had personally ordered Mei's prohibition after receiving a nod from the prime minister. But he promised, once my present matter had been satisfactorily settled, the ISD could assist in smoothing her eventual return to Singapore if it was informed beforehand, initially, for short visits on special passes, which could gradually be extended to normal social visits.

"Why was she declared a prohibited immigrant? What had she done? Was it not because of me?" I indignantly questioned him. "I cannot see any reason other than the fact that she is very close to me and that they are trying to hit at me through her," hastily proceeding to answer those questions myself.

"We do not know the reasons but, all I can say is, that it was a mistake," the deputy director, surprisingly, revealed.

"If it was a mistake, surely, it should be rectified immediately."

"As the case is now before Justice Sinnathuray, it would not be proper for us to intervene in the matter. If, however, a verdict is delivered in her favour, then, it will end there but, if it goes against her, we will still be able to assist in the matter."

I told him that I would hold him to his word. But he replied that only if I were to "behave" after my release and not create any problems for them, could I count on their assistance. There was a perceptible shift in the ISD stance. They urged that I "should renounce politics, marry her, and live happily ever after." There was very little to gain by going into national politics, especially at my age, and leave politics to younger men.

At other times, they asked me which constituency I would be standing in. "The Bedok constituency," I unhesitatingly replied. Although they knew the reason why, they nevertheless asked me why the Bedok constituency, in particular. By most accounts, the present incumbent, S. Jayakumar, was reputedly unpopular and disliked by his constituents but, whether it was true or not, I had no means of knowing. Jayakumar was the minister whose ministry was responsible for prohibiting Mei from entering Singapore. They maintained that the Bedok constituency should be the last of all the constituencies for me to contest in because Jayakumar might not be sympathetic to any application for Mei's return to Singapore. And so, this idle bantering went on day in and day out, night in and almost night out in the company of one or more ISD baby-sitters.

I was reminded times out of number that my case was not an ordinary one and that, before any decision could be taken, it had to go up to, and be approved by "the old man." On one occasion, an officer could not resist telling me:

"Well, you would not have created all this problem for yourself, if you had not confronted him in the Select Committee."[5] Such a remark presupposed that I had deliberately sought a confrontation with the prime minister and his government. This could not be further from the truth. As already related, I was subpoenaed a reluctant witness to appear before the Select Committee. So were the other members of my Council. We went there in the *bona fide* belief that we were going to debate the relative merits of the proposed Legal Profession (Amendment) bill, but none of us had anticipated the vicious *ad hominem* attack on Council members. Every now and again, an officer unctuously opined that the ISD had done all that it could for me—and the matter of my continued detention now lay in the laps of their political superiors but, as my case was a special one, it had to go even higher up for a decision. This continual avowal annoyed me for it belied the prime minister's oft touted claim that he had nothing to do with the arrests because the second echelon leaders were running the country. But when I reminded the officer of this claim, he just shrugged his shoulders. He wished me for my pains a world of sighs that, if it were at all possible, "the old man," Devan, and I, the three of us, should be locked up together in a room and each be given a pair of boxing gloves to slog it out and so save them all a lot of trouble. This little episode revealed more than anything else that my detention under the ISA had little to do with the American connexion or with national security.

Looking back, it is possible to see that, given his paranoia about America and Americans and his deeply suspicious nature, the prime minister imagined that he had a plausible case of an American black operations from a few stray straws in the wind. In an over zealous attempt to instruct his younger colleagues on how to handle a perceived dispute with a superpower, he overrode their better judgment and the ISD's report and recommendation and blew it out of all proportions from nothing to an American black conspiracy. Upon the realization that there was nothing more to it than his merest suspicions, he downplayed the allegations in Parliament by a novel

---

5. Select Committee on the Legal Profession (Amendment) bill, (Bill No 20/86) October 9–14, 1986.

suggestion that they be referred to an independent committee of three international experts knowing full well that no self-respecting nation would ever agree to it and, *ergo*, the matter would, hopefully, fade quietly away.

In the meanwhile, my law firm required the use of the books of accounts, the files, and documents seized by the ISD. After repeated requests, they finally agreed to return them. I was quite relieved because my accounts clerk, Serlene Ng, had been pestering Ashleigh and me to request for their return. Coincidence of coincidences, on the very day and at the very time the books of accounts were returned to my office, the Inland Revenue officials were waiting there for them. Suspecting that they were working in cahoots with one another, Ashleigh refused to accept the books from the ISD and suggested that the ISD hand them directly to the Inland Revenue officers. But the ISD officers however strenuously denied the collusion, claiming the day and time of their arrival were purely coincidental. The Inland Revenue officials insisted, on the other hand, that the books of accounts be returned first to the firm. And so, they were ceremoniously handed over to Ashleigh only to have them taken away within seconds later by the tax department. My accounts clerk Serlene was no better off in possession of her account books than before.

18

On the Eve of the Day

> It is the professionalism and the integrity of the ISD which is crucial ...
>
> —Lee Kuan Yew[1]

Friday, July 15, 1988, at about 8:30 a.m., whilst I was in the shower, a Gurkha guard rapped lustily at the door and called out through the peep hole in halting English to dress up because I was wanted at the office. I thought the day of release had come. My heart leapt up. I hurriedly completed my shower, changed, and accompanied him there. I was disappointed to be taken to a room to be photographed with number 1-406-661, finger- and palm-printed, after which I was returned to my cell. This procedure is amongst the preliminaries attended to when one is first admitted as an honoured house guest of the prime minister and the ISD.

The afternoon of that day dragged ever so slowly by.

According to the routine, which was by now well-established, I would be in the interrogation room in the company of one or more officers daily until about 8 p.m., when I would be escorted back to my cell for the night. It was part of the so-called rehabilitative procedure. At times, other ISD officers would stop by a while for a chat. On this particular evening, Director Tjong dropped in. I hailed him with the customary question whether he had any good news for me. On this occasion, poker-faced, he answered: "Bad news." My

---

1. *The Straits Times*, May 28, 1988.

heart sank. He then asked me when the advisory board was due to meet on my representations. I told him, "On Saturday next." Sphinx-like, he remarked somewhat self-evidently, that if I was going to be released, there was not much point for the advisory board to meet on my representation, because Justice Sinnathuray was overburdened with work, having sat on the recent Tun Mohamed Salleh Abas tribunal in Malaysia,[2] (which recommended his dismissal from office as Lord President of Malaysia). I was perplexed. To my further inquiry as to whether he had any indication of the probable date of my release, he pompously replied: "Well, use the date of the sitting of the advisory board as a bench-mark and work it out yourself." I was not quite sure what to make out of his statement. My inner feelings, however, cried out loud that the day of release was close at hand, which seemed to be borne out by his next remark that it would be in my best interest not to issue any press statements after my release from the Centre; and, strangely I thought, pressed me for an immediate agreement to it. I had earlier promised S.K. Tan that, immediately after my release, I intended to leave for Malaysia and, whilst there or on any foreign soil, I would not issue any press statement. He commented that I should not issue any press statement at all, as it might create further complications that might result in my rearrest and return to the Centre.

"Once released, I have not the slightest intention of ever returning to it."

"In that case, you would be wise to heed my advice, and eschew politics altogether because, in my honest opinion, you would get nowhere."

"I will chew over your advice on not issuing press statements."

"You are trying to fob me off with your reply," he responded. "Well then, chew it over the night and let my officer know tomorrow."

With that final remark, he ended a perplexingly brief conversation which however bristled with hope; he left us, accompanied by his

---

2. See *May Day for Justice* by Tun Mohamed Salleh Abas, Magnus Books, Kuala Lumpur. Cf. *Judicial Misconduct* by Peter A. Williams, Q.C., Pelanduk Publications (M) Sdn. Bhd.

usual entourage of officers. He had never been as cryptic as this before.

Left to ourselves, the ISD officers and I had a lively speculation for the next hour or so on his remarks which seemed pregnant with promise, revolving around the probable dates of release. I gleaned from our discussion that the prime minister was not in Singapore and had gone on an official visit to Korea, Japan, and Taiwan. My release required his specific approval. They stressed again for the umptieth time that my case was not an ordinary one. They had dropped all pretence as to who was the directing force behind my arrest and upon whose critical goodwill my release now depended. He would, however, be returning to Singapore on the night of Thursday, July 14, 1988. And, as if I was not appreciative of that fact, they laid great stress that, "He is a busy man." The second generation leaders were supposed to be in charge and should therefore be in the position to determine my release. But I was stonewalled once more with the monotonous refrain that my case was not an ordinary one. It was idle to pursue the matter.

I went back to my cell that night, my senses all a-tingling that something positive was finally afoot, and that the day of my release was imminent. But the tantalizing question was: Would I be released in time to celebrate with Mei her birthday in Kuala Lumpur?

19

A Summer Bird—July 16, 1988

> O Westmoreland, thou art a summer bird,
> Which ever in the haunch of Winter sings
> The lifting up of day.
>
> —William Shakespeare, *Henry IV,*
> *Part 2*, Act IV, sc. 4, 91

I had spent an uneasy, restless night. My mind kept straying back to Mei and Director Tjong's equivocal words the night before. They did seem promising enough then but, as the morning dawned, his words and the prospects of release did not look as promising. As the morning hours crept on, I became more and more resigned to the fact I might not be released after all and would not be able to be in Kuala Lumpur the next day. I thought of writing Mei a note that I might perhaps be out soon when we could have a belated birthday celebration.

At about 10:40 a.m., I was escorted by a Gurkha guard to the interrogation room. Because Saturday was a half day, the fact that I was in the interrogation room a little earlier than usual did not strike me as odd. All the familiar faces were there. We exchanged the usual pleasantries and chatted on matters of inconsequence. We were going through the daily ritual of ordering lunch *à la carte* when, at about 11:00 a.m. or so, Deputy Director Sim walked in.

"Well, you are being released today," said Smiley Sim, with the characteristically broad smile on his well-tanned face.

Strange as it might seem, I, who had been longing for release, was not ready for it when it came. I had pestered my captors daily with the ritual question, "When will I be released?" And yet, now that I was told it, I was terribly afraid it might not be true. I could not believe my ears. It might be a cruel hoax. I stared at him and in what seemed like eternity blurted out,

> "You are not joking, are you?"

> Still smiling benignly, he replied: "This is too serious a thing for a joke. I am telling you, you are being released today, but subject to restrictions."

I sat there momentarily bereft of words. Then joy and jubilation swept over me. It was good, heady news, great news. I would be released at 1:00 p.m.

A MHA press release would be issued at 3:00 p.m., but embargoed for publication until 5:00 p.m., which should give me sufficient time to avoid the press corps and make a quiet and uneventful retreat to Kuala Lumpur. With his face still creased in smiles, he said:

> "You see, I have not forgotten Mei's birthday. This is the best birthday present for her."

There and then, I applied for permission to depart Singapore for Kuala Lumpur. It was telefaxed to Phoenix Park, where the Internal Security Department now has its main office, and, within the hour, permission was received. I could hardly suppress my feelings of joy from bubbling all over. Smiley Sim reiterated that he had remembered July 17 was Mei's birthday and had tried to secure my release before then. In this respect, he observed that the prime minister, who had just returned from a long and apparently successful overseas journey, could have easily put aside the question of my release until much later, but that he had not done so. I did not know whether I was supposed to be grateful or not, but I held my counsel.

They tried to contact Ashleigh to come over to the Centre at 12:00 p.m., ostensibly for a special family visit; but, in truth, to execute a bond for the suspension of the order of detention. As they could not locate him, they contacted my brother, George, instead.

They managed later to contact and inform Ashleigh of my release that day and requested him to come with his wife, Eliza, to the Centre to execute a bond in a sum of one thousand dollars, subject to two conditions:

    (i) that I shall not travel beyond the limits of Singapore without the prior written approval of the Director, Internal Security Department, Singapore;

    (ii) that I shall not associate, or be in communication, with any foreign diplomat or representatives of any foreign government whether in or outside Singapore.

Ashleigh and Eliza both executed the necessary documents but, because the processing took some time, they were asked to return at 2:15 p.m., with the injunction not to disclose the news of my release to any one yet. When the ISD officers later discovered that my mother was not in favour of my descending into the political arena, they wished they had known of it earlier for they would have preferred her as guarantor. Just fancy that!

In the meantime, the ISD officers gave me a farewell luncheon during which a senior officer said:

> "Our advice to you is not to go into politics," adding, as an after-thought, "But, if you do and win, remember you will still need the ISD."

It was a comment with which I was not entirely in disagreement. 2:15 p.m. came; but Ashleigh was nowhere to be seen, which gave us, especially me, some anxious moments. I wanted to put as much distance as I could between the Centre and me in the shortest possible time. It transpired that he had been caught in a traffic gridlock, delaying his return to the Centre. Most of the ISD officers were there to see me off. It was weird and unreal, as if I were going off on a long official sojourn with all the household staff out in the driveway in attendance. I, for my part, was not unhappy to shake the dust of Whitley Detention Centre from off my feet.

At 5 p.m., a terse MHA press statement stated:

> The Government has today released Francis Seow on a Suspension Direction with two restrictive conditions. [As mentioned above.] The Suspension Direction will be revoked if Seow acts in any manner prejudicial to the security of Singapore or breaches any restrictive condition.

CHAPTER 19

My hair had overgrown during my enforced stay in the Centre, as I had declined the services of the prison barber in whose tonsorial skill I reposed no great confidence whatsoever. Without disclosing my identity, Ashleigh had thoughtfully made an appointment with my longtime hairdresser that afternoon. When I walked into his salon, my hairdresser was glad but not surprised to see me. He uncannily had suspected that the appointment was for me.

Thereafter I hurried over to Beverly Mai, gathered a few necessary things together, went over to Ashleigh's apartment, and made the necessary phone calls to inform my dear wife, Marjatta, in London of my release; she was delirious with joy at the news. I then made a beeline for Changi International Airport. As a precautionary move, Ashleigh thought he should accompany me. Whilst we were in the airport MAS Golden Lounge waiting for departure, he mixed a glass of Johnny Walker Black Label whisky and soda with lots of ice in just the way I liked it. It stood there until near to departure time. When I finally brought myself to take a sip, the taste was wondrous strange. It had been seventy-two days too long!

Epilogue

> If we are to survive as a free democracy, then we must be prepared, in principle, to concede to our enemies—even those who do not subscribe to our views—as much [sic] constitutional rights as you concede yourself.
>
> —Lee Kuan Yew[1]

Like baying bloodhounds in full cry, the media tracked me down to Shah Alam, Selangor, Malaysia, where I was recuperating at Mei's brother's home from the black hole of Singapore. But, mindful of the promise I had made on the eve of my release to soon-to-be-promoted-and-decorated S.K. Tan that I would make no political statement on this special occasion whilst on foreign soil, I declined comments.

On August 1, 1988, I returned to Singapore where I found an A.R. Registered ten-page letter dated July 20, 1988 from the Inland Revenue department. It had been date-stamped "received" on July 30 by my law firm in my absence. The letter directed me to answer certain queries concerning my previous twelve years' tax returns within 35 days from the date of receipt, that is to say, by September 3, 1988, failing which "legal proceedings may be instituted against you under section 94 of the Income Tax Act." The prime minister was keeping the pressure on. No one, save the prime minister, knew that the general election was just weeks away, or that polling day

---

1. Legislative Assembly Debates, September 21, 1955, Vol. 1, col. 726.

had been fixed on September 5. My ISD inquisitors knew, and through them he, that I intended to participate in the next general election, despite all their efforts to dissuade me from it. Thus, if I were kept preoccupied with answering tax queries, there would be precious little time for me to wage any meaningful campaign. And better yet still, if I were charged in court with tax offences, much valuable political capital could be made out of them without troublesome human rights groups breathing down the neck of the authorities crying out "foul." It would be a tax summons case by itself. But the artful author-protagonist of this scenario was conspicuously absent from view, like Hamlet without the Prince.

On August 5, I sought the private and informal advice of my former accountants, who were anxious they were not known as still being associated professionally with me and my firm. On their advice, I wrote to the Inland Revenue department that—

> ... I have just been released from detention. My office is in complete disarray as a result of the ISD search. I have to put it back to businesslike and working order.
>
> As regards your queries, it is absolutely necessary for me to go through the voluminous records, as well as my mental recollections to reply adequately to you. As you are well aware, all the accounts books of the firm have been taken away by you. In this connexion, I shall, also, need the assistance of my present and former accountants to assist me.
>
> In the circumstances, and subject to my accountants' availability for inspection of the accounts books and discussions thereon, I shall appreciate if you will let me have an extension of 3 months to clear the above matter.

I also sought professional advice from my current firm of accountants who confirmed that the request for a period of 3 months was not unreasonable in the circumstances bearing in mind that the firm's account books had been seized by the ISD and then by the Inland Revenue department (which had refused to return them.) Time and again, members of my staff were inconvenienced by having to go to the department to seek clarifications on past accounts or to take copies of them. To say that the firm was inconvenienced by the department's unnecessary detention of its books of accounts was a gross understatement. It was another price to pay for being in bad odour with the paramount leader and his government.

On August 6, I issued a press statement on my arrest and detention:

> The Internal Security Act (ISA) was introduced to prevent subversion and suppress organized violence by communists or other persons who intend to overthrow a lawfully constituted government. It was never intended to suppress or stifle legitimate and honest voices of dissent, criticism or comment, however unpalatable and unpleasant, of government policy or action. It was never intended to besmirch the good name and reputation of any person for party political purposes. It was never intended to perpetuate the rule of any political party or as a means to obtain information on any persons for party political ends. It was, in fact, intended to safe-guard the security of the realm. Unfortunately, recent events tend to indicate the ISA has been much abused. For well is it truly said that security is like liberty in whose name many crimes are committed. Therefore, it behooves every Singaporean to scrutinize government statements justifying arbitrary arrests and detentions—the price of liberty is eternal vigilance. ...
>
> It is a well-known fact that the ISD is provided with an awesome arsenal of weapons in the war against subversion and organized violence. Therefore, the ISD has the grave responsibility to use them with scrupulous restraint. But, more importantly, Singaporeans should be ever alert that these weapons are not misused politically to the detriment of the honest critic or dissenter. ...
>
> Following my first public criticism of Government legislation—the Newspaper and Printing Presses (Amendment) bill—several government departments began to take an interest in my affairs and, most recently, the Comptroller of Income Tax invoked his powers under the Income Tax Act, and requested particulars of my assets and liabilities for the last twelve years. A formidable undertaking by any standard! A firm of accountants declined to act half way necessitating a change of accountants. Investigations such as these, of persons who may aspire to political office, are seen to be an unworthy way to discourage political criticism or aspirations. ...
>
> The Government has extended to me an invitation to contest the next General Election. It would be truly churlish not to accept the invitation even though the Government has mined the road there with obstacles and hazards.

On August 10, the Comptroller of Income Tax, feigning umbrage at the above statement, replied that—

> The facts clearly show that your application for another three months is groundless. *Additionally, you have by your statement to the Press [dated August 6] shown that you have no intention of complying.* [Emphasis added]

How on earth he could come to that erudite conclusion without ever having spoken to me baffles me to this very day! Be that as it may, on August 11, *The Straits Times* published a letter from an agitated Inland Revenue department:

> The political leadership has never been involved. This is the essence of tax philosophy and tax administration.

A wry statement in the circumstances! I wondered then, and, in the tranquillity of academic Harvard some years removed from those turbulent days, I still wonder: who was kidding whom? That same morning, I had scarcely turned over the last sports page of the morning's newspapers when into my office walked a court process server, accompanied by an underling from the Income Tax department. They rudely served me with summonses to appear before the subordinate courts to answer six alleged tax evasion charges, when only 14 days into the aforesaid period of 35 days had barely elapsed. The impatient department had unilaterally rescinded the time within which it had given me to answer its queries. It was most irregular. And, in my long experience in the administration of justice on either side of the bar, such arrogant bureaucratic conduct and behaviour were wholly unprecedented. The return day on the summonses was August 16, 1988—only five days away! This was certainly not a case of justice being delayed, but rather a case of justice being hastened and denied—for nefarious political ends!

On August 12, 1990, I issued a press statement setting out the chronological events of my encounter with the Inland Revenue department culminating in those tax evasion charges, and ended with these questions:

> Why has the department served summonses on me before I even have had a chance to reply to them within the period stated by them? Who ordered that the 35 days' period be cancelled without even letting me know? Why has the department's case against me been suddenly accelerated for no apparent reason? Why do they appear no longer to be interested in my reply? Why does a civil servant refer to my press statement (made on political matters) as the reason why no extension of time will be given to me and my accountants? Why does he consider my issuing a political statement to be an indication that I will not comply with a legitimate departmental request?

In hindsight, all the answers point clearly to and end at Government Hill. On the same day, I sent another letter to the Inland Revenue department (to which I never received a reply) that—

> ... I am advised that my request for an extension of time is a reasonable one in the circumstances. It should not be you who decide what documents are relevant for my defence and I may want to look through all the firms's account books and records in addition to those photocopies which you have sent me.
>
> I am also at a loss to understand the last sentence of your letter [of August 10]. On what grounds do you reach the conclusion that I will not comply with your department's request, when I have already written to you on the very matter?
>
> I trust that you will reconsider and provide me with the requested extension of three (3) months.

On August 16, at 9 a.m., pursuant to the judicial summons, I attended Court No. 13 with my counsel, Vinod K. Dube, an impassionate and knowledgeable Indian lawyer. The court was packed with press reporters, alerted by the tax department officials. Contrary to normal procedure, the prosecutor, State Counsel Jiang Siew Ming, pressed the judge with a vehemence rarely seen in court for the charges to be read out, a plea to be taken on them, and early dates to be set for trial. Dube objected to this prosecuting zeal, submitted no plea should be taken at that stage of the proceedings, and the case adjourned for mention to a later date, so as to enable the defence, amongst other things, to consult professional advisors. After listening to submissions from both the prosecution and the defence, the youthful Daniel, nodding in agreement, ordered that no plea be taken and adjourned the case for three weeks to September 6, for mention again before him in Court No 13. Judicial wisdom and independence had momentarily triumphed. The matter having ended, Dube and I left the courtroom and I, the building. I proceeded to the High Court and to another appointment.

The magistrate's decision to adjourn the case for mention to September 6 had inadvertently upset the prime minister's carefully laid out election plans. He had earmarked September 3 as polling day. And if no plea was taken until past polling day, it would be rather awkward to capitalize on it in the forthcoming hustings. Wherefore it was necessary to reverse the morning tide of events, for, before the day was well out, we were to witness unparalleled drama in court. Shades of executive interference fell darkly across the scene!

About an hour later, at about 10:30 a.m., Dube was still relaxing in the bar room of the Subordinate Courts' Building, savouring the morning's forensic encounter, when a registry clerk approached him to say that Alfonso Ang, the registrar of the Subordinate Court, a senior judicial officer, wished to see him in his chambers. Puzzled at this request, Dube went to see Ang, who informed him that he [Ang] had been *"directed"* to tell him that he was to appear again, together with me, in Court No. 13 at 2:15 p.m., the same day. He stressed it was an order, lest we misunderstood it as a casual invitation. No reason was given. My counsel was taken aback and, suspicious and uneasy at what this singular order might portend, tried to locate me without success. An unseen sinister hand was at work.

At 2:15 p.m., Dube duly appeared alone to inform the magistrate of his and my law firm's inability to reach me. The magistrate stood the case down to 4 p.m. so as to allow him further time to contact me. I was, however, in another part of the city blissfully unaware of this strange and disturbing turn of events. Promptly at 4 p.m., the court reconvened, and the zesty tax prosecutor forcefully renewed his morning's application that the charges be read out and a plea taken. Confronted with such an unusual request, the discomforted magistrate asked him the purpose of reading the charges in my absence. Ordinarily, this unexceptional, modest chore belongs to the usher of the court, who would read out the charges in his town-crier's best across the void of the court room to the defendant, who is asked how he pleads to them. The prosecutor's insistence over the strenuous objections of the defence carried the day. Overwhelmed by the exuberance of executive authority as personified in the prosecution, justice reclined painfully back to witness the sorry spectacle of a quixotic prosecutor usurping the usher's role by reading out aloud the charges to an absent and invisible defendant, and then asking him as to how he pleaded to them. The resulting silence was reportedly deafening. A comic performance capable of rivalling the best of Gilbert and Sullivan! But, alas, it speaks volumes on the administration of justice in Singapore!

Epilogue

Emboldened by the success of his forensic skirmish, the prosecutor next instructed the magistrate that the mention date should be changed and brought forward to August 18 in Court No. 13 at 2:30 p.m., despite my counsel's vigorous objections that the court earlier had already fixed September 6 as the mention date. The court was *functus officio*, and for the court to reverse itself was to create an unhealthy, if not illegal, precedent. Dube was terribly upset that the prosecutor was virtually directing the court what to do. And, alas, for the defence, the court yielded to the demands of the overbearing prosecutor and, in a vain attempt to repair his shattered authority, told my counsel that if I did not attend court on the new date and time, he would issue a warrant for my arrest.

My counsel had beheld a judicial somersault of no mean proportions. In striking contrast, the tax summonses of other defendants that day were adjourned for mention or trial to about the middle of the new year. I was being singled out for this unsought honour of a swift and speedy trial to the absurd extent that the bumbling prosecutor was able to brush aside all legal niceties and procedure. The court had acted in a highly unusual manner and contrary to the criminal procedure code and the accepted norms of practice. That same evening, upon being made aware of the incident, I instantly instructed my counsel to petition the High Court for a revision of the magistrate's decision.

On the next day, August 17, Dube and I went to the Supreme Court Registry to file the petition for revision which threw the registry staff into a state of nervous excitement and tension as to whether it was in order to accept it. Eventually, after some to-ing and fro-ing, the petition was accepted by the registry for filing. Dube and I then waited for a free judge to hear the application but, notwithstanding its urgency, not one judge was reportedly free. The emergency duty judge that day was Justice Sinnathuray; he was not immediately available. After being assured we would be informed when he was able to hear it, we left the Registry. We heard nothing throughout the whole day, even though we had held ourselves out ready to appear in court at a moment's notice. Upon inquiry the *next* morning, we were informed the petition had been dismissed by Justice Sinnathuray. No reason was given for the dismissal. Justice can be as swift and as summary, without even the presence of the applicant, when circumstances warrant it.

On August 18, I appeared in the magistrate's court with Dube. The usher of the court read out the charges and asked me to plead. I protested at the gross procedural irregularity of the court reversing its own order in my absence and refused to plead until my accountants and I had a full opportunity to study all the relevant books and documents (which were still in the possession of the Inland Revenue department), when I would be in a better position to plead. In view of my stand, the court recorded a plea of "not guilty." When the prosecutor, no doubt acting on specific instructions, applied for the case to be transferred to Court No. 14 for trial in a district court (which has powers of imposing harsher penalties), it was granted forthwith without argument.

There, the prosecution astounded us further by requesting for the trial to take place in the waning thirteen days left of August, as it was, after all, he airily claimed, "a straightforward case." This was fortunately impossible. Perusing hard the court's calendar, the Registrar first asked the prosecutor for dates convenient to the prosecution, and without further ado set the case down for hearing on December 5–23, 1988, the earliest dates available, over my counsel's vigorous objections at the prosecution's obscene haste for an early trial. Given the egregious pressure on the Subordinate Courts' calendar, it was a superlative achievement, a remarkable juggling of dates and cases, as cases were being set down for hearing well into the next year. The reason for this unseemly haste became all too clear—when, within a few days thereafter, Parliament was dissolved and the general election announced. Polling day was fixed on September 3!

Considering the above, my faith in the integrity and independence of the judiciary, already shaken, was completely shattered. Regrettably, I instructed my counsel to apply for the trial to be transferred from the District Court to the High Court where, unlike trials commenced in the subordinate courts, the avenue of appeal leads up to the august Judicial Committee of the Privy Council, Singapore's own ultimate and independent court of appeal in London. Wherefore in this context, it is most apposite to recall the infallible advice of the prime minister to future governments, whether PAP or no:

> *I can only express the hope that faith in the judicial system will never be diminished, and I am sure it will not, so long as we allow a review of the judicial processes that takes place here in some other tribunal where obviously undue influence cannot be brought to bear. As long as governments are wise enough to leave alone the rights of appeal to some superior body outside Singapore, then there must be a higher degree of confidence in the integrity of our judicial process. This is most important.*[2] [Italics added]

What pearls of wisdom! What rare prescience! What prophetic vision! With his unique "over-the-horizon radar vision"[3]—since upgraded to satellite vision—the prime minister had foreseen that "undue influence" could be brought to bear on our courts, and rightly sounded the warning on judicial integrity and independence! The situation has not changed. In truth, it has become more critical than ever to restore and maintain a superior judicial body outside Singapore to do justice between the state and the people, and vice versa. To digress for a moment. When Singapore was a constituent state within the Federation of Malaysia, I recall an apprehensive prime minister telling Singapore law officers to resist any attempts by the federal government to abolish appeals to the Privy Council, of which he then stood in genuine dread. We were told it was the last independent judicial bulwark which Singapore and its leaders had against any encroachment by the federal government on the Constitution and the fundamental freedoms. Events in Singapore since the utterance of those memorable words have only served to reinforce the profundity of that statement.

Fearful of executive influence and confident that I would be convicted in any event by a pliant court, I had laid great store on this important avenue of appeal to the Privy Council in London, "where obviously undue influence cannot be brought to bear," and where true and unsullied justice can still be expected. Thus, on or about November 25, 1988, my counsel moved the High Court for the transfer of the case to itself, but Justice Lai Kew Chai held, dismissing the

---

2. Parliamentary Debates, March 15, 1967, cols. 1294–5.
3. See Parliamentary Debates on the Group Representation Constituency bill, March, 1988.

application, that "district judges are perfectly competent" to try such cases and that "all accused persons should be treated equally regardless of status."[4] We were not discussing judicial competence or equality before the law—an elementary legal principle which all law students learned at law school—but, not necessarily, the keen difference between theory and practice with all its myriad nuances!

Knowing that the prime minister was or might be interested in a case, it would take a brave and courageous judge—some would even say reckless—to do real justice to the parties. A statement made by Soviet Deputy Vladimir I. Denisov of President Mikhail Gorbachev, then at the acme of his political power, before the Supreme Soviet might not be out of context here:

> No Supreme Court judge in this country would dream of judging against him in his worst nightmare.[5]

I have been too long in the service of the state not to know the consequences of an unexpected decision by a free and independent judge. There is no need to dwell on the permutations of governmental action in such a phenomenon. The recent case of Senior District Judge Michael Khoo, a judge of Supreme Court timbre, who was unwittingly dragged into the political amphitheatre by opposition MP J.B. Jeyaretnam following a reversal of judgment in his favour only to be cruelly derided by the prime minister for alleged judicial incompetence, is an object case in point. Khoo was subsequently vindicated by the Privy Council, but the judgment came too late, for he resigned the legal service to enter private law practice.

As long as their lordships in the Judicial Committee of the Privy Council delivered decisions favourable to the PAP government, the merits and advantages of an independent Privy Council in Singapore's judicial system continued to be extolled by the government. When, however, on November 21, 1988, they allowed the appeal of the prime minister's *bête noire*, lawyer and former opposition MP J.B. Jeyaretnam, and delivered a judgment critical of the decision of the Supreme Court, I knew the fate of the Judicial Committee of the Privy Council had been sealed. To the intense discomfiture of the

---

4. [1990] 3 Malayan Law Journal 410.
5. See *The New York Times*, Wednesday, February 28, 1990.

Singapore judiciary and the government, their lordships recorded "their deep disquiet that by a series of misjudgments the appellant [Jeyaretnam] and his co-accused suffered a grievous injustice. They had been fined, imprisoned and disgraced for offences of which they were not guilty."[6] Less than two months thereafter, the law minister moved in Parliament the abolition of appeals to the Privy Council by errant lawyers on the spurious and specious ground that their Lordships in London "were out of touch with local conditions." This selfsame minister, as late as January 1986, had unabashedly lavished undiluted praise on it as "the litmus test of our judicial system's independence."[7] At about the same time, the government acted to remove the supervisory jurisdiction of the courts in ISA cases which, in the words of the attorney general, is "one of the most important safeguards against the arbitrary exercise of power." It is useful to recall his sonorous remarks before a full bench of judges of the Supreme Court and the bar at the ceremonial opening of the 1977 legal year, on the unquestioned value of judicial review:

> Your lordships' impartial and unbiased administration of the law in all matters, particularly in respect of those matters requiring strict observance of the rules of natural justice, and in respect of matters where the exercise of administrative discretion has been challenged, is ... the corner-stone upon which our system of justice has been constructed.
>
> Those charged with the functions of the government, in all their wide diversity, know full well that ultimately there can be recourse to these courts to correct irregularities and injustices in governmental administration. ...
>
> *As in all countries where the rule of law prevails, it is your lordships' exercise of the court's supervisory jurisdiction that provides one of the most important safeguards against the arbitrary exercise of power.*[8] [Emphasis added]

As if in mockery of his earlier injunction, this selfsame attorney general was responsible for the drafting of those egregious amendments to the equally egregious Internal Security Act by removing from the court its supervisory jurisdiction.

---

6. Jeyaretnam v The Law Society of Singapore, *Daily Telegraph*, Friday, January 6, 1989.

7. Parliamentary debates, January 10, 1986, col. 718.

8. See [1977] 1 *Malayan Law Journal*, xx.

Forewarned by the ISD of my electoral intention which had been garnered during my incarceration, the longtime prime minister nonpareil and his government planned the sabotage of my electoral prospects by capitalizing on the negative publicity flowing from the tax charges preferred against me. The ISD officers had repeatedly warned me that, if I went into politics notwithstanding their advice, I had better expect "the old man" would throw all the dirt the ISD scavengers could dig on me. And, melancholy as it is to record, in this machination the prime minister succeeded, aided and abetted by a short-sighted and selfish leadership of the Workers' Party, under whose banner owing to the narrow casement of time I had chosen to run.

On Wednesday, August 24, 1988, at the Eastview Secondary School premises, I filed my nomination papers to stand as a Workers' Party candidate for the Eunos Group Representation Constituencies (GRC) together with genial, veteran politician, Dr. Lee Siew Choh, and Malay radio and musical star, Inche Mohamed Khalit bin Baboo, as teammates. The Group Representation Constituencies is a political contrivance ostensibly to institutionalize multiracial representation in Parliament and to compel political parties to take a noncommunal, multiracial approach when they contend for the right to form the government. But, in actual fact, it is designed to hinder the political opposition in any contention for political power. I had intended to stand in the Bedok GRC where Law Minister Jayakumar was standing but, as belated complications set in regarding the distribution of constituencies among the Workers' Party candidates, I opted for the Eunos GRC. Reports had it that Jayakumar's worry-lined dark face broke into wide smiles of relief when told that I had not chosen his constituency after all.

The prime minister had devised a contingency plan to field a candidate of ministerial rank to confront me in any chosen constituency save that he did not know which constituency. As soon as we walked into the nomination centre for the Eunos GRC, a PAP candidate was immediately withdrawn from the PAP GRC team and replaced by Minister of State, Dr. Tay Eng Soon, who was originally slated to stand at the single Tanglin constituency.

It was a rich, inspirational experience, as the short days of the campaign sped swiftly by, to see the breathtaking presence of huge, surging crowds of people turning up nightly to hear me. I had neither seen nor addressed such large enthusiastic crowds before. They swelled into ever greater numbers, whose motor vehicles caused a bumper-to-bumper gridlock for miles all the way to the rally ground, until the eve of polling day when the reluctant riot police had to be brought in for crowd and traffic control. Until then, only the ISD officers were visible in swarms recording candidates' speeches and crowd reaction. My speeches and the crowd attendances at my rallies were sparsely covered by the controlled media. It did not publish when or where I would be speaking. And, yet, by word of mouth alone, all my rallies without exception were attended by exuberant overflowing crowds. Small wonder, then, that my dear prime minister had to stoop to low-down, shameless negative stratagems.

During the campaign, the government, as forewarned by the ISD and grossly misusing the information hereinbefore extracted, plummeted to a new low in gutter politics—in what may be more aptly described as PAP slime, sleaze, and smears—by circulating three scurrilous, scandalous, and spiteful news sheets thus revealing the true aim and object underlying my arrest and detention. The myth of the American connexion had somehow vanished—and the near-hysterical orchestrated campaign against the alleged American and foreign involvement in Singapore's domestic politics conveniently consigned into the limbo of history.

My teammates and I came within an ace of capturing the Eunos GRC. We obtained 49.1 per cent of the popular votes cast. Given the political mine-field and only nine days for campaigning by the wily prime minister, it was "a jolly good show," a gallant effort. By being however "the highest polling losers," Dr. Lee Siew Choh and I were offered two seats as nonconstituency members of Parliament under the Parliamentary Elections Act. Given the Workers' Party's former stance and hubris, the government thought we would reject the seats. But my teammate, Dr. Lee Siew Choh, and I decided to accept them. But to ensure however that I did not take my place in Parliament, the government deliberately temporized in convening

Parliament until well into the new year, by which time through the agency of the courts, I was disqualified from taking my seat because of the convictions and fines imposed *in absentia*. Thereafter, the government announced that Parliament would be convened on January 9, 1989. I was then in New York at the time attending the tenth anniversary celebrations of the Human Rights Watch, New York, and undergoing treatment by an American arrhythmia specialist.

I conclude this dismal tale by recalling an apposite rhetoric of my dear prime minister:

> Has there been a denial or a negation of the spirit of reasonableness and tolerance which is the essence of a democratic system?[9]

Given the above, the answer can only resound in an impassioned affirmative—too many innocent lives have already been sacrificed upon the altar of vague Marxism to propitiate the false god of security for the prolongation of the authoritarian rule of Prime Minister Harry Lee Kuan Yew and his PAP government. In another part of the world in another milieu, the celebrated theologian, Dr. Reinhold Niebuhr, warned about "the depth of evil to which individuals and communities may sink ... when they try to play the role of God to history." Singaporeans, too, especially Harry Lee Kuan Yew and his successor in title, can profit from this warning.

---

9. Legislative Assembly Debates, October 14, 1959, col. 691.

Appendices

Appendix 1

STATEMENT OF EX-DETAINEES OF OPERATION "SPECTRUM"
Embargoed until 10 a.m. 18th April 1988

PREAMBLE

We, the undersigned, were detained by the Internal Security Department (ISD) on 21 May and 20 June 1987 and released in stages under Suspension Directives and/or Restriction Orders in June, September and December 1987.

While we had privately always maintained our innocence and kept a rueful and fearful silence on the unjust treatment we were subjected to, and would have been inclined to keep our silence, the Government has since repeatedly raised the issue of our arrests and detention and made false and damaging statements about us.

On the one hand we had been intimidated by implicit and explicit threats against our safety should we speak up on our arrests and detention. On the other hand the Government and its spokesmen have continued to make bold and untruthful statements regarding the reasons for our arrests and detention and have denied that any of us had been subjected to ill-treatment or torture.

We make this statement now because of this constant barrage of Government taunts and its public invitation to speak the truth on the conditions we were subjected to under arrest and detention.

We make this statement as principled men and women who will speak the truth and state our position for the record.

In making this statement, we do not intend to challenge the Government; we do not desire any official response; neither is there any desire to make "political capital" of this. Our sole purpose in making this statement is to clear our names.

STATEMENT

We are accused of being involved in an alleged "Marxist conspiracy to subvert the existing social and political system in Singapore, using communist united front tactics, with a view to establishing a Marxist state."

We categorically DENY the Government's accusation against us.

We have never been Marxist conspirators involved in any conspiracy.

We were never a clandestine communist or Marxist network and many of us did not even know or know of one another before the arrests.

We were rather community and Church workers, legal reformers, amateur dramatists, helpers of the Workers' Party, professionals and ordinary citizens exercising our constitutional rights to freedom of expression and association in Singapore.

We have never propagated, in words or in action, a communist state for Singapore. Rather, we had, through open and legitimate organizations and legitimate means, advocated more democracy, less elitism, protection of individual freedoms and civil rights, greater concern for the poor and the less privileged, and less interference in the private lives of citizens.

We hold completely the beliefs expressed by fellow ex-detainee Chew Kheng Chuan in his representation to the ISA Advisory Board, where he stated and we paraphrase: "... (we are believers) in an open and democratic polity and in the virtues of an open and accountable government. (We) strongly believe that for a society to be meaningfully called democratic, interest and action in politics cannot be the sole prerogative of the professional politician. A citizen of a democracy, to be worthy of that society, has not just the right, but indeed the duty to participate in the political life of his or her society. It is a grave danger to democracy to suggest that for one to comment on political and social issues or to hold differing political opinions, one should go and form a political party to take on the government! Has the citizen no political voice, other than a vote once in every four years, that cannot be articulated freely and responsibly, but only through the medium of a professional politician? Such is a situation even worse than that of the common man's crippling dependency on 'experts'—whether plumber or temple medium. It will lead to a society where only the authorized, registered, professionally-affiliated expert can comment on the subject under his or her purview."

We believe that as with the case of the individual citizen, so too has an organization this same legitimate role to play in the democratic life of our country.

Absurdly, it seemed to us that we were arrested and detained for the legitimate exercise of our rights as citizens through registered and open organizations. We did not infiltrate these organizations, but joined them as members, volunteers, and full-time workers. Neither did we use these organizations as fronts to propagate subversive activities. All activities carried out by these organizations are legitimate, open and approved by elected executive committees, whose numbers clearly stand in their own right as capable, autonomous and intelligent individuals.

Neither were we "instructed" by any person or organization, not Tan Wah Piow, Paul Lim, nor Vincent Cheng, nor any political party to do what we did in our respective activities or groups.

TREATMENT DURING DETENTION

During our detention, we were subjected to treatment which should never be meted out to any person under interrogation.

Following our sudden arrests, we were subjected to harsh and intensive interrogation, deprived of sleep and rest, some of us for as long as 70 hours inside freezing cold rooms. All of us were stripped of our personal clothing, including spectacles, footwear and underwear and made to change into prisoners' uniforms.

Most of us were made to stand continually during interrogation, some of us for over 20 hours and under the full blast of air-conditioning turned to a very low temperature.

Under these conditions, one of us was repeatedly doused with cold water during interrogation.

Most of us were hit hard in the face, some of us for not less than 50 times, while others were assaulted on other parts of the body, during the first three days of interrogation.

We were threatened with more physical abuse during interrogation. We were threatened with the arrests, assault and battery of our spouses, loved ones and friends. We were threatened with INDEFINITE detention without trial. Chia Thye Poh, who is still in detention after twenty years, was cited as an example. We were told that no one could help us unless we "cooperated" with the ISD.

These threats were constantly on our minds during the time we wrote our respective "statements" in detention.

We were actively discouraged from engaging legal counsel and advised to discharge our lawyers and against taking legal action (including making representations to the ISA Advisory Board) so as not to jeopardise our chances of release.

We were compelled to appear on television and warned that our release would depend on our performances on television. We were coerced to make statements such as "I am Marxist-inclined. …;" "My ideal society is a classless society. ...;" "so-and-so is my mentor. ...;" "I was made use of by so-and-so. ..." in order to incriminate ourselves and other detainees.

What we said on television was grossly distorted and misrepresented by editing and commentaries which attributed highly sinister motives to our actions and associations.

We state once more clearly and unequivocally, we never acted in any way to subvert the security of our country; we were never a part of any Marxist conspiracy to bring about a communist state. If necessary, we would be willing to prove our innocence in an open trial.

We consider ourselves nothing less than some of the most loyal and responsible citizens of Singapore. We greatly regret not our past actions but the fact that our Government felt it necessary to malign our good names and arrest, detain, and abuse us for what we did or did not do.

Sgd. TANG LAY LEE   Sgd. YAP HON NGIAN

Sgd. KENNETH TSANG   Sgd. WONG SOUK YEE

Sgd. TEO SOH LUNG   Sgd. KEVIN DE SOUZA

Sgd. NG BEE LENG   Sgd. f.TANG FONG HAR

Sgd. CHNG SUAN TZE

Appendix 2

FLOOR PLAN OF WHITLEY DENTION CENTRE AND CELLS

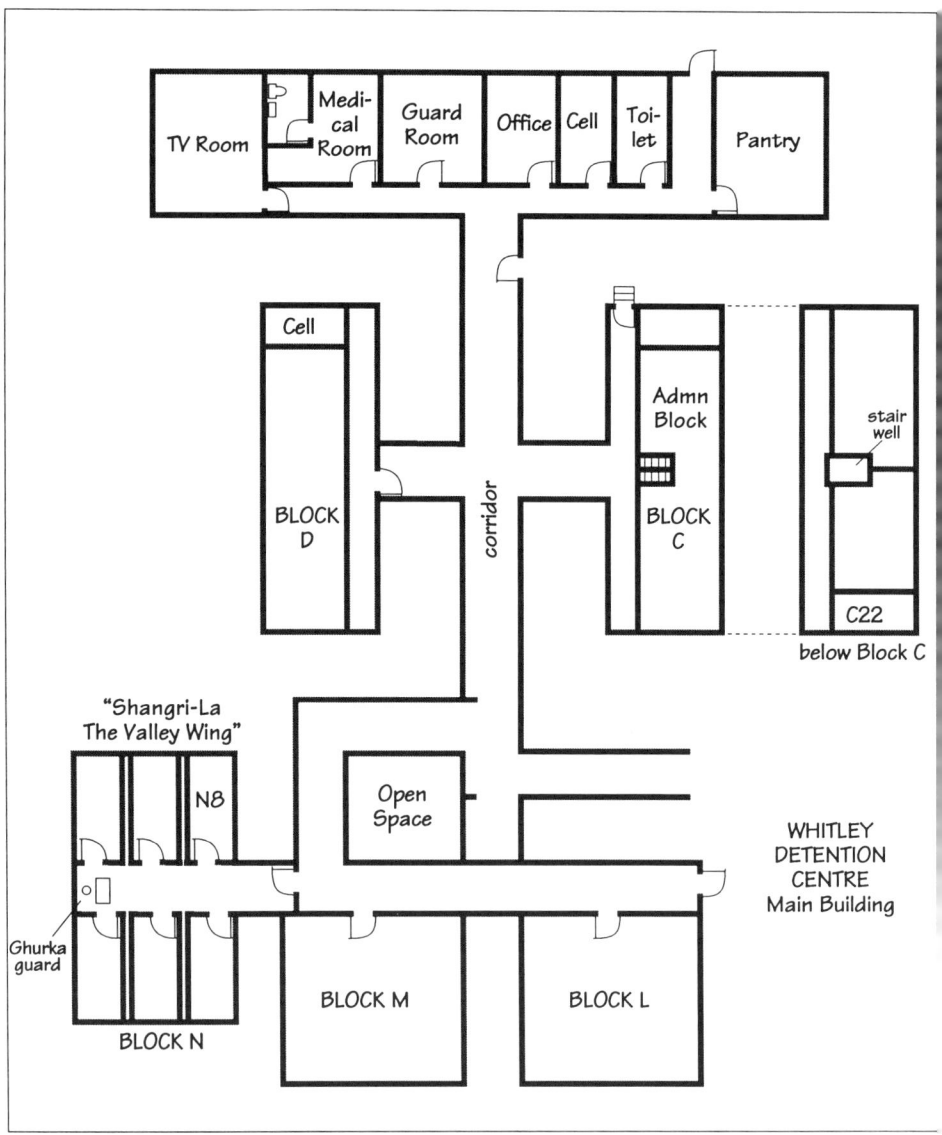

Floor Plan of Whitley Detention Centre and Cells

DETAILS OF SELECTED AREAS

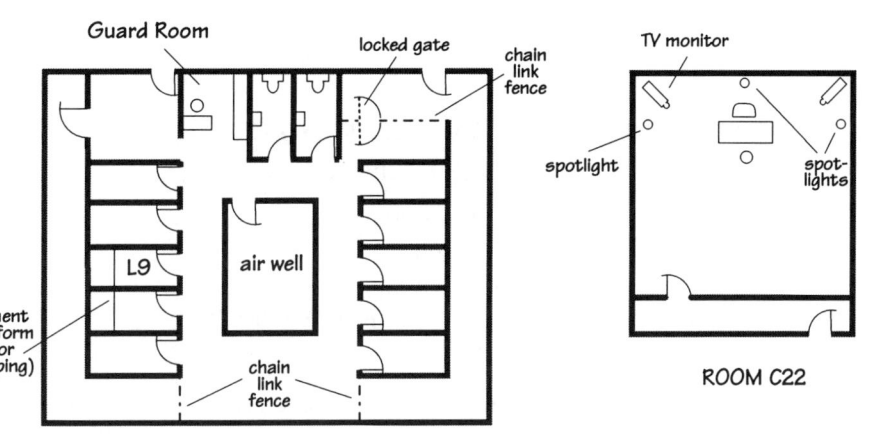

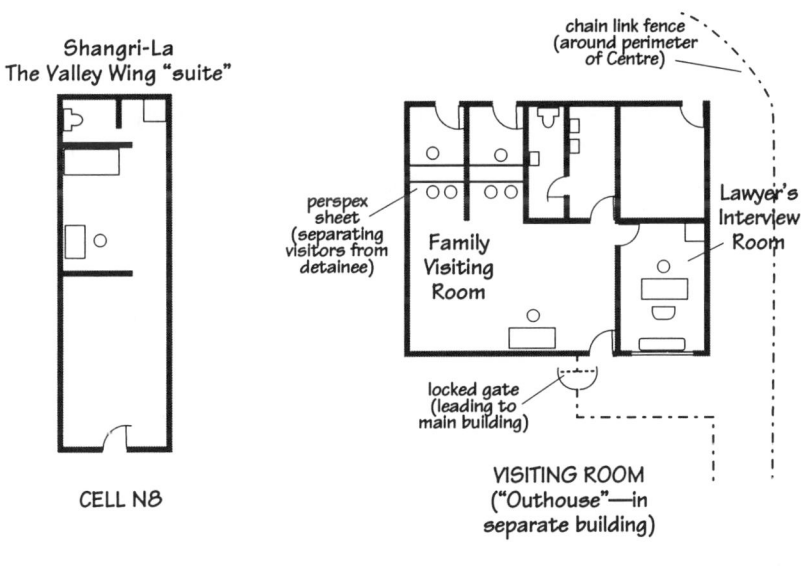

Appendix 3

STATEMENT OF GROUNDS OF DETENTION

THE INTERNAL SECURITY ACT
(CHAPTER 143, 1985 Ed)
s 11(2)(a)
and
The Internal Security
(Detained Persons Advisory Board) Rules, 1964
Rule 3 (1)

In accordance with paragraph (a) of subsection (2) of section 11 of the Internal Security Act and paragraph 1 of rule 3 of the Internal Security (Detained Persons Advisory Board) Rules, 1964, I hereby inform you that you are entitled to make representations in connection with the order of detention dated the 5th day of June 1988 which was served on you on the 5th day of June 1988, by forwarding your representations within fourteen days of the date hereof to the Chairman of the Advisory Board.

Your representations should be in the form, a copy of which is attached herewith.

Dated this 17th day of June 1988.

Sgd.

(Signature of officer in charge of place of detention)

Lim Chin Ow
(Name)

Ag. D.S.P,
Designation)

STATEMENT REQUIRED UNDER SECTION 11 (2) OF
THE INTERNAL SECURITY ACT, CAP 143, 1985 ED

DETAINEE'S NAME: FRANCIS T. SEOW

GROUNDS ON WHICH A DETENTION ORDER IS MADE

Your actions between September 1986 and May 1988 showed that you had made yourself a willing party to acts of interference in Singapore's internal affairs by representatives of a foreign power, thereby rendering yourself vulnerable to foreign manipulation which would undermine the integrity of the political system of Singapore and pose a grave threat to the independence and sovereignty of Singapore and a Detention Order is made to prevent you from acting in a manner prejudicial to the security of Singapore.

ALLEGATIONS OF FACT

That you had met with representatives of a foreign power, namely the United States of America, Mr. Hank Hendrickson, 1st Secretary of the U.S. Embassy, Mr. Joseph Snyder, Special Assistant to Gaston Sigur who is the Assistant Secretary of State for East Asian and Pacific Affairs, State Department, and had on your own admissions (contained in your Statutory Declaration dated 16 May 88, particular references to which have been set hereunder,) discussed your entry into politics in Singapore; that your plans to contest the next general elections was finalised after their instigation, encouragement and advice and after you "felt comforted" that there were friendly faces in the State Department who were "supportive" of your plans and who would be "willing to help secure refuge" for you when needed, and that in doing so you had allowed yourself to be made use of for whatever purpose these representatives of the U.S.A. may have had in espousing your cause. You consorted with the U.S. diplomat and officials to foster your own political objectives and in doing so you rendered yourself obligated to them.

References to your admissions in the Statutory Declaration made by you on 16 May 1988 and annexed hereto.

a) In Nov 86 you met Mr. Joseph Snyder and Mr. Colin Helmer in Washington U.S. As stated by you in your SD:

> "I was then contemplating entering politics and it would then be useful for me to build up my relationship with State Department officials if anything should happen to me in that eventuality. By then I had already raised the subject of seeking asylum in the U.K. with Sir Ham, the British High Commissioner then, but got a negative answer. I thus wanted to look up Joe to renew

our acquaintance and to size up his disposition towards and usefulness to me." (Para 7 of SD)

b) You stated that Mr. Snyder "expressed certain critical opinions on Singapore. He thought that it was 'horrendous' that a law could be passed just to oust me as President from the Law Society. He also brought up the Newspaper and Printing Presses (Amendment) bill. We then discussed politics." You then stated in your SD:

"Joe asked me whether I was in fact entering politics and I said that I was considering it. He wanted to know, in that event, whether I was going in alone or through a party. I said probably as an independent because I did not think much of the opposition parties. My thinking was to get as many professionals as possible to come in with me. He was pleased and generally supportive of it. He liked my style of approach and saw me as a potential leading opposition personality. I sensed that Joe was well disposed towards me and my political intentions, and that he would help me to emigrate to U.S. should I ever want to do so." (Para 9 of SD)

c) You also stated in your SD that:

"I felt comforted that I had friendly faces in the State Department who were supportive of my plans and willing to help secure refuge for me when needed." (Para 10 of SD)

d) You stated in your SD that:

"The idea of taking part in politics at the coming election congealed in my mind" after your return from this trip to the U.S. (Para 123 of SD)

e) You stated that you subsequently recounted your meeting with Mr. Snyder to Mr. Devan Nair in mid-1987 as follows:

"Their response to my intention to enter politics were very encouraging. I sensed that they would help me to secure refuge in the U.S. if and when I needed it. I cannot recall what else I told Devan but I could have given him the impression that I had the backing of the State Department. Amongst other things, I gave Devan the address and telephone number of Joe and Colin. I said that both of them were useful chaps to know when he (Devan) was back in the U.S. because they might be able to get things done for him; if one required asylum, they might be able to help." (Para 94 of SD)

f) On 13 Nov 1987 you met Mr. Hank Hendrickson at the Tai Pan Hotel for lunch at your initiation. At this meeting you discussed with him your plans to contest the next general election. As stated by you in your SD:

"He said that I should play a more positive role to lead the opposition. He remarked that after Ben Jeyaretnam's disqualification, there was no credible opposition and he thought that I could fulfill the role left vacant by Ben. Hank also said that from the pick of available opposition candidates I was probably the best person to lead them because I was able to reason and argue with the PM at the Select Committee hearings, had the facility of language and the ability to think on my feet. Hank emphasized the need to recruit more young professionals into the opposition. He said that this would pave the way for the establishment of a more effective opposition in Parliament." (Para 17 of SD)

g) You then stated in your SD as follows:

"I was of course pleased with what Hank said and in my mind, I set about to identify persons to approach to join me in contesting the next elections." (Para 17 of SD)

h) You stated:

"In fact, it was only from the start of this year or the end of 1987 that I began to seriously set about making concrete plans. I worked out a list of professionals to approach to join me to take part in the election." (Para 117 of SD)

i) You also said:

"I found Hank to be a pleasant person. I maintained cordial relationship with him as he had been supportive of my political intentions, which I found most encouraging. Having a direct line to a diplomat in the U.S. Embassy here would also be helpful in case things should turn sour after I enter politics, and I need assistance to settle in the U.S. expeditiously. In retrospect, I would say that Hank's interest in me was extraordinary compared to that of other diplomats I had come into contact with in Singapore. But this did not occur to me earlier because I was keen to cultivate his friendship just as he was keen to seek me out." (Para 23 of SD)

By the Direction of the Minister for Home Affairs

Sgd. Tan Chin Tiong
BG (Res) TAN CHIN TIONG
Permanent Secretary
Ministry of Home Affairs
Singapore

Appendix 4

REPRESENTATIONS

THE SCHEDULE
FORM I
Rule 3(2)

Internal Security (Detained Persons Advisory Board) Rules, 1964

REPRESENTATIONS IN CONNECTION WITH DETENTION ORDER

To the Chairman, Advisory Board

Name in full	FRANCIS TIANG-SIEW SEOW
Race	CHINESE
Occupation	Advocate & Solicitor
Language in which representations will be made	ENGLISH
Permanent Residence	#11–35 TOMLINSON ROAD, S'PORE 1024
Place of Detention	WHITLEY ROAD DETENTION CENTRE
Date and Place of Arrest	6TH MAY 1988, WHITLEY ROAD DETENTION CENTRE

I, the abovenamed FRANCIS TIANG-SIEW SEOW hereby make representations regarding the Order for my detention made under section 8 of the Internal Security Act, Cap. 143, 1985 Ed., as follows:

THE REPRESENTATIONS OF 8 PAGES ARE ANNEXED HERETO AND SIGNED BY MY SOLICITORS, M/S MURPHY & DUNBAR OF 585 NORTH BRIDGE ROAD, #10–03 BLANCO COURT, S'PORE 0718

Dated this 25th day of June 1988.

Sgd. Francis T. Seow
Signature or Mark

REPRESENTATIONS MADE BY FRANCIS TIANG-SIEW SEOW PURSUANT TO SECTION 11 OF THE INTERNAL SECURITY ACT

The preamble to the Internal Security Act states that the purpose of the Act is to provide for the internal security of Singapore, the prevention of subversion, the suppression of organized violence against persons and property in specified areas of Singapore, and for matters incidental thereto.

It is submitted that it well accepted that preventative detention under the Act is not conceived as punishment. The purpose is to detain a person who either is or poses a potential risk to the internal security of Singapore so that the risk is contained.

It follows from this that such a risk must be a real and present risk. It is obvious from the framework of the Act that when the President is satisfied that the person detained no longer is a threat to the internal security of Singapore nor is likely to revert to being such a threat, that person ought to be released. In the instant case, the allegations made of Francis Seow initially was that he had exposed himself and made himself a willing party to acts of interference in Singapore's internal affairs by representatives of a foreign power, and it was suggested that as he had within the last two years paid off large personal debts that he was being funded, by inference, by some foreign power. As presented by the media and by some Ministers, the double thrust made Francis Seow an internal security risk because he had thereby become obligated to some foreign power and rendered himself vulnerable to foreign manipulations which would undermine the integrity of the political system of Singapore and pose a grave threat to the independence and sovereignty of Singapore.

In the Statement required under Section 11(2) of the Internal Security Act, the grounds on which the detention order was made now makes no reference whatsoever to the possible funding of Francis Seow by a foreign power. It is submitted that the case against him therefore has been weakened considerably because the remaining thrust would now appear to be far less likely if there was no funding.

The allegations of facts set out the proposition that a First Secretary of the United States Embassy and other State officials instigated, encouraged and advised Francis Seow in connection with his entry into politics in Singapore, so that Francis Seow felt "comforted that there were friendly faces in the State Department who were supportive of his plans and who would be willing to secure refuge for him when needed." It should be pointed out that the only occasion when the question of asylum was raised was when it was raised with the British High

Commissioner. The question of asylum was never, in fact, raised at all with any American Ambassadorial or State officials. The fact that Francis Seow may or may not have felt comforted because of his cordial relationship with these people, and that, Francis Seow may have thought that an approach for asylum might be granted by the United States clouds the fact that asylum was never discussed with these people at all and certainly never offered. This is aside from the point that it does not follow that to seek asylum necessarily implies that one intends to engage in subversive activities.

Put bluntly the case against Francis Seow raises the supposition that one of the Great Powers which has always been particularly friendly and helpful to the Republic of Singapore would seek to recruit a prominent lawyer and an ex-Solicitor General of the Republic, so that he could be used, presumably, by the United States to achieve some purpose of its own. That purpose is not disclosed in the Allegations of Fact and it is submitted that divorced from the stress of media coverage, the proposition itself is really unrealistic and untenable. What benefit there could be to the United States to have the stability of the Government of Singapore, perhaps the strongest bastion of stability in the Far East apart from Japan, disrupted is hard to conceive. Still more difficult is it to grasp what purpose there would be in endangering the internal security of Singapore. And in this connection it should be stressed that the Government of Singapore is not the Republic of Singapore.

FACTS

First, it is denied that Francis Seow was a willing party to acts of interference by representatives of a foreign power. The truth of the matter is that, although, Francis Seow has admitted meeting with Mr. Hank Hendrickson, a First Secretary of the United States Embassy on four or five occasions of which one concerned Hank Hendrickson's own personal legal matter, what really took place was that Francis Seow disclosed to him the possibility only of his standing for election. Whereupon Hank Hendrickson told him that he, Hank Hendrickson, thought Francis Seow would make a good opposition candidate because of his facility of language and his ability to think on his feet. The fact that Hank Hendrickson may have emphasized the need "to recruit more young professionals into the opposition" can hardly cause any internal security risk to Singapore. Such emphasis as there may have been emanating from Hank Hendrickson or even if the suggestion first came from Francis Seow was the recruitment of young professionals as future Parliamentarians. It should not be lost in the heat of the argument that professionals are by nature far more cautious than the average man in the street. A professional may be more vocal, but he is trained to think logically and is therefore, much less likely to indulge in organized violence or open or clandestine subversion. In other words such discussion as there was, was to urge on Francis Seow to choose responsible candidates. It might be the cause of a challenge to the incumbent Government of Singapore. Is it an internal security risk for Francis Seow to seek professional recruits to stand as candidates? A reasonable interpretation of what Hank Hendrickson said could be that a lone voice in Parliament such as was Mr. J.B. Jeyaretnam, could achieve little and, therefore, emphasized the need to recruit more young professionals into the opposition. It is difficult to accept such suggestions as being subversive.

With regard to the meeting of Mr. Joe Snyder, this meeting occurred during a weekend visit to Washington by Francis Seow. The discussion occurred at a fastfood restaurant over a period of under an hour and a half. There was only the one meeting and the conversation was general. Again it is difficult to conceive of anything that Mr. Snyder said as set out in the references to Francis Seow's admissions in his Statutory Declaration as being subversive. It must be stressed that in the passage quoted (para. 9 of Statutory Declaration,) Francis Seow set out his own impression of the impact on him of the meeting with Joe Snyder. There is nothing to suggest that the phrase "generally supportive ..." indicates that Joe Snyder gave any specific advice to Francis Seow with regard to Francis Seow's political intentions.

With regard to all the meetings, it should be noted that they were held openly and not in conspiratorial seclusion or manner. These were not the actions of anyone plotting to subvert the State.

If one examines in detail each of the passages of Francis Seow's Statutory Declaration referred to in the Statement, the only suggestion there is is that Francis Seow would make an able Member of Parliament and suggested further that he picks carefully the candidates to stand. This hardly amounts to an interference in Singapore's internal affairs by a foreign power to the extent that their actions amounted to a security risk. Certainly there is nothing to suggest that Francis Seow or the United States had contemplated foreign manipulation which would undermine the integrity of the political system of Singapore and pose a grave threat to its independence and sovereignty. At worst, what can be suggested from a plain reading of the Statement of Facts was that Francis Seow would make a good candidate and a good Parliamentarian because of his facility of speech and his ability to think quickly on his feet. This could possibly pose some threat to the People's Action Party but surely not to the independence, integrity and sovereignty of Singapore.

It should be pointed out that Mr. Goh Chok Tong, the First Deputy Prime Minister, stated in a meeting of three ministers with the Press as reported in *The Straits Times* of Tuesday, the 24th day of May 1988 after the arrest of Francis Seow that Francis Seow "was such a flawed character that it was preposterous to consider him a political threat." At a later stage, it was reported and presumably was the gist of what Mr. Goh Chok Tong had said that, "Unless the ruling People's Action Party was inept in handling its election campaign, Seow would not stand a chance of being elected." The headline of the article reads with regard to Francis Seow, "He is so flawed he stands no chance of getting elected." It is submitted that if the three ministers of the Singapore Government are of the view that Francis Seow poses no threat politically, then he can really pose no threat at all to the internal security of Singapore.

From what the Ministers have said and from the reports in the Press, it appears that after stringent investigations, Francis Seow was not assisted financially by foreign powers, is not a Marxist and there appears to be no evidence to suggest that he imposes any risk to the security of Singapore. If there had been such evidence, there should be no thought of Francis Seow being released shortly.

Sgd. Murphy & Dunbar

MURPHY & DUNBAR

Solicitors for Francis T. Seow

Dated the 25th day of June 1988

Appendix 5

C.V. DEVAN NAIR
c/o Miss K. Nair
12 Leigh Road
London, N5.
8 July, 1988.

AN OPEN LETTER TO LEE KUAN YEW

For The Editor
The Straits Times
Singapore.

Kuan Yew,

I will come to the crux of my case against you straight away. What is it that you are afraid of, and that impelled you to such a massive public exercise in the total denigration of a comrade of nearly thirty years? What prompted you to stoop so low to an utterly shameless demolition effort, by way of the incredibly sordid White Paper tabled before Parliament on 29 June?

Your statement in Parliament the same day gave you away. It made it abundantly clear that you were motivated by political revenge. For you referred to my recent public statements on political developments in Singapore as having made necessary what you did. But legitimate political comment calls for a rational political response, not for political revenge by way of a revolting descent into the gutter. The entire exercise reeks of revenge, a motive which enabled you to throw overboard all ethical considerations, medical ethics, Confucianist, Christian, Hindu ethics, the whole lot.

According to your own panel of doctors, I suffered from a medical condition, not a moral or political one. Clinical tests clearly indicated a much enlarged liver, resulting in a state of acute confusion, bouts of giddiness, exhaustion and fainting spells, admittedly erratic conduct, and amnesia. We may differ about the diagnosis. Several doctor friends of mine in Singapore, let alone in the United States, have quite other notions about the diagnosis. For now, we will let that be.

But where in the civilized world is sordid political capital so shamelessly squeezed out of a medical condition? Where else would self-respecting politicians count obviously transient behaviour, proceeding from a critical medical condition, as a fundamental moral or political lapse? And where else is the sacrosanct confidentiality of medical reports, and of doctor-patient relations, so outrageously violated for a purely political purpose? You know the answers. Only in a society governed by a man like you.

All my comrades in party, trade unions and government, including you, have always known me (you often extolled me), as a highly moral man over nearly three decades of intimate comradeship in a common struggle for a common cause—the building of a nation. How does a clearly transient condition transform me overnight into a hopeless alcoholic, womaniser, wife-beater, among other lurid depictions of depravity?

The data presented in the White Paper, in the form of my letters to you just before and after my resignation, and of Dr. Nagulendran's psychiatric report[1] to you (the use of which constitutes the most disgusting outrage on medical ethics imaginable), can only be seen in undistorted perspective, in the light of the most crucial data of all which, of course, has been carefully omitted. You know very well that all this was done or took place when I was under extraordinarily heavy sedation, 125 mgs (yes, one hundred and twenty-five mgs) of valium daily, to be precise, for some ten days. Thereafter, I was subjected to a slowly graduated decline in the dosage, until it ceased when I left for New York a few weeks later. My son Janadas [Nair] knew of this, but he was persuaded that this was normal for cases like mine. But doctors in the United States were astounded when I told them of this. Even Dr. Gitlow[2] who looked after me in New York, was not told of the kind of sedation I was under, although he had asked for the information.

Such excessive sedation, enough to dope an elephant, makes not for clarity, but for hallucination and disorientation, and you had successfully pontificated to a man rendered highly suggestible by a psychotropic (mood-altering and mind-changing) drug. Further, psychiatric examination and assessment by Dr. Nagulendran was conducted when I was in a highly sedated state. In other modern societies it would have been an impartial medical inquiry that would have been called for, rather than a political White Paper, and the Government, not the patient, would have been in the dock for the scandalous appropriation of medical reports on a patient as state documents for shameless political use. In addition, I believe that I would have been able to sue my Singapore

---

1. Dr. R. Nagulendran, Consultant Psychiatrist, Ministry of Health.
2. Dr. Stanley E. Gitlow is a consultant to the U.S. State Department and a specialist in New York in the treatment of addictive diseases.

doctors, in particular Dr. Nagulendran and Dr. Tambyah, alleging gross violation of medical ethics.

May I state, in addition, that neither I nor any member of my immediate family were ever shown any of the medical reports on me, with the outstanding exception of Dr. Gitlow who took pains to show me every single report of his, and to discuss them with me. He also took care to obtain my written consent to send his evaluations and test results to Singapore. But none of the doctors in Singapore bothered, at any stage of my illness, to show me their reports, nor to obtain my consent before they forwarded them to the prime minister. Indeed, the first time I saw these reports was in the White Paper. And thereby hangs a sadly significant tale.

Drug-induced confusion and suggestibility was enhanced by the near-absolute trust and confidence I had then reposed in the infallibility of your own judgments and actions. It is in this light that my letters to you reproduced in the White Paper should be seen. How wrong I was, I know now.

A very good friend of mine, the Indian physiotherapist who accompanied me to Kuching, Mr. Kalu Sarkar, has been quoted against me in the White Paper. Again, a stupendous omission, equivalent to the omission of the Pacific Ocean from the map of the world. It was not revealed that Mr. Sarkar had been arrested, detained, cruelly treated, and released for return to India only after the ISD secured from him statements about me which he knew to be untrue. I discovered this when I met him in India on my way to the United States in 1985. Among other things, Mr. Sarkar vouched for the fact that when in Sarawak, I only rarely drink liquor in the daytime. Only in the evenings did I have my customary drinks. He therefore did not attribute my erratic conduct in the mornings and afternoons to alcohol. I learn that Mr. Sarkar, who is a respected member of his community, is preparing his own affidavit now, as a free man, and not as one of your detainees.

I have publicly acknowledged that my erratic behaviour in Kuching, although proceeding from a medical condition, was nonetheless unbecoming of a Head of State, and have more than once humbly apologised to the people of Singapore for having failed them. But the salacious slant of many of the reports in the White Paper is vividly illustrated by what my wife and son Janamitra discovered during a visit to Kuching in November 1985, in order to check on reports of my conduct there. This refers to the allegation repeated in the White Paper that I had made sexually suggestive remarks to Mrs. George Chan, wife of an assistant minister. I quote from Mitra's report to me: "I told him (Dr.

George Chan) about the report that you had propositioned someone's wife while you were in Sarawak. He said this was the first time that he had heard this. He asked whose wife you were supposed to have propositioned. I replied, 'Yours!'"

"Dr. Chan was surprised. He stated that you had been rude to his wife. But he dismissed the whole incident as 'small.' He said that you had called him the next day and asked to speak to his wife, whom you promptly apologised to. He said his wife never thought anything about it. He also said that as a doctor, he knew there was something wrong with you, and those times in which you behaved strangely and in confusion were completely uncharacteristic."

A humane response to the deviant behaviour of a sick man also came from Tun Abdul-Rahman bin Ya'kub, the then Governor of Sarawak, in whose residence I was a guest during my visit, and whom I met in London in November 1985. He told me that he had flown hurriedly to Singapore on hearing of my hospitalisation in order to see me. He was not allowed to do so. Instead, he was taken to your office, where you wanted to know whether he had any complaints to make. He told you quite categorically that I had done nothing to complain about.

When I asked the Tun to tell me frankly whether there was any substance to rumours that I had molested ladies in Kuching, he assured me that no such report had come to his attention. But he said that he was very concerned for me as a very ill person, as evidenced by clearly uncharacteristic erratic speech and conduct. For example, he was startled when I wanted the Malay orchestra to play Indian music. I don't recall this at all.

The Tun also vigorously denied rumours circulating in official circles in Singapore to the effect that the Malaysian Government had complained to the Government of Singapore about my behaviour in Kuching. He said that this was entirely baseless, for the good reason that there was nothing to complain about. They were only concerned about the obviously ill visiting President they had on their hands. Dato Musa Hitam, the Deputy Prime Minister of Malaysia at the time, confirmed this when I met him in Manila in November 1986.

Next, what disturbed me most about the visit to the Iban longhouse was not so much lubricious reports about having fondled Iban ladies on my lap, but the fact that I have only the haziest recollection of the visit. Understandable, because I was told that I had collapsed at least twice on my way there, and once in the longhouse itself. As for the Iban ladies, Tun Abdul-Rahman bin Ya'kub told me that there was nothing untoward about what was reported to have happened. It was customary longhouse practice. But you know that customary practice or not, I would not have allowed it if I had been in a normal condition. In any case, I had not spent the night in the longhouse, as many other visiting dignitaries had done, including Mr. Malcolm Macdonald, the Governor-General of the British South East Asia in colonial times.

Other reports in the White Paper allege uncharacteristically crude behaviour on my part with nurses and other ladies. I have no means of checking on the veracity or otherwise of these allegations. I simply cannot recognize myself in them. It may be that in the deplorable amnesic condition I was in, I did perhaps behave offensively. All that I can do is apologise for the unpremeditated behaviour of an amnesic person. I offered apologies to Tun Abdul-Rahman bin Ya'kub when I met him in London if I had behaved offensively to anyone. His response was that no apologies were necessary from a man who was as obviously unwell as I was. But I would still apologize as I did to the people of Singapore.

The White Paper has maligned a thoroughly respectable married German lady with children, whom I had first come to know in Europe several years ago. Incidentally, she had nothing whatever to do with the Friedrich Ebert Foundation, one of the numerous misstatements of simple facts in the White Paper. I had only helped her with an academic assignment, as I had helped so many others, and I am angered by the suggestion, without proof whatsoever, that my relations with the lady were improper in any manner. I never went into her room at the hotel where she first stayed. I only rang for her from the lobby where she joined me. Nor did anything improper happen between us when I visited her in a private home, nor in Changi Cottage where I had taken her for a swim. My wife will speak for herself on this and other matters in which she has been so unpardonably misinterpreted. But you do jump to the worst possible conclusions about people, specially if you have fallen out with them.

The way you dramatically embellish your facts when it suits you takes some beating. Where on earth did you get the idea that I had consumed a bottle of whisky every night for a few months before my visit to Kuching? The *Istana* wine cellar count you had asked for surely revealed to you that I did not order anywhere near 120 bottles of whisky over a period of, say, 4 months. And I never did buy any liquor from outside the *Istana*. How could you have brought yourself to make such an obviously misleading statement? Even on the occasions I had abused alcohol, polishing off one bottle at one sitting at any time is a feat which I could not possibly have managed. And every night for months in succession? Come off it, please!

In the eagerness to prove that my powers of perception and judgment have suffered permanent impairment as a result of irreparable brain damage, the final authoritative evaluation by Dr. Gitlow of all the test results he presided over in New York is pointedly ignored or understated. Before forwarding his evaluation to Singapore, which was with my explicit consent, Dr. Gitlow informed me that the psychometric tests showed that I was "inordinately bright," with an exceptional command of language. And his considered professional evaluation of all the test results was that all my brain functions were within the range of normality for a person of my age, He also wrote to me later that "it is essentially an evaluation that fails to reveal any significant abnormality." He also told me in writing: "Medical personnel are not only trained to note minutiae, but to realize simultaneously where they properly fit within the variable limits of 'normal.'"

But I have noted a mischievous and certainly politically inspired interpretation in the *Straits Times* of July 2, of the brain scan done in New York on June 17, 1985 by Dr. Robin J. Mithick. Dr. Mithick said the scan showed "frontal and mild cerebellar atrophy." The interpretation did not come from Dr. Gitlow, but from somebody in Singapore. Perhaps you might know who planted this "expert." This is how the politically motivated interpretation goes: "This (*brain scan*) means that the brain tissue in the front part of the brain (the cerebrum), which controls the higher faculties such as language, reasoning and judgment, had deteriorated. There was also mild degeneration of brain tissue at the rear part of the brain (cerebellum) which controls the sense of balance, and co-ordination of physical functions. The degeneration is permanent and irreversible." Who said so? I challenge you to show that Dr. Gitlow said anything like this. In fact, all this was the "minutiae" Dr. Gitlow referred to in his letter to me. Deterioration in language? Dr. Gitlow told me that the finding of another test was exactly the opposite.

I now understand why Brigadier General Lee told the BBC in a recent interview that my recent political criticism of the Government "showed impaired judgment." So legitimate criticisms of some of your disastrous policies are the result of the impairment of perception and judgment on the part of the critics? In which case innumerable Singaporeans who feel the same way as I do, not to mention your growing number of critics elsewhere, are all loony bins? Again, come off it, please!

Talking about "command of language," Dr. Nagulendran's psychiatric assessment could have avoided grievous errors of interpretation if he had some command of language himself. His rendition of the Tamil word my wife used, "*thattu*," meaning a light tap on the head, was "hit."

This was how I came to "hit" my wife once. You improved considerably on the psychiatrist by saying that I "beat her often," a vivid example of the geometric progression of exaggeration in your hands.

You want another example? To the psychiatric's question whether members of my family drank, my wife's answer was "yes." This became in your hands, "Your two brothers and three sisters, your father, your mother, and two uncles, they all had alcoholism." This atrocious libel on an entire family was later retracted, according to James Fu's letter[3] to the *Far Eastern Economic Review*, which stated that the prime minister "withdraws ... unreservedly" his "lay rendering of the family-history part of the medical report on Nair" (*FEER*, 5 March 1987). You no doubt consider it safe now to resuscitate the libel in the White Paper, under cover of parliamentary privilege.

A few words about the alcoholism diagnosis. I do not blame Dr. Gitlow at all for reporting that the "presumptive" diagnosis was alcoholism. He could not have done otherwise, for two reasons. One, I was sent to him for treatment, not for diagnosis, which was done in Singapore. Two, the patient was yet to liberate himself from the enormous influence you still exercised on his thinking and attitudes, and was convinced that his amnesic condition and breakdown in Kuching could only be explained by the diagnosis of alcoholism. Nothing more was needed for Dr. Gitlow's "presumptive" diagnosis. Only a few months later did the scales begin to fall from my eyes, slowly and painfully. There was a direct correspondence between my discovery of myself and my discovery of you.

The final certitude that I was never an alcoholic only came when I went to reside in Indiana as a Fellow of the Institute for Advanced Studies in Indiana University. I asked for and obtained a copy of the medical report of the extensive and thorough-going medical examination I had undergone in 1984 (about a year before my Kuching visit) in the Indiana University Teaching Hospital—clinical, radiological, neurological, brain scans including an NMR scan, the whole works. The Dean of the Medical School, Dr. Ward B. Moore and another doctor who went through the entire report told me that they found nothing to suggest alcoholism, nor did they discover any sign of brain damage. They also expressed the view that it was not credible to suggest that I had become an alcoholic or had suffered brain damage within a year of such comprehensive tests. Experiential knowledge since has also convinced me that the alcoholism diagnosis you continue to cherish no longer holds water.

---

3. James Fu Chiao San, Press Secretary to the Prime Minister.

You delude yourself if you believe that the disgusting concoction of misinterpreted truths, half-truths, and untruths, not to speak of gaping omissions, in your parliamentary statement and in the White Paper, will enjoy more than a passing season. Nearly thirty years of struggle and effort in the service of the people of Singapore, in intimate comradeship with you and others, are not wiped out so easily. Not even the formidable intimidatory apparatus of power and systematic misinformation you have assembled can forever stifle the truth. What will ultimately prevail is the season of truth. And the total truth, many-sided and whole, will include the virtues and defects, successes and failures, prides and shames of all of us, including you and me. In short, total truth has an infallible way of debunking the debunkers.

Your genius for sticking labels on people does Singapore no good. The truth of things often requires the removal of the labels on them. Nowhere more so than in the brand of politics you have developed. Thanks to you, Singapore has rapidly become a vivid illustration of the political adage: "Give a dog a bad name and hang it."

If our nation is to survive as a credible entity in the modern world, we need to unstick the labels you have so tirelessly fixed on people and opinions you disapprove of. Honest, educated young professionals, who had the temerity to develop social ideas of their own, suddenly found themselves arrested and labelled "Marxist conspirators." A former solicitor-general who entertained rather nebulous notions of leading a small opposition group in Parliament was labelled an instrument of an unlikely Machiavelli in the U.S. Embassy. Now I am the latest victim of your label-fixing genius—brain-damaged alcoholic, wife-beater and what not.

Memorable words of your own, uttered 27 years ago, will attest to the fact that this is not the first time I have been the victim of a total smear, a furious attempt at utter demolition. I quote from a radio talk you gave to Singaporeans in 1961, when you and I were fighting real enemies, and not tilting at windmills as you are doing today.

> Lim Chin Siong ... (the most important open-front leader the M.C.P.[4] had built up) ... was once Devan Nair's closest open-front comrade. Devan Nair was his constant guide. But when Devan Nair decided that the M.C.P. was wrong in continuing the armed struggle after independence in the Federation and not coming to terms with Malayan nationalism, Lim began to fight Devan Nair relentlessly and ruthless, by fair or unfair methods, by smears and intimidation, to destroy every influence that Devan Nair had with the workers and in the unions. His

---

4. Malayan Communist Party.

personal friendship for Devan Nair meant nothing. I knew that this was what one must expect of a good Communist.

Well, the Lim Chin Siong of 1961 turns out to be an incompetent juvenile in the art of demolition compared to the awesome efficiency displayed by the Lee Kuan Yew of 1988.

If I had been less naïve and gullible than I was, I might perhaps have perceived a possible danger signal in an informal and personal exchange that took place between us some three or four months before I resigned as President in March 1985. You will recall that I had made it clear to you then that I did not wish to renew my presidency when my term expired in October 1985. I was surprised to learn from you that it was not considered desirable for me to retire in Singapore after I stepped down as President. You suggested that I accept an ambassadorship. I declined, saying that I did not relish the life-style of an ambassador, involving as it did the treading of an endless cocktail circuit, picking up the latest gossip, and sending it off as a despatch to the Foreign Ministry. I told you that I would prefer a readership in the National University instead, which would enable me to do my own writing and to relate to our students. You did not seem to particularly like this prospect.

When we met again the following week, you told me that the younger ministers were disappointed that I had rejected an ambassadorship. Surprised, I asked why. I was dismayed to learn that some of them thought that if I remained in Singapore, I might be tempted to interfere in the political process. I assured you that I would not interfere in any way, and certainly not with the trade unions, which was probably what some persons might have been nervous about. In any case, I had believed what you told me. Indeed, I was prone to repose uncritical belief in you most of the time. I no longer do. I was perhaps blind then to what might have been an unmistakable writing on the wall for me.

It is not possible, in the course of a single letter, to reply in full to the massive public onslaught you unleashed on me with your speech on 29 June, and the accompanying White Paper, which I am confident will be judged by history as a product of acute political dementia. Some might even say a terminally diseased spiritual condition. The political disvalues you have come to pursue, the perils that the nation faces as a result, the circumstances of my resignation, and above all what I consider the betrayal of the multiracial revolutionary movement which made Singapore, are the subjects of a book I am writing on.

I am most grieved by the wrong you and Dr. Nagulendran have done to my wife, than by the harm done to me. She has been shockingly and disgustingly misrepresented as a witness against her own husband. In your system, it seems that anything goes. Members of a single family are made to bear witness against each other, not to speak of doctors bearing witness against their patients. Are these the "Confucianist" values you prescribe for Singaporeans? My wife will make her own response. My sons, too, who were witnesses of the circumstances surrounding my resignation, will bear their own witness to the unfolding truth as they saw it.

For the rest, we have not seen the end of the play. The last Act of the tragi-comedy you began has yet to be played out. I wish you good luck.

(Sgd.) C.V. DEVAN NAIR

N.B. For your information, I have distributed this to certain other journals and international news agencies.

Index

Abas, Tun Mohamed Salleh, 237
Abdul Rahman Putra al-Haj, Tungku, xxvi, 4–5, 49, 181–82
Abdul Rahman bin Ya'kub, Tun, 276–77
Accountants, 61, 187, 244–46
Act
　Income Tax, 243, 245
　Internal Security, ix–x, xxiv–xxix, 68, 73, 96, 176, 185, 186, 187, 190–91, 245, 253, 257–60, 258–61, 264–65, 268–72
　Legal Profession, 58–59
　Parliamentary Elections, 127–28, 255
　Pensions, 48–49
　Prisons, 10–11, 35
　Societies, 170
Aeschylus, 229
Amara Hotel, 125
American Bar Association, 101
America
　American plot, 98, 126–28, 149, 156, 162, 182–83, 188, 234
　American Society of Newspaper Editors, 173, 177
Amnesty International, 90, 100, 109, 160, 217–18
Anandan, Subhas, 77, 81–83, 89, 98
Anderton, Jim, 101
Ang, Alfonso, 248
Ang, Sunny. *See* P.P. v Sunny Ang
Anti-British League, xix, 167. *See also* C.V. Devan Nair and communists
Aquino, Corazón, 158, 218
Arotcarena, Fr. Guillaume, 70. *See also* Marxist conspiracy
Asia Watch, xxiv, 89–90, 100, 160
Asian Wall Street Journal, The, xxviii, 148, 169, 173, 185–86, 188
Assistant Official Assignee, 18
Asylum. *See* C.V. Devan Nair and Jocelyn Seong
Attorney General. *See* respective holders: C.H. Butterfield,

Murray Buttrose, Ernest P. Shanks, Q.C., Tan Boon Teik
Attorney General's chambers, a.k.a. AG's chambers, 13, 16, 19, 21, 28, 43, 54, 106, 197–98
Australia, xvii, 39, 71, 226
Australian, The, 6
Automobile Association of Singapore, 140–41

Baba, Roslina binte, 91, 98, 104, 106, 108–9
Baboo, Khalid bin, 254
Baey, Lian Peck, 119
Bangkok Bank, Bangkok, 180
Banque Nationale de Paris. *See* Mei Siah
Barker, Eddie W., 47, 50–52, 141–42, 196
Barisan Sosialis—Socialist Front, 3–4, 10, 28–29, 34–35, 68, 207
Bedok GRC. *See* Constituency and elections
Bertrand, M. *See* P.P. v Sunny Ang
Beverly Mai, 85, 111–13, 115, 242
Bill
　Group Representation Constituency, 251
　Legal Profession (Amendment), 59, 63, 66, 159, 189, 234
　Maintenance of Religious Harmony, 80
　Newspaper and Printing Presses (Amendment), 58, 76, 159, 164, 245, 266
Black operations, 132, 234. *See also* American plot
Blom-Cooper, Louis, Q.C., 214
Bogaars, George E., 45, 54
Brunei, Sultanate of, 11, 136
Bukit Turf Club. *See* Singapore Turf Club
Butler, Samuel, 229
Butterfield, C.H., Q.C., 15, 21
Buttrose, Murray, 15–16

Cafe de Luxe, 17
Caldwell, Dr. Malcolm, 74
Cashin, Howard, 94, 214–15
Central Intelligence Agency (CIA), 58, 97, 157–58, 179, 181
Centres of detention, xx–xxi. *See also* Detention
   Central Police Station, top floor, 35
   Changi Prison, xxiii, 10, 46
   holding centres, 8, 35
   Moon Crescent Detention Centre, 10, 35
   Whitley Detention Centre. *See* Whitley Detention Centre
Chacko, Jacob, 138
Chan, Dr. George, 275–76
Chancery Lane, 113–15
Changi Cottage, 277
Cheng, Vincent, 69–73, 260. *See also* Marxist conspiracy
Chew, Kheng Chuan, a.k.a. K.C. Chew, 67, 86, 95–96, 210, 212–13, 231, 259. *See also* Marxist conspiracy
Chia, Thye Poh, xiii, xxviii–xxix, 10, 68, 231, 260
Chiam, See Tong, 66, 187
Chiang, Wee Tiong, 134
Chinese
   chauvinism, 6
   language and culture, 32–33, 36, 139
   schools, 28, 33–34, 37–38, 204
   secondary IV examinations boycott, 33, 43, 203
Chinese Chamber of Commerce, 33, 36
Chng, Suan Tze, 261. *See also* Marxist conspiracy
Choor Singh, Justice, 31, 45
Chua, Robert, 157
Chua, Sian Chin, 34, 204
Civil servants. *See* Singapore Civil Service
Coblentz, William K., 101
Cohen, Jerome A., xxiv, 100, 107
Colonial Secretariat, 14, 17, 197
Commissions of Inquiry into:
   allegations of corruption and nepotism, 26–27
   allegations of Executive interference in the subordinate judiciary, 56–59
Chinese secondary IV examinations boycott, 36–38, 43, 203
4th term of reference, Law Society's interest in, 57
prison conditions, xx
Commissioner for Oaths, 178
Committee of Privileges, 57
Comptroller of Income Tax. *See* Inland Revenue
Communism. *See* Communist
Communist, xix–xx, xxv–xxvi, xxix–xxx, 9–10, 28, 32–34, 36–38, 47, 67–68, 167, 174, 181, 203, 207, 226, 230, 245, 258–59, 261, 280–81
Communist Party of Malaya (CPM), a.k.a Malayan Communist Party (MCP), xix, 34, 203, 280. *See also* Communist
Confessions. *See* Marxist conspiracy
Confucianism. *See* Confucius
Confucius, xiii, xxvii, 124, 176, 194
Confucian conformity, xxvi–xxvii, 176
Constituency
   Bedok, 233, 254
   Bedok GRC, 254
   Eunos Group Representation (GRC), 94, 254
   Tanglin, 254
Constitution of the Republic of Singapore, 73, 89–90
Coomarasamy, Justice Punch, 125
Cornell University, 166, 168, 217
Corrupt Practices Investigation Bureau (CPIB), 19, 50–51, 141
Criminal District and Magistrates' Courts, 19, 27, 31, 247. *See also* Subordinate Courts
Crown Counsel and Deputy Public Prosecutor, 13, 15–16, 19, 34, 40, 50, 54
Cumaraswamy, Param, 137

D'Aniello, Reverend Giovanni, 70. *See also* Marxist conspiracy
Davies, Derek Gwyn, 175
Daily Telegraph, The, 253

Denisov, Vladimir I., 252
Detainees. *See* Detention
Detention
   interrogation and interrogators, xxii, 131–32, 142–44, 150–51, 154–55, 159, 171–73
   interrogation room, xxi–xxii, 121–22, 179
   prison clothes, 116, 152, 216
   "softening-up" period, 156
   solitary confinement, xxii–xxiii, 65, 208, 212–13
   treatment during
     abuses, threats, xxi–xxii, 95, 182
     "psychological pressures," xxiii–xxiv, 129
     sleep deprivation, xxi–xxiii, 88, 104, 169
     without trial, xiv, xxv–xxvii, 68, 184, 226, 260
D'Souza, Fr. Edgar, 70–71. *See also* Marxist conspiracy
De Souza, Kevin, 73, 87, 213, 261. *See also* Marxist conspiracy
Devan, Janamitra 168, 182, 275
Devan, Sabrina, 168
Dhanabalan, S., 57, 169
"Digits," Singaporeans as, xiii, 6
Dube, Vinod K. 247–50. *See also* Inland Revenue Department
Dutch Labour Party, xx. *See* Socialist International

East Asian Legal Studies, 100
East India Company, 1–2
Eisenhower administration, 97
Emergency Committee for Human Rights in Singapore, a.k.a Echris, 90, 101
Emergency Regulations. *See* Preservation of Public Security Ordinance
Economist, The, xviii
Elections
   by-election, Hong Lim Anson, 27, 74, 79
   general elections, 2, 5, 21–22, 27, 32, 79, 93, 124, 127–29, 133–36, 168, 170, 243–45, 250, 267, 270–71
Elias, Harry, 63

Elliott, Professor T.H., xx
Emigration, 163, 165
English-educated, 22
Eunos GRC. *See* Constituency and elections
Ex-detainee. *See* Detainee

Fajar, 21
Far Eastern Economic Review, xxviii, 70, 134, 166–67, 193, 279
Feed-back unit, 65
Fernandez, Geoffrey. *See* P.P. v Geoffrey Fernandez
Frankfurter Allgemeine, 100
Friedrich Ebert Foundation, 277
Fu, Chiao Sian, James, 279

Geylang Catholic Welfare Centre, 69, 73–74. *See also* Marxist conspiracy
Ghows, Abdul Wahab, 20
Giam, Chin Toon, 218
Gitlow, Dr. Stanley E., 274–75, 278–79
Goh, Chok Tong, xii, 66, 87, 98, 100, 120, 169, 183, 193–94, 272
Goh, Keng Swee Dr., 49, 196
Goh, Fr. Patrick, 70. *See also* Marxist conspiracy
Goodwood Park Hotel, 103, 155
Government
   "administration by intimidation," 7
   British/United Kingdom —, 2–3, 5, 34, 165
   Labour Front —, 3, 21, 71, 97
   Lee PAP —, x, xviii, xx, xxiii–xxv, 5, 7, 10, 22–25, 28, 38, 53, 96, 132, 174, 181–82, 185–86, 198, 252, 256
   Malaysian —, 60, 181, 276
   Singapore —, xxiii–xxiv, xxvii, 4, 58, 60, 75, 78, 83–84, 96, 132, 137, 160, 166, 183–84, 186, 191, 217, 245, 253, 270–72, 276
Government House, 15, 17–18. See also *Istana*
Group Representation Constituency (GRC) bill, 251. *See also* Elections

Gurkha guards, xxi, 11–12, 52, 104–6, 116–19, 121–22, 142, 146, 150, 152–55, 205, 209, 211, 214, 216, 236, 239. *See also* Singapore Police force

habeas corpus applications, 92, 98, 100, 102–3, 177
Hammer, The, 79. *See also* Marxist conspiracy
Harvard Law School, 60, 100
Helmer, Colin, 126, 136, 161, 180, 183, 265. *See also* Hank Hendrickson
Hendrickson, E. Mason, a.k.a. Hank, 89, 91–92, 98, 123, 125, 127, 136, 144–45, 156–59, 163, 165, 183–86, 192, 265–67, 270–71. *See also* Patrick Seong and Francis Seow
Ho, Fr. Joseph, 70. *See also* Marxist conspiracy
Hongkong Bank, 189
Hong Leong Securities Company, 134–35
Hoog, John, 89
Human Rights Watch, New York, 256

Ideology, national, xii–xiv
Immigration Department, 84
Income Tax Department. *See* Inland Revenue Department
Indians, 13, 15, 20, 27–28, 34, 55, 81, 109, 131–32, 139, 175, 218, 247
Inland Revenue
  Comptroller of Income Tax, 245
  Department of, xvi, 60–62, 142, 188, 235, 243–44, 246–47, 250
  press statement dd. August 6, 1988, 245
Internal Security Act (ISA)
  Advisory Board, 77, 193, 259
  arrest under, 68, 91, 99, 106, 197, 219, 245
  detention under, xxv, xxvii, 68, 77, 137, 182, 197, 219, 234, 245, 264–65, 268–69
  judicial review of, xxvii, 253
Internal Security Council, 4, 31
Internal Security Department (ISD), xii, xvi, xxi, 8–11, 30, 34–35, 59, 67, 69–70, 73, 76–78, 81–82, 84–85, 87–88, 90–93, 95–96, 98–100, 102–6, 108–20, 122–23, 126–27, 131–32, 135–40, 143–44, 146–48, 150–51, 154–57, 159–60, 162–66, 168–72, 173, 177–80, 183–84, 187–92, 196–97, 199, 203–4, 206–9, 212, 215–16, 219, 226, 228, 231–36, 238, 240–41, 244–45, 254–55, 258, 260, 275
Internal Security (Detained Persons) Rules, 1960, 10, 264, 268. *See also* Prisons Regulations, 1938.
Internal Security (Detained Persons Advisory Board) Rules, 1964, 264, 268
International Commission of Jurists, (ICJ), 100, 160
International Committee for Artists' Freedom, 78
Interrogation. *See* Detention
Ismail bin Abdul Rahman, Tun, Dr., 39
Israelis, 9
Istana Annexe, 52, 100, 107

Jamit Singh, 29–31
Janz, Udo, 100
Japan, 2, 6, 50, 118, 175, 238, 270
Japanese military forces, 2
Jayakumar S., 65, 119, 229, 233, 254
Jek, Yuen Tong, 195
Jeyaretnam, Joshua Benjamin, a.k.a. J.B. Jeyaretnam, xxvii, 19, 49, 56–57, 66, 74, 79, 159, 252–53, 267, 271
  district judge, 19, 74
  member of Parliament, 57, 159
  WP's secretary general, 74
Jiang, Siew Ming, 247
Johore
  Straits of, 51, 232
  Sultan of, 1
John, Margaret, 217
Johnson, President Lyndon B., 10, 98

Kennedy administration, 97
Khoo, Michael, 252

Index 287

Khoo, Warren, 138–39
Khosa, Jernail Singh, 63–64
Ko, Teck Kin, 36–38
Koh, Bock Thye, 45
Koh, Gene. *See* P.P. v Freddy Tan
Koh, Ruby, 189
Koh, Tommy, 162, 186
Kwa, Soon Bee, Dr., 147

Lai, Kew Chai, Justice, 91, 251
Lambertson, David, 98, 126–27, 180, 183
Lawasia biennial conference, 137, 219
Law Society of Singapore, xxviii, 54–59, 62–64, 73–74, 76, 85, 89, 100, 109, 125, 136, 138, 164, 187, 203, 218, 266
  council members, 64, 109, 138
  Criminal Legal Aid Scheme, 74
  extraordinary general meeting, 59
  Select Committee on Legal Profession (Amendment) bill, 62, 136, 138
  Special Assignments (Civil Legislation) Subcommittee, 62
Lee and Lee, 34
Lee, Chiaw Meng, Dr., 119
Lee, Harry. *See* Lee Kuan Yew
Lee, Hsien Loong, Brigadier General, a.k.a. B.G. Lee, 129, 145, 159, 169, 193, 228, 278
Lee, Kuan Yew
  address, American Society of Newspaper Editors, 173
  arrests of Roman Catholic activists, 69–71
  Istana meeting, 71, 100, 107, 230
  "bag of political tricks," 96–98
  blitzkrieg on D.V. Devan Nair, 193. *See also* White Paper, Command 8 of 1988
  C.V. Devan Nair, defamation writ against, 183
  C.V. Devan Nair's open letter dd July 8, 1988. *See* Appendix 5
  Commission of Inquiry into secondary IV examinations boycott, 32–33
  Committee of Privileges, 57
  Constitution, observations on, xxv, 89–90
  Derek Davies *et al.* in Suit No. 3336 of 1987, 71
  Fajar trial, 21
  Malay press conference, 137
  May 1959 general elections, 21
  P.P. v Freddy Tan, 45–46
  P.P. v Geoffrey Fernandez, 51
  PAP assemblyman, 16, 19
  parliamentary motion on arrest and U.S. involvement, 185–87
  Privy Council, observations on, 251–52
  salary of prime minister, 23
  Select Committee on Legal Profession (Amendment) bill, 62–66
  Senior Minister, xiv
  Solicitor General's appointment, 42–44
  speech, NUS forum, 119–20
  statements, required prior approval of, 177, 225, 226
Lee, Siew Choh, Dr., 35, 254–55
Legal Service Commission, 43, 56
Legal Profession (Amendment) bill. *See under* Bill
Lester, Anthony, Q.C, 154
Lewis, Flora, 12
Lim, Benny, 157, 159, 227
Lim, Chin Siong, 71, 207, 280–81
Lim, Chor Pee, 65
Lim, Huat Chye, Paul, 76, 230–31, 260. *See also* Marxist conspiracy
Lim, Li Kok Teresa, 72. *See also* Marxist conspiracy
Liu Qing, 91
Lockwood, Christopher, xxix
Looi-Seow, Clare, 217
Looi, Colin, 217
Looi, Mark, 217
Looi, Susan, 217

Macdonald, Malcolm, 277
Mahoney, Tom, 16–17
Maintenance of Religious Harmony bill. *See under* Bill
Malacca, Settlement of. *See* Straits Settlements
Malay *ultras*, 5, 183

Malayan Union, 2
Malaysia, Federation of, 4, 52, 181, 183, 251
Malaysian Singapore Airlines (MSA), 49
mandamus proceedings, 91
Mandela, Nelson, xiv, xxix
Marco Polo Hotel, 164
Marshall, David Saul
  law partnership with, 52
  Lee Kuan Yew's fear of, 33, 53
  P.P. v Sunny Ang, 42
  suspension from practice, 54
  vocal critic, 52–53
  Workers' Party founder-chairman, 73–74
Marxist conspiracy, 69–70, 76, 98, 230–31, 258, 261. *See also* Centres of detention
Media, xxviii, 6, 9, 26, 45, 71, 94, 96, 100, 124, 138, 158, 173–75, 179–80, 184, 187–88, 228, 243, 255
Merican, Noor Mohamed a.k.a. Sammy Davis, Jr., 55
Method of recording. *See* Centres of detention
Minister for Education, 37, 97, 119, 169
—Finance, 37, 97, 135
—Home Affairs, 36, 39, 70, 77, 103, 119, 148, 190, 214, 232, 267
Ministry for Community Development, 78
—Home Affairs, 11, 69–70, 79
Mithick, Dr. Robin J., 278
Mohan, Chandra, 138
Mohan Das Naidu, 138
Moore, Dr. Ward B., 279
Mahbubani, Kishore, 186
Murphy and Dunbar, 187, 193, 268, 272
Musa Hitam, Datuk, 276

Nagulendran, Dr. R., 274–75, 278, 282
Nair, C.V. Devan
  allegations of alcoholism, 167, 193
  asylum, 163, 165, 167–69
  Chairman, Prisons Inquiry Commission, xx, 116
  confidant of Lee Kuan Yew, 3
  detention under P.P.S.O., xix
  encomia by Lee Kuan Yew, 206–7
  house "bugged", 168
  National Trade Unions Congress (NTUC), secretary general, 74, 206
  op-ed article, "The closing society," 173–94
  opposition parties and politics, observations on, 170
  President of Singapore, 3, 9, 52, 68, 119, 166–67, 174, 194
  press statement dd May 21, 1988, criticizing arrest, 181
  —dd May 22, 1988, 181
  letter from Lee Kuan Yew dd March 5, 1985, 167
  —open letter to Lee Kuan Yew dd July 8, 1988. *See* Appendix 5
  resignation as President of Singapore, 167, 274, 281–82
  Sarawak visit, 9
  Socialist International speech, xix–xx
  speech, NUS, 139
  U.S. meetings, 166–67
  wedding guest, 119
Nair, Janadas, 274
Namazie, Mirza, 63, 138
Nanyang University, 33, 38
Nathan, Patrick, 125
National Day, xviii, 25–26. *See also* H.M. Queen's Birthday
National Solidarity Party (NSP), 66
National Trade Unions Congress (NTUC), 74, 206
National University of Singapore (NUS), 65, 74, 119, 139
Nepal, Kingdom of, 11
New York Times, The, 12, 217, 252
Newspaper and Printing Presses bill. *See under* Bill
Ng, Bee Leng, 261. *See also* Marxist conspiracy
Ng, Hong Leong, 134
Ng, Serlene, 235
Ngoh, Dr., 116, 150–51

Official Assignee's chambers, 18–21
Ong, Eng Guan, 26, 27, 61–62

Ong, Kian Tong, 32
Ong, Pang Boon, 195
Ong, Thiam Hock, 201
Onraet, René, 8, 11
Operation Cold Store, 31
Operation Spectrum. *See* Marxist conspiracy
Ordoñez, Sedfrey, 138
Ordinance. *See* respective ordinances; *See also* Acts
  Preservation of Public Security (PPSO), 3, 21, 31, 71, 138
  Official Secrets, 97

Parliamentary Select Committee on the Legal Profession (Amendment) bill, 62–66
Party
  Barisan Sosialis, 3–4, 10, 28–29, 34–35, 68, 207
  Labour Party, 2
  Malayan Chinese Association (MCA), 3
  National Solidarity Party (NSP), 66
  People's Action Party (PAP), x–xi, xvi, xix–xx, xxiv–xxv, xxvii, xxix, 3, 5, 7, 10, 16, 19, 21–28, 32, 38, 53, 55, 57, 62, 68, 71, 74–75, 79, 96–97, 132, 139–41, 175, 182–83, 185–86, 193, 195–98, 206, 208, 251–52, 254–56, 271–72
  Progressive Party, 13
  Singapore Democratic Party, 66, 170
  United Malays National Organization (UMNO), 3
  United National Front, 32
  United People's Party (UPP), 27
  Workers' Party, 32, 66, 73, 74, 76, 79, 169–70, 254–55, 258
Pavilion Intercontinental Hotel, 81, 119
Penang, a.k.a Prince of Wales Island. *See* Straits Settlements
Phay, Seng Huat, Dr., 43, 75
Phey, Yew Kok, 75
Politics, gutter, 26, 193, 207, 255
Political Study Centre, 25

Port of Singapore Authority Employees Union, 31
P.P. v Geoffrey Fernandez, 49–52
P.P. v Sunny Ang, 40–42, 133
P.P. v Freddy Tan, 45–47
Preservation of Public Security (PPSO). *See under* Ordinance
President of Singapore. *See* C.V. Devan Nair
Press Conference, 71, 87, 98, 100, 120, 137–38
Prison
  Changi Prison. *See* Centres of detention
  Director of Prisons, 10, 46, 190
Prisons Act. *See under* Act
Prisons Regulations, 1938, as amended, xxii, 10–11. *See also* Internal Security (Detained Persons) Rules, 1960
Pritt, D.N., Q.C., 21
Privy Council, Judicial Committee of the, 42, 250–53
Province Wellesley. *See* Straits Settlements
Public Service Commission, 43. *See also* Legal Service Commission
Public Works Department (PWD). *See* Singapore Civil Service

Queen's Birthday, 24–25. *See also* National Day

Raffles, Sir Thomas Stamford, 1, 6, 40
Rajah, Justice A.P., 13, 15
Rajah, K.S., 50
Rajaratnam, S., 182, 208
Raman, Gopalan a.k.a. G. Raman, 73–74
Ramason, R., 138
Ramoo, P., 50
Reagan administration, 186
Registrar of Citizens, 83
—Societies, 73, 170
Rehabilitation, period of, 211, 213, 226–35. *See also* Detention and interrogation
Robertson, Dr. Jean, xx
Robots. *See* Digits

Roman Catholic Church, 8. *See also* Marxist conspiracy
Royal Federation of Malaya Police Force, 72
Royal Navy Underwater Demolition Team, 40. *See also* P.P. v Sunny Ang
Rusk, Dean, 97

Saint Andrew's School, 166
St. John's Island, xxiii. *See also* Centres of detention
Saint Joseph's Institution, 167
Salleh Misnin, 229
Samat Dupree, 229–30
Sarawak, 9, 275–76
Sarkar, Kalu, 9, 275
Savi, V.G., 11
Schwartz, Eric, 89
Schultz, George, 186
Scotsman, The, 78
Scotland Sunday, 78
Scott Thillagaratnam, 138
Scuba diving. *See* P.P. v Sunny Ang
Search and seizure, 112
Security
  national, xii, 112, 140, 182, 187, 197, 232, 234
  Whitley Detention Centre, 8, 11, 68
Select Committee. *See* Parliamentary Select Committee
Sentosa Island. *See* Chia Thye Poh
Seong, Patrick, 55, 84, 87, 89, 91, 99, 107, 120, 123, 126, 231
Seong, Jocelyn, 89, 91, 99
Seow, Francis
  Century Park Sheraton Hotel meeting, 89
  Commission of Inquiry into allegations of corruption etc, 26
  Commission of Inquiry into allegations of Executive interference in the subordinate judiciary, 56
  Commission of Inquiry into the secondary IV examinations boycott, 36–38, 43, 203
  Committee of Privileges, 57
  Council member, Law Society, 55
  Crown Counsel, 13, 15–16
  Assistant Official Assignee, 19
  return to AG's chambers, 21
  transfer to the courts, 27–28, 75
  promotion, 43–44
  private law practice, 53–54
  relations with AG, 197–204
  resignation from service, 22, 47–49, 52–54
  Eunos GRC, 254
  habeas corpus applications, 92, 98, 100, 102–3, 177
  tax request for assets/liabilities, 60–61
  tax investigations, 178
  tax proceedings, 243–50
  New Legal Year address, 56
  Non-constituency Member of Parliament, 255
  President of the Law Society, xxviii, 56, 58, 60, 64, 76, 125, 136, 164, 187, 218
  press statement dd August 6, 1988, 245
  press statement dd August 12, 1988, 246
  release
    conditions of, bond, 241
  Select Committee on the Legal Profession (Amendment) bill, 64, 66, 159, 189, 234
  Singapore Town Club, 93
  Solicitor General, 43–44, 123, 130, 136
  statutory declarations, 177, 180–81, 184, 191, 196
  suspension from practice, 54
  Tan, Rajah, and Cheah, 13, 89
  U.N. conference on the law of treaties, 47
Seow, André, 133, 219
Seow, Eliza, 241
Seow, Francesca, 114
Seow, Ingrid Annalisa, 217
Seow, Ashleigh, 89, 99, 104, 109–10, 112–15, 133, 148, 167, 185, 188, 206, 214, 217, 219, 235, 240–42
Seow, Caroline, 219
Seow, George, 22, 219, 240
Seow, Gerald, 164, 219
Seow, Marjatta, 18, 110, 118, 203–4, 217–18, 242

Shanks, Ernest P., Q.C., 21
Sharma, P.V., 167
Siah, Mei, 38, 59–60, 83–85, 87, 110, 113, 118, 125–26, 132, 134–35, 148, 150, 161–62, 164–66, 188, 219, 232–33, 238–40, 243
Sigur, Gaston, 265
Sim, Poh Heng, 82, 85, 133, 159, 171–73, 176–77, 215, 228, 231–32, 239–40,
Singapore
  Crown colony, 2
  independence of, 30, 37, 265, 269, 271
Singapore Alliance Party (SAP). *See under* Party
Singapore Civil Service, xv, 22–26, 42, 45, 48, 52, 96–97, 119, 192, 197, 199, 228, 246
Singapore Country Peoples' Association (SCPA), 33
Singapore Cricket Club, 17
Singapore Democratic Party (SDP). *See under* Party
Singapore General Hospital, bill from, 148
Singapore Harbour Board Staff Association, 29–31
Singapore Inc., 8
Singapore Legal Service, 13, 16, 22, 28
Singapore Legislative Assembly debates, 13, 67, 71, 102, 173, 195, 226, 243, 256
Singapore Pioneer Industries Employees' Union (SPIEU), 74
Singapore Police Force. *See also* Internal Security Department
  Criminal Investigations Division, (CID)
  Special Investigations Service (SIS), 40
  Commercial Crimes Branch, (CCB), 187, 214–15
  Gurkha Police Contingent, 11
Singapore Polytechnic Students' Union, 73
Singapore Polytechnic Catholic Students' Union, 73. *See also* Marxist conspiracy

Singapore Rural Residents' Association (SRRA), 33
Singapore Town Club, 93
Singapore Turf Club, 141–42
Singapore Year Book
  1963, 4
  1965, 5
Sinnathuray, T.S., 56, 75, 77, 84, 194, 233, 237, 249
Sivasubramaniam, Bahma, 219
Sleep deprivation. *See* Detention
Smith, Colin, 72
Socialist International Bureau meeting. *See* C.V. Devan Nair
Speaker of Parliament, 13, 57, 62
Special Assignments (Civil Legislation) subcommittee. *See* Law Society
Special Branch, Singapore, xvii, xxiii, 11, 31, 34–36, 39, 97. *See also* Internal Security Department (ISD)
Special Branch, Hongkong, 180
Special Branch, Malaysia, 110
Spruce, Jill, 100
Standard Chartered Bank, H.K., 179, 187
State Advocate General, 22, 26, 28, 33, 40. *See also* Attorney General
Statement. *See also* Detention and respective declarants
  MHA —dd. May 21, 1987 on Marxists arrest, 67
  MHA —dd. May 26, 1987 detailing conspiracy, 69
  joint press —dd April 18, 1988. *See* Appendix 1
  U.S. Embassy —dd April 22, 1988, of concern on rearrests, 91
  MHA —dd May 7, 1988, 144
  Devan Nair's press —dd May 21, 1988, 181
  —dd May 22, 1988, 181
  MHA —dd May 23, 1988, 182
  U.S. Embassy —dd May 26, 1988, denying involvement, 183
  ISD —, investigations "inconclusive," 184
  MHA —dd June 5, 1988 on detention, 191

Statement (*continued*)
  MHA —dd July 16, 1988, 241
  press —dd August 6, 1988 on arrest, 245
  —dd August 12, 1988, 246
statutory declaration, xxi, xxiv, xxvi–xxvii, 96, 182
  Patrick Seong dd April 23 and 28, May 3, 1988, 87, 92–93, 99, 144–45, 158, 179
  Francis Seow dd May 20 and May 28, 1988, 177, 180–82, 184, 191
Straits Settlements, 2, 11
Straits Times, The, xxiii, 37, 46, 50, 69, 94, 120, 138, 144, 158, 177, 181–82, 185, 193–94, 206, 208, 230, 236, 246, 272–73, 278
subordinate courts, 28, 55–56, 178, 247–50
Suleiman bin Abdul Rahman, Datuk, 39
Sunday Daily Telegraph, The, xxxvi, xxix, 253
Sunday Observer, The, 72
Sunday Times, The, 56
Snyder, Joseph, 125, 136, 161, 180, 183, 265–66, 271

Tai Pan Hotel, 266
Tambyah, Dr. John A., 275
Tan, Ah Tah, Justice, 19, 38
Tan, Professor Arthur, 147
Tan, Boon Teik, 25, 40, 44, 54, 63, 197–204
Tan, C.C., 89
Tan, Chin Tiong, 190, 267
Tan, Eric, 115, 178–79
Tan, Freddy. *See* P.P. v Freddy Tan
Tan, Kheng Sun, 95
Tan, Rajah & Cheah, 13, 89
Tan, S.K., 106, 109, 111–14, 150, 156, 178, 189, 227, 237, 243
Tan, Dr. Tony, 169
Tan, Wah Piow, 69–70, 73–76, 165, 230–31, 260. *See also* Marxist conspiracy
Tan, Wee Kian, 34
Tang, Fong Har, 59, 65–66, 76, 230, 260. *See also* Marxist conspiracy

Tang, Lay Lee, 260. *See also* Marxist conspiracy
Tang, Tuck Wah, 187, 214
Tsang, Kenneth, 260. *See also* Marxist conspiracy
Tay, Beng Swee, 201
Tay, Boon Woo, 32
Tay, Eng Soon, Dr., 254
Teehankee, Claudio, 218
Temasek, 1
Teo, Eng Seng, 88
Teo, Joo Lai, Julius, 188
Teo, Soh Lung, 55, 57–59, 65–67, 73–77, 81–85, 87–89, 91–93, 95, 98, 100, 104–6, 108–9, 123, 138, 144, 154, 212, 214, 230–31, 260
Teo Teck Huat Co. Ltd.. *See* Julius Teo
Third Stage. *See* Marxist conspiracy
Tjong, Yik Min, 150, 180, 189–91, 227, 236, 239
Toa Payoh General Hospital, 130
Toh, Chin Chye, Dr., xxvii, 7, 119, 169–70, 183, 195–97
Torture. *See* centres of detention
Traverse Theatre
  "Oh Singapore!", 78

UMNO-MCA Alliance, 3
United Malayan Banking Corporation, 180
United National Front. *See under* Party. *See also* R.Vetrivelu
United Nations
  conference of the law of treaties, 47
  seminar on the role of the police in the protection of human rights, 39
United People's Party (UPP). *See under* Party
University of Cambridge, 3, 65
University of Singapore, Students' Union, 73–74. *See also* National University of Singapore
U.S. embassy, 89, 91, 98, 125, 159–60, 163, 183, 265, 267, 280
U.S. State Department, 97, 125–26, 136, 145, 156–58, 163, 165, 181, 274

Vaswant, Dr. Kuldip Singh, 143
Vetrivelu, R., 32
visitors' book, 17, 105

Wee, A.S.K., 145, 203
Wee, Cho Yaw, 203
Wee, Chong Jin, 38, 54, 218
Wee, H.L., 203
Wee, Robert, 199–202
Whitley, Major N.H.P., M.C., 11
Whitley Detention Centre, 8–11, 104, 121
  Block C, xxi, 119, 121, 142, 213
  Cell L9 Block L, 116, 153, 205–7, 209, 211
  interrogation room, C-22, xxi–xxii, 121–22, 132, 142–44, 150–51, 154–55, 159, 171, 173, 179, 215–16, 227–28, 236, 239
  interview room
    counsel, 105
    family, 105
  medical room, 115, 118, 143–44, 152
  security, 212–14
  sketches of. *See* Appendix 2
  under ISD, 8–9, 10–11

Valley Wing, 209–11, 213
visits, 91, 214, 215, 240
White Paper, Command 8 of 1988, 9, 193, 207, 273–75, 277, 279–81.
  See also C.V. Devan Nair
Whyte, Sir Hamilton, 164–65
Williams, Peter A., Q.C., 237
Wilson, Harold, 5
Wong, Souk Yee, 72, 87, 260. *See also* Marxist conspiracy
Wong, Yip Chong, Dr., 45–46
Woodbridge Mental Hospital, 45
Workers' Party. *See under* Party
Workers' Party Alliance, 170
Yang di-Pertuan Negara, 25
Yap, William. *See* Marxist conspiracy
Yeow, Fook Yuen, 29, 31
Yong, Archbishop Gregory, 69, 71, 137, 230. *See also* Marxist conspiracy
Yong, Nguk Lin, 37. *See also* Commission of Inquiry into the Secondary IV examinations boycott
Yong, Pung How, 49
Yoong, Siew Wah, 50
Zainuddin, *Datuk Paduka* Daim, 135

*Design, illustrations, maps,
and typography by*

METAGLYPHICS

Hamden, Connecticut USA